MC
SOCIETY FOR RESEARCH IN
CHILD DEVELOPMENT

Serial No. 227, Vol. 57, Nos. 2–3, 1992

COPING WITH MARITAL TRANSITIONS: A FAMILY SYSTEMS PERSPECTIVE

E. Mavis Hetherington
W. Glenn Clingempeel

IN COLLABORATION WITH
Edward R. Anderson
James E. Deal
Margaret Stanley Hagan
E. Ann Hollier
Marjorie S. Lindner

WITH COMMENTARY BY
Eleanor E. Maccoby

MONOGRAPHS OF THE SOCIETY FOR RESEARCH IN CHILD DEVELOPMENT
Serial No. 227, Vol. 57, Nos. 2–3, 1992

CONTENTS

ABSTRACT

Hetherington, E. Mavis, and Clingempeel, W. Glenn, in collaboration with Anderson, Edward R.; Deal, James E.; Stanley Hagan, Margaret; Hollier, E. Ann; and Lindner, Marjorie S. Coping with Marital Transitions: A Family Systems Perspective. With Commentary by Eleanor E. Maccoby. *Monographs of the Society for Research in Child Development,* 1992, **57**(2–3, Serial No. 227).

Almost half the children born in the last decade will experience the divorce of their parents, and many of these children will also go through the changes associated with their custodial parent's remarriage. Most children initially experience their parents' marital rearrangements as stressful; however, children's responses to their parents' marital transitions are diverse and are likely to vary with the age of the child and to change over time as family members adjust to their new circumstances. This longitudinal study examined family relationships and adolescents' adjustment during the transition to remarriage. Three groups of families were studied: stepfamilies with a divorced custodial mother who was in the first months of a remarriage; families with a divorced custodial mother who had not remarried; and nondivorced families. Families were assessed three times during a 26-month period, and there were approximately equal numbers of early adolescent male and female target children in each family type. Family relationships and children's adjustment were assessed using interview measures obtained from multiple perspectives and from observational measures of family interactions in the home. This *Monograph* examined differences between the three family groups in children's adjustment, marital relationships, parent-child relationships, and sibling relationships as the children were moving through early adolescence and as stepfamilies were coping with a new remarriage. Authoritative child rearing was associated with positive adjustment in children in all family groups. Children in nondivorced families were more competent and exhibited fewer behavior problems than children in divorced or remarried families. Unlike the findings with younger children, few gender × family-type interactions were obtained, and no adjustment to the remarriage over the 26 months of the study was found in stepfather-stepchild relations or in the adjustment of stepchildren.

PREFACE

This research was supported by a grant from the John D. and Catherine T. MacArthur Foundation, and the authors express their appreciation for the support throughout this study.

So many other individuals have played critical and important roles in this endeavor that it is not possible to list them all by name. Eight graduate students at Temple University were involved in the difficult task of data collection, recruitment, scheduling, and interviewing families. Over 80 undergraduates and 15 graduate students at the University of Virginia have been involved in the development and use of a complex observation coding system, data entry, and data analyses over the course of the study. The Virginia team was responsible for the data analysis and writing of this *Monograph.* We especially wish to thank the graduate students, many of whom have moved on to new academic posts, who labored through multiple revisions of this *Monograph.* Without their dedication, patience, and support, this *Monograph* would never have been completed. Their names are listed on the chapters to which they made major contributions. However, this research project is a group effort, in which undergraduates, graduate students, and the senior investigators functioned as a collaborative team. We are grateful for the opportunity to have worked with and learned from such a gifted and dedicated group of young scholars.

Finally, we wish to thank our reviewers, James Bray and Eleanor Maccoby, who have provided thoughtful and helpful critiques.

E. Mavis Hetherington
W. Glenn Clingempeel

Please address correspondence to E. Mavis Hetherington, James M. Page Professor of Psychology, Department of Psychology, Gilmer Hall, University of Virginia, Charlottesville, VA 22903.

I. COPING WITH MARITAL TRANSITIONS: A FAMILY SYSTEMS PERSPECTIVE

E. Mavis Hetherington

Family reorganizations associated with divorce and remarriage have become increasingly common experiences in the lives of parents and children. The rate of divorce doubled in the two decades following 1960. In spite of a modest decline in the divorce rate since 1979 (Hernandez, 1988), it is estimated that half of couples married after 1970 will eventually divorce. Almost 50% of all children are expected to experience the divorce of their parents and to spend an average of 5 years in a single-parent household (Glick & Lin, 1986). It has been said, however, that the period in a single-parent household can be viewed as a way station rather than a destination because 72% of women and 80% of men remarry (Glick, 1989a). Women with children, women over 35, and blacks are much less likely to remarry than white, younger, childless divorced women. Furthermore, the remarriage rate decreased sharply in the 1970s and has continued to decrease more gradually during the 1980s (London, 1991). Remarriage rates for adults divorcing in the last decade will be substantially lower than those in earlier cohorts. However, it is still projected that 40 percent of adults currently in first marriages will become members of stepfamilies before their youngest child reaches 18 years of age (Glick, 1988, 1989b). Furthermore, because the divorce rate is slightly higher for second than for first marriages, many adults and children are exposed to a series of marital transitions and household reorganizations. It is estimated that one out of every 10 children will experience two divorces of the custodial parent before he or she turns 16 (Furstenberg, 1988).

Much early research involved static notions of divorce and remarriage and contrasted the adjustment of family members in traditional nuclear nondivorced and in nontraditional families at a single point in time. The focus of such studies was on family structure and on divorce and remarriage as events occurring at a single point in time. More recently, divorce and remarriage have been viewed as nonnormative transitions involving changing adaptive challenges to family members and alterations in family functioning over time. The diverse sequences of family reorganizations and experiences following divorce and remarriage and the patterning and timing of these experiences are critical for the long-term adjustment of adults and children. Furthermore, responses to a current marital or family situation will be influenced by the experiences that have preceded it. The response to divorce will be influenced by the predivorce family relationship and adjustment, and roles and relationships in the one-parent household will shape the family's subsequent response to the addition of a stepparent.

One of the main challenges confronting members of families in transition lies in defining and developing appropriate, acceptable, and fulfilling roles within different family relationships. This may be a particularly difficult task for nontraditional families, in which clearly prescribed normative roles are often lacking (Cherlin, 1981; Hetherington, Stanley Hagan, & Anderson, 1989). Both divorce and remarriage involve a complex series of changes that can affect all aspects of family relationships. Adaptation in one family subsystem can influence adaptation in another either positively or negatively (Hetherington, 1988; MacKinnon, 1989). Thus, the marital, sibling, and parent-child relationships will interact to affect the adjustment of all family members to marital transitions.

The longitudinal study presented in this *Monograph* examined the effects of transitions on the functioning of and interrelations among these family subsystems and on the adjustment of early adolescent children in nondivorced families, in single-parent households with a divorced custodial mother, and in newly remarried families with a custodial biological mother and a stepfather. Over the 2-year course of the study, all families were dealing with changes associated with the normative transition of early adolescence; however, the stepfamilies were additionally confronting the challenges of adapting to the early stages of a remarriage.

In order to set the background for the hypotheses we address and the analyses reported in this *Monograph,* I first summarize the main findings of previous research dealing with the effect of marital transitions on family functioning and on children's adjustment. In the following review of the literature, I focus on single-parent households with a divorced custodial mother and on remarried families with a custodial mother and a stepfather because these were the types of families involved in our study.

THE ADJUSTMENT OF CHILDREN IN DIVORCED AND REMARRIED FAMILIES

In both home and school settings, behavior, social, emotional, and learning problems have been found to be more characteristic of children from divorced and remarried families than of children from nondivorced families (Allison & Furstenberg, 1989; Baumrind, 1989; Bray, 1987, 1988; Guidubaldi, 1988; Hetherington, Cox, & Cox, 1985; Perry & Pfuhl, 1963; Rosenberg, 1965; Touliatos & Lindholm, 1980; Zill, 1988; Zimiles & Lee, 1991). However, such differences do not always emerge (Bohannon, 1975; Burchinal, 1964; Wilson, Zurcher, McAdams, & Curtis, 1975). Furthermore, several longitudinal studies of preadolescents found that many children who initially had demonstrated problems in adjustment gradually adapted to their new family situation with a concomitant decrease in problem behavior (Hetherington, 1989; Hetherington et al., 1985; Wallerstein & Kelly, 1980). In addition, children whose parents are later going to divorce show more behavior problems both before and after the divorce, which suggests that family conflict and an unhappy marital relationship may already be taking their toll before the divorce occurs (Block, Block, & Gjerde, 1986, 1988; Cherlin, Chase-Lansdale, Furstenberg, Kiernan, & Robins, 1991).

The effects of marital transitions on children's adjustment are most marked by increases in the frequency of externalizing, antisocial, noncompliant behavior (Bray, 1987, 1988; Camara & Resnick, 1988; Hetherington et al., 1985; Zill, 1988). While it has been speculated that girls may show more internalizing than boys in response to family conflict and their parents' marital transitions (Emery, 1982), research suggests that externalizing may in fact be the most common response of both boys and girls, although some of these findings may be age specific. For instance, Baumrind (1989) reported that, in contrast to her findings with younger children, adolescent girls in divorced mother custody families showed more externalizing than did adolescent boys. Wallerstein and her colleagues (Wallerstein, Corbin, & Lewis, 1988) reported elevated rates of depression in late adolescent and young adult females whose parents had divorced earlier; however, they had no comparison group of nondivorced families, and because depression in females has been found to increase in this age period, the findings may be attributable to developmental rather than marital change.

There is some controversy about whether the remarriage of a custodial parent exacerbates or attenuates the problems of children living in divorced, single-parent families. Although some studies report that children experiencing the first 2 years of their parents' remarriage often show more problems than do those in one-parent households (Hetherington et al., 1985), others find that children in single-parent households (Zill, 1988), particularly sons (Hetherington et al., 1985), exhibit as many problem behaviors as those in stepfamilies. Moreover, several studies have found that children in divorced households are more likely to have problems if they are in the custody of the opposite-sex parent (Santrock & Sitterle, 1987; Santrock, Warshak, Lindbergh, & Meadows, 1982; Zill, 1988). However, a recent study suggests that, as children move into adolescence, both sons and daughters exhibit more delinquency when they are in the custody of their father instead of their mother (Buchanan, Maccoby, & Dornbusch, in press). This may be because fathers monitor their children's behavior less carefully than mothers and because monitoring plays an increasing role in controlling antisocial behavior as children get older.

Some investigators (Furstenberg, 1988; Zill, 1988) have argued that the high incidence of behavior problems in stepchildren can be attributed to stresses that preceded the remarriage, to factors associated with an unsatisfactory first marriage, to the divorce itself, and to life in a one-parent family. Certainly, some of the legacy of past family experience is carried over into children's response to the custodial parent's remarriage; however, the remarriage itself also seems to contribute new adaptational challenges. Longitudinal studies find that, in both divorce and remarriage, adaptation to the new family situation occurs over time, in patterns that vary somewhat with children's gender and age (Hetherington, 1981, 1988, 1989; Hetherington et al., 1985; Wallerstein & Kelly, 1980, 1982).

Gender and Age Differences in Children's Adjustment to Their Parents' Marital Transitions

In adjusting to marital transitions, the complex interactions between the children's gender, their age at the time of the divorce or remarriage as well as at the time of assessment, the time since the divorce or remarriage occurred, custodial arrangements, and the type of structure in the one-parent family or stepfamily are not well understood. In general, preadolescent boys show more intense and enduring problems in response to their parents' divorce than do girls; most girls adapt to the divorce and to life in a single-parent, mother-custody household within 2–3 years unless they encounter sustained or additional stresses. There is, however, accumulating evidence that problems in heterosexual relationships, precocious sexual activities, and confrontational exchanges with the mother may emerge at adolescence in girls from divorced families (Baumrind, 1989; Hetherington, 1972, 1988; Udry, 1987; Udry, Talbert, & Morris, 1986; Wallerstein et al., 1988). In contrast to the response to divorce, girls are reported to have more difficulty than boys in adapting to the custodial parent's remarriage (Baumrind, 1989; Brand, Clingempeel, & Bowen-Woodward, 1988; Bray, 1987, 1988, 1990; Hetherington, 1988; Pink & Wampler, 1985; Santrock et al., 1982; Zaslow, 1988, 1989). Because boys often become involved in negative coercive relationships with their divorced custodial mother, they may have something to gain and little to lose by the introduction of a warm, supportive stepfather. In contrast, girls—who usually have a better relationship with their divorced mothers—may have more to lose in the remarriage and have been found to exhibit more enduring antagonism and resistance to the new stepfather. Although a recent survey study by Zill (1988) found few gender differences in response to divorce and remarriage, the studies cited previously that did find such differences used multiple and/or observational methods rather than relying solely on interview data, studied only single-parent families formed as a result of divorce, and did not combine families with divorced, unmarried, and remarried mothers (Zaslow, 1988).

Emery (1982) proposed that the reason boys appear to be more disturbed in response to divorce and marital conflict is that most investigators focus on externalizing, which boys are more likely to exhibit in response to family stress, whereas girls are more likely to internalize. However, in a careful review of the research on divorce, Zaslow (1989) concluded that, although externalizing is reported more often in boys than in girls following divorce, internalizing is found for both genders, and when remarriage has occurred, girls are more likely to show pervasive increases in both types of problem behaviors. Zaslow qualifies this assertion by noting that the age of the child at the time of the marital transition and at the time of assessment as well as time since the transition are also important factors in children's responses.

Following their parents' marital transitions, children of all ages show an initial increase in problem behaviors and disruptions in relationships with other family members (Bray, 1988; Hetherington et al., 1985). Although it has been proposed that the experience of divorce early in life has more adverse effects on children than it does later (Allison & Furstenberg, 1989; Kurdek, 1981; Kurdek, Blisk, & Siesky, 1981; Zaslow, 1989), this position is not consistently supported (Wallerstein et al., 1988). It seems more accurate to say that the effects vary qualitatively according to children's developmental status. Older children are more cognitively and socially skilled and have greater personal and extrafamilial resources for coping with their parents' marital transitions. About one-third of late preadolescents and adolescents cope by disengaging from the family and becoming involved in extrafamilial groups and activities; in some cases, they become attached to a friend's or neighbor's family, which serves them as a surrogate family (Hetherington, 1989; Wallerstein & Kelly, 1980, 1982; Weiss, 1979). Younger children do not have such an option, and their adjustment depends more on resources and experiences within their own family.

In contrast to the inconsistent support for the notion of a vulnerable period to adverse effects of divorce, the greatest difficulty in adjusting to remarriage consistently appears to occur in early adolescence. Unlike early adolescents, younger children appear better able eventually to become attached to and benefit from the presence of a competent stepparent (Bernard, 1972; Bowerman & Irish, 1962; Duberman, 1973, 1975; Hetherington et al., 1989; Lutz, 1983; Ransom, Schlesinger & Derdeyn, 1979). The developmental tasks confronting early adolescents may make adaptation to their parents' remarriage especially difficult (Brand et al., 1988; Hetherington, 1988, 1989; Hetherington & Anderson, 1987). Two key developmental tasks at this time are the development of autonomy and the need to cope with pubertal sexual fantasies and feelings. Children who have experienced precocious power and independence in a single-parent household may be particularly sensitive to infringements on their autonomy by a stepparent at this time, and coping with changing adolescent perceptions of parents and an increasing preoccupation with sexuality may render the presence of a biologically unrelated adult distressing. The introduction of a stepparent in early adolescence may result in troubles with intimacy, sexuality, and the appropriate display of affection between family members (Jones, 1978; Krantzler, 1975; Strother & Jacobs, 1984). In contrast, late adolescents may not be as averse to the entry of a stepparent into the family because they are anticipating leaving home and entering new young adult roles and relationships; in fact, the remarriage may relieve them of emotional and economic responsibilities for their custodial parent.

FAMILY RELATIONSHIPS IN DIVORCED AND REMARRIED FAMILIES

Mother-Child Relationships in Divorced Families

Following their parents' divorce most children reside with a custodial mother; about 11% live with a custodial father. During the period of separation and divorce and the first two years that follow, there is typically a marked disruption in parent-child relationships (Camara & Resnick, 1987, 1988; Hetherington, Cox, & Cox, 1982; Wallerstein et al., 1988). In this early period, a preoccupied and/or emotionally disturbed parent and a distressed, demanding child are likely to have difficulty supporting or consoling each other and may even exacerbate each other's problems. Custodial mothers frequently become temporarily erratic, uncommunicative, nonsupportive, and inconsistently punitive in dealing with their children. However, difficulty controlling and monitoring children's behavior is the most sustained parenting problem faced by divorced mothers (Bank, Forgatch, Patterson, & Fetrow, 1991; Forgatch, Patterson, & Skinner, 1988). This is unfortunate since Baumrind (1989) reported that firm control and monitoring by mothers—especially in divorced families—are particularly important for girls in the development of resilience, self-regulation, and social responsibility. There is some suggestion that higher levels of conflict and of attempted maternal control and monitoring in divorced families relative to nondivorced families may occur in adolescence as a response to daughters' acting out behavior (Hetherington, 1972). However, such reactive attempts at control by divorced mothers do not seem to be successful (Hetherington, 1972; Udry, 1987; Udry et al., 1986). The greater autonomy and decision-making power of children in mother-headed households may be associated either with earlier acceptance of responsibility and social maturity or with an unwillingness to accept parental direction and restraints in adolescence (Hetherington, 1989).

Disruptions in parent-child relationships are most marked and enduring for custodial mothers and their sons, who are likely to become involved in escalating coercive interchanges (Hetherington, 1988). In contrast, divorced mothers and their preadolescent daughters often form close, congenial relationships; however, these too may become conflictual in early adolescence, particularly if the mother remarries (Baumrind, 1989; Hetherington, 1989). In spite of the period of diminished parenting in the immediate aftermath of divorce, divorced mothers become increasingly competent and authoritative parents with time.

When there is little conflict between the divorced spouses, a warm, involved, stable noncustodial father can play a positive role in the adjustment of children, especially of sons. Most custodial fathers, however, become increasingly unavailable to their children (Furstenberg, 1988; Hetherington et al., 1982).

Marital and Parent-Child Relationships in Remarried Families

Although both divorce and remarriage involve family reorganization and changes in roles and relationships, the former results in separation from or loss of the noncustodial parent and the latter in the addition of a family member. The main tasks of a newly remarried family lie in incorporating the stepparent into its midst and in establishing some consensus among family members on what that stepparent's appropriate functions may be. The stepparent confronts the difficulties inherent in simultaneously establishing stable marital and functional parent-child relationships.

Marital relationships in stepfamilies.—A primary challenge to remarried families lies in developing and sustaining the marital bond in an instantly formed family with children. Spouses must establish their relationship within a family system that is structurally more complex than that experienced by couples in a first marriage and that may include ex-in-laws and noncustodial children as well as nonresidential parents and grandparents; thus, family boundaries are often not well marked (Ahrons, 1980; Albrecht, Bahr, & Goodman, 1983). Our society provides few norms to guide remarried family members in adjusting to these complex roles and relationships

(Peek, Bell, Waldren, & Sorrell, 1988). Moreover, family members bring with them previous histories and experiences of marriage and family life that can affect their adjustment to the new marriage (Hetherington & Camara, 1984). As Papernow (1984, p. 346) has noted, the typical starting point for the remarried couple—"a weak couple subsystem, a tightly-bonded parent-child alliance, and potential 'interference' in family functioning from an 'outsider' "—would be considered pathological in a newly married pair.

In most first marriages, a close marital relationship serves as the foundation for positive relationships among other family members (Belsky, 1984) and may promote the psychological well-being of the spouses (Cowan, Cowan, Heming, & Miller, 1991; Cowan, Cowan, Schultz, & Heming, in press; Cox, Owen, Lewis, & Henderson, 1989). Especially in the early stage of remarriage, however, a positive marital relationship has sometimes been associated with behavior problems in the children and difficulties in parent-child interaction (Brand et al., 1988; Bray, 1987, 1988; Hetherington, 1988, 1989). Stepchildren often view the new stepparent as a competitor for the affection and attention of their biological parent and resent a close marital relationship. It is not surprising, therefore, that, among married couples in stepfamilies, the most frequently reported area of stress, and the one that interferes most with marital satisfaction, is that of parent-child relationships. Additionally, remarried couples report many more overall life stressors, particularly negative ones, than do couples in nondivorced families (Bray, 1987, 1988; Hetherington et al., 1985).

With a previous disrupted marital experience and elevated levels of stress, it might be expected that the quality of the marital relationship and interactions would differ in remarriages. However, owing in part to measurement and methodological differences across studies, the results of studies examining the similarities and differences between first and second marriages have been inconsistent (Albrecht et al., 1983). Some studies have found no differences in marital satisfaction between couples in first marriages and those in remarriages (Anderson & White, 1986; Pink & Wampler, 1985). Other investigators have reported that newly remarried couples are more coercive, less positive, and less skilled in communicating than are nondivorced, longer-married couples (Bray, 1988). In contrast, other researchers have described a "honeymoon period" early in remarriage during which spouses report higher marital satisfaction and are observed to be less negative and more positive than couples in stabilized first marriages (Hetherington, 1988).

When remarried couples describe and compare their first and second marriages, they typically report many differences. The second marriage is seen as more pragmatic and less romantic, more open in communication with a greater willingness to confront conflict, and more egalitarian with respect to child-rearing and housekeeping roles (Centers, Raven, & Rodrigues, 1971; Furstenberg, 1979, 1982; Giles-Sims, 1984, 1987; Weingarten, 1980). Such views may help couples who fear a second marital failure perceive their remarriages as different from their previous one; however, there is little research or observational data to corroborate these self-reports—in fact, there is some evidence that marital relationships within stabilized remarried families and nondivorced families are more similar than different (Hetherington, 1988).

A substantial research literature is now available that describes the characteristics of first marriages and the correlates of marital satisfaction in the marriages. However, there has as yet been little research on the specific qualities of a remarriage that are associated with marital satisfaction or with the psychological well-being of the spouses. These are two issues that were examined in the present study.

Comparisons of distressed and nondistressed couples in first marriages have shown that negative emotions and the escalation of negative affect are better predictors of later levels of marital satisfaction and stability than are positive emotions (Gottman & Levenson, 1988; Levenson & Gottman, 1985; Raush, Barry, Hertel, & Swain, 1974). However, such results must be qualified in view of recent findings of gender differences in husbands' and wives' responses to conflictual or negative marital interactions, at least in first marriages. Whereas husbands try to avoid, withdraw from, or deescalate conflict and to conceal feelings in the face of acrimonious exchanges, wives are more eager to confront and discuss problems and more willing to tolerate, provoke, or escalate conflicts (Gottman & Levenson, 1988; Raush et al., 1974; Rubin, 1979). Gottman and Levenson (1988) have associated this with gender differences in patterns of autonomic and endocrine arousal. In the face of confrontations, men's arousal is greater and more sustained than women's. Men try to withdraw emotionally to reduce conflict and attain a comfortable level of physiological arousal. Thus, high negativity and conflict in marital interactions is associated with lower marital satisfaction in men than in women in first marriages. No information is available as to whether this pattern of gender differences is also found in second marriages.

Gender differences have also been reported in the relation between marital satisfaction and depression. Both Cowan, Cowan, and Heming (1989) and Cox et al. (1989) found that marital satisfaction and depression were closely negatively related for women. For men this relation has been less consistently found. Cox et al. (1989) found no such association. In contrast, Cowan et al. (1989) reported that, although husbands' depression related to marital conflict, it was not associated with current marital satisfaction; however, depression did predict subsequent declines in the husbands' marital satisfaction. Finally, Biglan, Hops, Sherman, Arthur, and Osteen (1985) found that, if one spouse showed signs of depression, the marriage was characterized by less positive observed interactions and more negative conflictual aggressive behavior between parents. The presence of such associations has not been explored in remarried families.

In summary, most family theorists view the quality of the marital relationship and the couple's satisfaction with it as having pervasive effects on other family relationships as well as on the adjustment of individual family members. Little is known about these associations in remarried families.

Parent-child relationships in stepfamilies.—Perhaps the most difficult interpersonal challenge in stepfamilies lies in developing a constructive relationship between parents and children. This includes renegotiating the relationship with the biological custodial parent and establishing a new relationship with the stepparent. Most investigators find that, although there may be a temporary period of disruption and an increase in conflict and negativity between the custodial mother and children immediately following remarriage, these aversive interactions diminish with time. Two years after remarriage, few differences are found between the relationships of nondivorced mothers and their children and the relationships of remarried mothers and their children except for scattered reports of less effective control and monitoring by the remarried mothers (Bray, 1987, 1988; Hetherington, 1988, 1989; Pink & Wampler, 1985).

The pattern is quite different, however, between the stepparent and the stepchild. Family members experience considerable confusion and ambivalence about what the relationship between these two should be. Research findings suggest that this ambiguity is reflected in such problematic family processes as less cohesiveness, poorer communication and parental discipline, less control and monitoring, and more disengagement on the part of the stepparent (Brand et al., 1988; Bray, 1988; Hetherington, 1988, 1989). Moreover, after initial attempts to form a positive relationship with the stepchild and to enhance the new family unit, many stepparents become increasingly disengaged from their stepchildren (Hetherington, 1988, 1989). Stepmothers are less able to disengage than stepfathers since they are more likely to have to remain involved in routine child care. The stepparents' disengagement and eventual withdrawal may be a response to persistent resentment and resistance on the part of some stepchildren.

With younger children, the most successful strategy for a new stepparent is to build a warm, involved relationship with the stepchildren initially and to support the discipline of the biological parent but to avoid taking over the role of a controlling disciplinarian rapidly. Even authoritative stepparenting (involving high warmth, effective communication, and firm but responsive control)—which is salutary in nondivorced families (Baumrind, 1973)—may at first lead to resentment and resistance on the part of stepchildren (Hetherington, 1988, 1989). It has been suggested that the move to authoritative parenting should be gradual and that, with some stepchildren, it may remain undesirable or impossible (Hetherington, 1988).

Sibling Relationships in Divorced and Remarried Families

Sibling relationships are unique because they combine the affective intensity and reciprocity of peer relationships with many of the complementary processes associated with parent-child relationships, the latter due to age differences in siblings (Dunn, 1983). Sibling relationships are characterized by an intense affective tone, with high levels of both empathically supportive and antagonistic behavior, and this ambivalence is found in both younger and older sibling pairs (Dunn, 1983). Siblings often serve as role models, teachers, nurturers, and antagonists.

Studies examining the effects of birth order, gender, and developmental changes on sibling relationships have produced inconsistent findings. In general, girls are likely to demonstrate more nurturant prosocial behavior but not necessarily less antisocial behavior toward their siblings than are boys (Bryant, 1982; Dunn, 1983). Teaching younger siblings is more commonly found in older sisters than in older brothers (Dunn, 1983; Hetherington, 1988). Some studies report that negative behaviors are more common in both older brothers and older sisters than in younger siblings (Dunn, 1983); others find this only for older brothers (Hetherington, 1988; MacKinnon, 1989). As siblings grow older, levels of negative behavior appear to increase, with younger children becoming more aggressive toward older siblings (Dunn, 1983). Little is known about how sibling relations change during the transition to adolescence.

The research on gender composition of sibling pairs also is inconsistent, with some studies showing that the relationship between same-sex dyads, especially those involving boys, is less positive (Abramovitch, Pepler, & Corter, 1982; Stoneman, Brody, & MacKinnon, 1986). Others find the relationship between older boy/younger girl dyads to be less positive and more negative than that between same-sex male dyads (Dunn & Kendrick, 1982).

Scarr and Grajek (1982) concluded that such family structure variables as birth order, sibling spacing, and gender combinations did not explain differences between siblings adequately, and others have noted that these variables explain little of the variance in individual differences in adjustment (Daniels, Dunn, Furstenberg, & Plomin, 1985; Grotevant, Scarr, & Weinberg, 1977; Rodgers & Rowe, 1985; Schooler, 1972). Most investigators have concluded that the quality of relationships and the quality of interactions within the family are more likely to explain developmental outcome than sibling structural variables are (Furman & Buhrmester, 1985; Hetherington, 1988; MacKinnon, 1989).

The quality of the marital relationship may stimulate either competition or cohesion in sibling relationships. Moreover, the parent-child relationship and differential treatment of children by parents have been found to influence sibling relationships and the adjustment of children in nondivorced, divorced, and remarried families (Daniels, 1987; Dunn, 1983; Hetherington, 1988; Plomin & Daniels, 1987). Finally, the quality of sibling interactions contributes significantly to the adjustment of children. This is especially notable in the development of antisocial aggressive behavior, where coercive exchanges between siblings are associated with increased externalizing behavior (Hetherington, 1988; Patterson, 1982).

Little is known about sibling relationships in families with divorced or remarried parents. Of the two contrasting theoretical perspectives that have been proposed, one suggests that siblings will become increasingly rivalrous and hostile as they compete for the scarce resources of parental love and attention following their parents' divorce or remarriage. The alternative hypothesis is that, having experienced marital transitions, children will view relationships with adults as unreliable, unstable, and painful and will turn to each other for solace and support (Bank & Kahn, 1982a, 1982b; Ihinger-Tallman, 1987). The meager research available on this topic suggests that, following divorce and remarriage, rivalry, disengagement, and hostility among siblings are more likely than positive, mutually supportive behaviors (Hetherington, 1989; MacKinnon, 1989). However, during times of marital transition, sisters are more able than brothers to act as buffers for each other and to fill the emotional void left by an unresponsive parent. Brothers are less likely to be mutually supportive under such circumstances, and sisters are unlikely to be an emotional resource for brothers (Hetherington, 1988; Wallerstein et al., 1988).

OVERVIEW OF THE STUDY

We take a developmental family systems perspective in examining changes in life experiences, family process, and individual adjustment associated with marital transitions (Chase-Lansdale & Hetherington, 1990; McGoldrick & Carter, 1980; Whiteside, 1982; Williamson & Bray, 1988). That is, we expected that the effects of divorce and remarriage will vary according to the developmental status of family members and their stage in the life and family cycles. We see divorce and remarriage not as single events but as part of a series of changes in family organization, functioning, and life experiences, and we expect the factors that promote psychological well-being or problems in family members and relationships to vary over time. Each family member is viewed as part of an interactional, interdependent system in which the behavior of each individual or subsystem, such as the marital, parent-child, or sibling subsystem, modifies that of other subsystems. Thus, individuals and subsystems are linked in a network of feedback loops, and a change in one leads to changes in the others. Divorce and remarriage involve alterations in family organization and functioning that are associated with a period of disequilibrium followed by gradual restabilization of relationships in the new family system. These family transitions, especially when compounded by the changes associated with a marked normative transition such as adolescence, are often stressful but offer opportunities for individual and family growth as well as dysfunction (Hetherington & Anderson, 1987).

This longitudinal study examined transformations in marital, parent-child, and sibling relationships and the effects that these changes have on the adjustment of early adolescent children following the remarriage of a divorced custodial mother. In order to distinguish adjustment to remarriage from adjustment to prior stresses associated with divorce, a comparison group of families with a divorced nonremarried mother was included. This group was chosen to be comparable to the remarried group with respect to the time elapsed since the custodial mother's divorce; thus, on average, the nonremarried families had been living in single-parent homes for the same length of time as the remarried families had before the remarriage. A comparison group of nondivorced families was also assessed since changes in family functioning and children's adjustment associated with the normative transitions of early adolescence were equally of interest. Early adolescents were selected as the focus of study because of the many social, physical, emotional, and academic changes they face. It was thought that the challenge of coping with changes in family structure and relationships, in addition to confronting the normative developmental tasks of early adolescence, would make children of this age especially vulnerable to problems in adjustment.

Information on family functioning and children's adjustment was collected using multiple informants and multiple methods. These included interviews, questionnaires, checklists of behavior symptoms, and observational assessments. Because a diversity of perspectives was expected, information was sought from parents and target children as well as from the children's teachers in order to obtain a broader view of family and individual functioning.

Data were also collected on many factors outside the home, such as relationships with grandparents and nonresidential fathers, life stressors, legal decisions and custody settlements, etc. Although this report is limited to within-household relationships and children's adjustment, we are aware of the possible influences of these other factors on family functioning and children's behavior.

The sample was composed of white, largely middle-income families containing an early adolescent child of parents who had at least a high school education; results presented here may not generalize to other segments of the population. In addition, the sample was limited to households headed by a divorced mother and to remarried families containing only a stepfather and the custodial mother's children. Although these are by far the most prevalent forms of divorced and remarried families, marked differences in family and individual functioning would be expected in other family forms, such as divorced father-custody families, stepmother families, or blended families.

The goals of this study were to examine the following issues:

1. The adaptation of family members and changes in the functioning of family subsystems over the 26 months following remarriage and during the child's negotiation of early adolescence;
2. The differences in family relationships as well as in the behavior and adjustment of family members in remarried families containing a stepfather as compared to nondivorced families and to families with a divorced, nonremarried custodial mother;
3. Gender differences in patterns of family functioning and in the adjustment of the children in these three types of families; and
4. Family functioning variables associated with the adjustment of children in nondivorced, in divorced mother-custody, and in remarried families.

This *Monograph* continues with a methods chapter, followed by a chapter examining children's adjustment, three chapters dealing with, respectively, the marital, parent-child, and sibling family subsystems, a chapter examining the contribution of family relationships to the adjustment of children, and a final integrative summary.

II. METHOD

Margaret Stanley Hagan

Multiple methods and measures were used in each of three assessment waves to examine the relationships and adjustment of family members in three types of families. Stepfamilies were assessed at an average of 4.20 months (SD = 2.21), 17.00 months (SD = 3.06), and 26.34 months (SD = 5.43) after remarriage. Nondivorced and divorced single-mother families were assessed at equivalent time periods.[1]

SUBJECTS

Families were recruited through such diverse means as a review of marriage license records; random phone calls; radio, television, and newspaper features; public service organizations such as churches, synagogues, scout troops, YMCAs, and YWCAs; and special interest groups such as Parents without Partners and stepfamily associations. The number of families in each group with male and female children participating in each assessment wave is given in Table 1.

All families met the following criteria. Parents were Caucasian and had at least a high school education. Not more than four children resided at home. In stepfather families, the mother had been previously married and divorced only once, the stepfathers had either been married and divorced once or been single prior to the current marriage, and the children were from the mother's first marriage. At the time the study began, there were no children from the remarriages; one child was born to stepparents by Wave 2 and another to a different remarried couple by Wave 3.

[1] For ease of communication, the latter families are hereafter labeled simply "divorced."

TABLE 1

Number of Families and Target Children from the Longitudinal Sample Participating in Each Wave

	Nondivorced		Divorced		Remarried		
	Boys	Girls	Boys	Girls	Boys	Girls	Total
Wave 1	38	37	33	36	27	31	202
Wave 2	37	36	30	34	24	25	186
Wave 3	35	33	24	28	19	25	164

At the beginning of the study, one child between 9 and 13 years of age was designated the target child (M = 11 years, 5 months, SD = 1 year, 5 months). When more than one child in a family met the selection criterion, the child who helped maintain a relatively even age and gender balance across the three family groups was selected. Approximately three-fourths of these target children (153/202) had a brother or sister who was designated as the target sibling. When more than one potential target sibling existed, the child closest in age to the target child was selected. The mean age of the target siblings was 10 years, 10.5 months, with a range of 4 years, 7 months, to 17 years, 4 months. The mean age difference between the target sibling and the target child was 2 years, 8.5 months, with a range of 0 months to 7 years, 7 months. Although this is a wide age range, it should be noted that 95% of the siblings were within 5 years of age of the target children. Genders of the target siblings were approximately evenly distributed across family types and target boys and girls.

The three types of families were assessed for comparability on the demographic characteristics listed in Table 2. They proved similar in most respects except that parents in nondivorced families were slightly older and that the income of the one-parent households was lower even though their educational level was comparable. It seemed more reasonable to use single-mother families with an income typical of national figures than to seek a matched but atypical sample. Remarried and nonremarried mothers had been separated and divorced for approximately the same period of time, and the duration of that period was well past the initial 2-year transitional crisis period of divorce (Hetherington, 1989).

A higher proportion of nondivorced than divorced and remarried families had more than two children. This might be expected since the nondivorced women were married longer and thus had more time to have children. Thus, in terms of birth order, there was a larger percentage of first- and second-born target children in divorced and remarried families than in nondivorced families. The decision was made not to control for birth-order effects, however, because there is ample evidence to suggest

TABLE 2

DEMOGRAPHIC CHARACTERISTICS OF THE THREE TYPES OF FAMILIES

	NONDIVORCED		DIVORCED		REMARRIED		TOTAL SAMPLE	
	M	SD	*M*	SD	*M*	SD	*M*	SD
Mother's age[a]	38.3	4.46	36.5	3.99	34.6	3.97	36.7	4.38
Father's age[a]	40.2	5.62	...	...	35.5	6.62	38.2	6.45
Mother's education[a]	14.8	2.64	14.1	2.41	14.0	2.33	14.3	2.49
Father's education[a]	15.7	2.52	...	...	13.8	2.77	15.3	2.65
Total family income[b]	25–35		5–10		25–35		20–25	
Child's age[c] at:								
Final separation	...	...	6-6	2-6	5-10	2-8	6-8	2-5
Divorce	...	...	7-6	2-11	7-10	2-7	7-9	2-8
Remarriage	...	...	...	...	11-0	1-6	...	...
First interview	11-5	1-4	11-5	1-5	11-4	1-6	11-5	1-5
Time[c] between:								
Final separation and remarriage	...	...	...	...	5-1	2-1	...	...
Divorce and remarriage	...	...	...	...	3-1	2-7	...	...
Final separation and first interview	...	...	5-10	2-0	5-5	2-1	5-8	2-1
Divorce and first interview	...	...	3-11	2-9	3-5	2-0	3-8	2-5
Length of marriage at first interview[c]	17-11	5-6	...	...	0-4	0-2	...	...

[a] In years.
[b] In thousands on a categorical scale.
[c] In years-months.

that birth order alone accounts for only 1%–2% of the variance in many measures of children's adjustment (Plomin, 1986).

Eighty-one percent (*N* = 164) of the original 202 families were still involved in the study at Wave 3 (nondivorced, 90.66%; divorced, 75.36%; and remarried, 75.86%). Although the reasons for sample attrition varied (e.g., illness, problems, changes in custody, etc.), most families who left the study felt that the extensive interview and observational procedure took too much time and that scheduling these on consecutive evenings was difficult. This was particularly true of divorced families and stepfamilies, who were asked to complete a substantially larger battery of assessments.

Composite scores of positivity and negativity within family subsystem relationships as well as composite scores of child psychopathology and competence were examined to test for selective attrition. Despite the fact that the attrition rates for divorced families with boys (28%) and remarried families with boys (30%) were higher than the overall attrition rate (19%), measures of neither children's adjustment nor relationship negativity were found to contribute to attrition. A main effect was found for marital positivity. Married couples with lower positivity were more likely to drop out. However, as this proved to be the case across both nondivorced and remarried families, marital positivity was not considered to be a discriminating factor in attrition rates.

PROCEDURE

Each assessment wave involved structured interviews, observations, and standardized tests that required two to three sessions of 3 or more hours to complete, plus a battery of questionnaires and tests completed in the absence of interviewers. The parents were questioned jointly by a single interviewer. The interviewer read instructions, asked and answered questions, and guided the parents question by question through some of the more difficult questionnaires. Mothers and fathers recorded their responses independently on separate forms. The target children and target siblings were seen in a separate room by a second interviewer. All test items were read to younger children and children who had any reading problems. In one of the sessions families were videotaped during the dinner hour and in another during family problem-solving interactions.

In addition to the intrafamilial assessments, the biological fathers of children in single-parent and remarried families, the stepgrandparents of children in stepfamilies, and the grandparents of children in all family types were contacted by phone and mail whenever possible. Each respondent completed a battery of instruments assessing the frequency of contact and the quality of the relationship maintained with the target child. The biological fathers also completed measures of their parenting. Two of each target child's teachers, one in math or science and one in social studies or English, were contacted by phone or mail and asked to complete assessments of the child's cognitive, social, and personal competence as well as problem behaviors.

MEASURES

Measures were selected and constructed to collect similar information from different sources and through different methods. Some consisted of standardized tests or measures that had been used in previous research; some involved the modification of existing or unpublished scales or instruments; still others were developed for this study. Brief descriptions of the measures and the observational coding system used in analyses included in this *Monograph* are presented first. The description of each measure includes a summary of the standardized scales or the scales derived through data reduction if the measure was created or substantially modified. Cronbach's alphas for the latter scales are summarized in the text. A full table of alphas is available from the authors. The description of measures is followed by a detailed overview of the data reduction and analytic procedures employed.

The measures discussed in this report describe the marital, parent-child, and sibling relationships as well as individual adjustment. Appendix Table A1 contains a list of the instruments and derived measures discussed and includes respondents, assessment occasions, and factor information. Standardized measures are referenced and any modifications noted. A large set of other measures was used in the study but not included in the tables or analyses here. These measures included assessments of legal issues, conditions associated with the divorce and leading to the remarriage, the personality and mental health of the parents, stresses acting on and support systems available to parents and children, and extrafamilial relationships. Since this *Monograph* focuses on family relationships within the household, it does not include an analysis of the relationships with the noncustodial father/ex-spouse, although this information was collected.

Interview and Inventory Measures

Demographic and Historical Factors

Measures were constructed using items taken from the Zill and Furstenberg (1981) National Survey of Children, Wave 2. The eight measures provided social demographic information as well as information about each family's marital, financial, employment, residential, and child-care histories and religious preference (see Table A1, I).

Measures of Children's Adjustment

Measures of the target children's adjustment were selected and developed to allow for multiple assessments of behaviors indicative of internalizing or externalizing and of diverse aspects of social and cognitive/academic competence. A summary of the standardized child adjustment factors or the factors resulting from the data reduction conducted on modified measures, including persons reporting, availability at each wave, and factor information, is presented in Table A1, II.

Child Behavior Checklist.—This measure was developed by Achenbach and Edelbrock (Achenbach, 1978; Achenbach & Edelbrock, 1979, 1983; Edelbrock & Achenbach, 1984) as a way of assessing children's problem behaviors and competencies (see Table A1, IIA). Parents reported on the children's problem behaviors and competencies, while teachers reported only on problem behaviors. Test-retest reliabilities for the original measure based on a nonclinical sample have been shown to be .95 for the total behavior problems and .99 for the total competence score; interparental agreement has been shown to be .98 and .97, respectively (additional reliability information can be obtained from the *Manual for the Child Behavior Checklist,* Achenbach & Edelbrock, 1983).

The parent version of the checklist was slightly modified for this study in that 27 of the problem behavior items considered either to be inappropriate for children aged 9–13 or to be tapping extremely pathological behaviors were omitted. Following procedures suggested by Achenbach and Edelbrock (1983), raw scores on the 91 remaining items were converted to T scores on the basis of the broadband classifications of internalizing and externalizing. Clinical cutoffs of $T \geq 64$ for boys and $T \geq 63$ for girls for externalizing, $T \geq 64$ for internalizing, and $T \geq 64$ for total behavior problems were used.[2] In addition to the broadband problem behavior scores, a social competence score was calculated on the basis of mothers' and fathers' reports on the activities, social, and school scales. The total competence score was used as an assessment of overall social competence, and in some analyses the school scale was used by itself as a measure of scholastic competence. Teachers' reports of only internalizing and externalizing but not of competence were available for all children except those in divorced homes at Wave 3.

Child Competence Inventory.—This measure was derived from the Adolescent Q Sort developed by Baumrind (1979a). Children's self-reports were obtained using a modified format endorsed by Harter (1982). For each item, children were asked first to decide which of the descriptions of children's behaviors or beliefs they were most like and then to rate whether it was "sort of true" or "really true," resulting in a four-point scale. The items were presented to parents in the original Q-Sort format. Only 56 of Baumrind's original 96 items were included, as we believed that these would provide adequate coverage of the social and cognitive competencies of children in the 9–15 age range. Because this measure is substantially modified from the original, it is referred to as the Child Competence Inventory to distinguish it from Baumrind's original measure (see Table A1, IIB).

Factor analyses of children's responses identified four competence factors. The *social responsibility* scale loaded on items assessing how easily children got along with others, how dependable, understanding, honest, obedi-

[2] Because of the reduced number of items and the retention of Achenbach and Edelbrock's original T-score criteria, psychopathology in the target children may have been underestimated.

ent, and modest they were, and how much they conformed to adult values and expectations. The *cognitive agency* scale included items assessing how persistent, productive, self-controlled, well organized, and hard working the children were as well as how well they did in school and whether they sought intellectual challenges. The *sociability* scale included items measuring whether children were friendly to other children and adults, enjoyed social interactions, were poised and socially competent, and had a good sense of humor. The final scale, *energetic/attractive/popular,* included items that indicated whether children were involved in activities and were physically attractive, popular, physically fit, energetic, and graceful. These four competence factors were replicated with both mothers' and fathers' data.

Cronbach's alphas for the social responsibility, cognitive agency, sociability, and energetic/attractive/popular factors were found to range across family members' reports and across waves from .59 to .72 (M = .66), from .75 to .84 (M = .79), from .44 to .70 (M = .60), and from .60 to .75 (M = .65), respectively. Thirty-two of the 36 (89%) internal reliability alphas were .60 or above. Test-retest reliabilities for the child and parent versions of the Child Competence Inventory were calculated on a separate sample of families for 80 mothers, 54 fathers, and 80 children in the same age range as those who participated in this study. Test-retest reliabilities based on two administrations of the test 2 months apart for the social responsibility, cognitive agency, sociability, and energetic/attractive/popular scales were, respectively, .84, .77, .75, and .68 for mothers' reports, .80, .71, .74, and .65 for fathers' reports, and .76, .67, .69, and .72 for children's self-reports.

Perceived Competence Scale for Children.—This 28-item teacher version of Harter's (1982) Perceived Competence Scale for Children summarized children's cognitive, social, and physical competencies and general self-worth as perceived by their teachers. The original standardized scores were used here. Internal consistency reliabilities for teachers' ratings for the scales have been shown to be .96, .93, .94, and .93, respectively (Harter, 1982; see Table A1, IIC).

Behavior Events Inventory.—This 32-item inventory is a modified version of a checklist devised by Patterson (1982) to assess coercive family processes by focusing on coercive and antisocial behaviors. In contrast to Patterson's original scale, the expanded version used in this study placed additional emphasis on prosocial behaviors such as kindness, empathy, and constructive activities. It also included items dealing with depression, loneliness, and physical complaints. Prior to each interview, parents and children were asked to indicate whether children had demonstrated these behaviors within the past 24 hours (see Table A1, IID).

Through factor analyses, four scales were identified from children's self-reports and three from parents' reports. Analysis of the children's self-reports revealed a *prosocial* scale, which assessed whether children had shared with someone, helped someone, studied, and demonstrated sympathy, empathy, or affection in the last 24 hours; a *coercive behavior* scale, which assessed whether children had whined, nagged, been noncompliant or verbally aggressive, or had a temper tantrum; a *depression* scale, which summarized evidence of loneliness, unhappiness, fear, or psychosomatic complaints; and a *delinquent behavior* scale, which included reports of stealing, physical aggression, sexuality, drug and alcohol use, and truancy.

The analysis of mothers' and fathers' reports revealed prosocial behavior, coercive behavior, and depression scales identical in structure to those derived from the children's self-ratings. However, the delinquent behavior scale could not be identified in parents' reports owing to the extremely low frequency of reports of such behaviors. It seems likely that parents did not know that their children were involved in these activities. Across waves and across persons reporting, the Cronbach's alphas for the prosocial behavior, coercive behavior, and depression scales ranged from .61 to .79 (M = .69), from .65 to .85 (M = .74), and from .52 to .69 (M = .62), respectively. The range of alphas for the children's reports of delinquent behavior was from .58 to .70 (M = .64). All but three (90%) of the alphas were at or above .60. Two-month test-retest reliabilities on the prosocial behavior, coercive behavior, and depression scales have been shown to be, respectively, .89, .92, and .69 for mothers' reports; .86, .87, and .65 for fathers' reports; and .78, .72, and .83 for children's reports. For children's delinquent behavior, 2-month test-retest reliability was .85.

Adult Depression

The 21-item Beck Depression Inventory (1967) was used as an index of parental depression. A single score assessing level of depression was obtained for each parent by summing each parent's responses on the 21 items (see Table A1, III).

Family Process: Marital Relationship

Measures of the marital relationship were selected to assess relationship satisfaction and conflict as well as the degree to which spouses shared household responsibilities. Husbands and wives in nondivorced and remarried families completed the full set of measures. A summary of the standardized scales and of the scales resulting from the factor analyses of new or modified measures, and including person reporting and availability at each wave, is presented in Table A1, IV.

Dyadic Adjustment scale.—Spanier's (1976) standardized Dyadic Adjustment scale was used to assess the harmony of the marital relationship on four subscales—satisfaction, expressiveness, cohesiveness, and consensus—and on a total marital adjustment scale. Internal reliability for the total marital adjustment scale has been shown to be .96, while the coefficient alphas for the four subscales vary from .73 to .94 (see Table A1, IVA).

Child-rearing Issues: Self and Spouse.—On this 22-item questionnaire constructed for this study, husbands and wives used a seven-point scale to rate an important aspect of the marital relationship not assessed by the Dyadic Adjustment scale, namely, the frequency of spousal disagreements over child-rearing issues (see Table A1, IVB). Two spousal conflict scales were identified through factor analysis: conflict over target children's performance of *daily routines* and conflict over *adolescent issues.* The daily routines scale indexed the frequency of spousal conflict over the target children's responses to parental authority and the children's compliance with the daily routines of chores, homework, bedtime, manners, etc. The adolescent issues scale assessed the frequency of conflict over matters such as the children's curfew, activities when away from home, dating behavior, and use of cigarettes, alcohol, or drugs. Across waves and across husbands' and wives' reports, Cronbach's alphas ranged from .79 to .94 (M = .87) for the daily routines scale and from .70 to .78 (M = .75) for the adolescent issues scale.

In addition to the Child-rearing Issues measure, a *Family Conflict* questionnaire, which included twelve items from the Zill and Furstenberg (1981) National Survey of Children, Wave 2, was administered to family members. A single five-point item from this questionnaire was used to assess the frequency of marital disagreements not related to child rearing.

Child-rearing Roles and Housekeeping Roles.—Two seven-item assessments of husbands' and wives' roles were taken from Baumrind's (1979b) longitudinal study of the familial antecedents of substance abuse (see Table A1, IVC, IVD). Only one five-point item from each measure was used in the analyses reported here. Each asked the responding spouse to indicate the degree to which he or she assumed responsibility for child rearing and housekeeping. High ratings (4, 5) on these items indicated that the husbands assumed most of the responsibility, low scores (1, 2) the wives; a rating of 3 meant that the respondent believed that both husband and wife shared the responsibility about equally.

Measures of the Parent-Child Relationship

Measures of parenting were selected and developed to allow for multiple assessments of the dimensions of warmth, negativity, control, monitoring, and discipline, which have been shown in previous research to be related to children's adjustment (Patterson, 1989; for a review of this literature, see Maccoby & Martin, 1983), and to distinguish between nondivorced,

divorced, and remarried families (Hetherington, 1988, 1989; for a review, see Hetherington et al., 1989). In addition, measures of the frequency of parent-child conflict were administered. Parents and children completed corresponding versions of the same questionnaires assessing the parent-child relationship. Each parent or stepparent completed the full set of parenting measures describing his or her relationship with the target child. Each also completed the Assessment of Child Monitoring, Parenting Practices, and Assessment of Parent and Child questionnaires describing his or her spouse's relationship with the child. Target children completed each measure twice, once for their relationship with the mother and once for their relationship with the father or stepfather. In addition, mothers and target children in single-parent and remarried families completed the Assessment of Parent and Child indices regarding the children's relationships with the nonresidential fathers.

The data reduction conducted on the parent-child relationship measures resulted in 11 scales: three factors reflecting aspects of parental warmth and involvement and two each reflecting control, monitoring, discipline, and parent-child conflict. A summary of these scales, including person reporting and waves available, is presented in Table A1, V.

Expression of Affection.—This 19-item instrument was adapted from one used by Patterson (1982) in his research on families of coercive and antisocial children. The form asks the parents and children to rate the frequency with which they have jointly engaged in various activities or behaviors in the past week or month on a seven-point scale (see Table A1, VA). Factor analyses identified an expressive affection and an instrumental affection scale. The former measured how often the parent hugged, spent time alone with, or laughed, talked, or joked with the child; the latter assessed how frequently the parent engaged in joint activities with the child. Cronbach's alphas across parents' and children's reports and across waves ranged from .75 to .86 (M = .82) for the expressive affection scale and from .62 to .80 (M = .72) for the instrumental affection scale. Two-month test-retest reliabilities across parents' reports have been shown to range from .78 to .87 for the former and from .76 to .83 for the latter.

Assessment of Child Monitoring.—The 21-item Assessment of Child Monitoring measure was based directly on items in the parental authority-directiveness dimension of Baumrind's (1978, 1979b) parental behavior Q Sort. However, rather than using the Q-Sort card method, the items were presented in the form of five-point rating scales. The items assessed the extent to which parents were aware of, attempted to control, and succeeded in controlling seven domains of the target children's behavior (see Table A1, VB). Four factors emerged from factor analyses of this instrument. The first two reflected two dimensions of parental monitoring and the second two tapped corresponding dimensions of parental control. The first monitoring scale assessed the extent of parents' knowledge of behaviors related to their children's *character development,* including who their friends were, how and what children were doing in school, and children's intellectual interests. The second assessed parents' awareness of any *deviant behaviors* engaged in by target children. The two corresponding control scales measured how much influence parents had in shaping behaviors related to the children's *character development* and in discouraging the children's *deviant behavior.* Cronbach's alphas across parents' and children's reports and across waves ranged from .49 to .87 (M = .71) for the monitoring scales and from .47 to .90 (M = .76) for the control scales. Overall, 87.5% of the internal reliability alphas were .60 or above. Two-month test-retest reliabilities have been shown to range from .68 to .81 for the monitoring scales and from .70 to .77 for the control scales.

Child-rearing Issues: Parent and Child.—This 37-item questionnaire was constructed for this study to assess parent-child agreement on rules and disciplinary practices. The first 22 items corresponded to the items on the Child-rearing Issues: Self and Spouse measure; the parent and child used a seven-point scale to rate the frequency of parent-child conflict in the past week or month. On the remaining 15 items, parents and children used the same seven-point scale to rate the frequency of each parent's use of different discipline techniques (see Table A1, VC).

Factor analyses revealed two factors of parent-child conflict and two of parental discipline style. The two conflict factors were identical to the two spousal conflict factors. The *daily routines* scale reflected the frequency of conflict over parental authority and children's compliance with the daily routines of chores, homework, bedtime, manners, etc. The *adolescent issues* scale assessed the frequency of parent-child conflict over such matters as curfew, activities when away from home, dating behavior, and children's use of cigarettes, alcohol, and drugs. A *nagging communication* about discipline scale indexed how frequently parents talked with children about what they had done wrong, explained why rules are important, etc., and a second discipline scale, *negative sanctions,* assessed how frequently parents used such measures as yelling, physical punishment, or the removal of privileges. Cronbach's alphas across parents' and children's reports and across waves ranged from .58 to .91 (M = .77) for the conflict factors and from .64 to .88 (M = .79) for the discipline factors. Overall, 97.9% of the internal reliability alphas were .60 or above. Two-month test-retest reliabilities across persons' reports have been shown to range from .63 to .72 for the parent-child conflict scales and from .65 to .88 for the discipline style scales.

Parenting Practices.—The Parenting Practices scale constructed for this study assessed different aspects of parenting style, including warmth, quality of communication, and involvement. Both mothers and fathers were asked to rate these items for the current period; additionally, single and remarried mothers rated them for the period immediately following the divorce and the latter also for the period immediately preceding the remarriage. The measure consists of 10 identical seven-point rating scales for each time period assessed; only results pertaining to the current parent-child relationship are discussed here (see Table A1, VD).

The single factor to emerge from factor analyses of the items assessing the current parenting style tapped the dimension of parent-child *rapport* and included global assessments of the level of each parent's involvement with the target child, how affectionate and responsive the parent was, how well the parent communicated with the child, and how much he or she enjoyed being the child's parent. One additional item—how well the parent got along with the child, taken from the Zill and Furstenberg (1981) National Survey of Children, Wave 2—was included in the rapport scale since both the mothers' and the fathers' responses proved to be highly correlated with the six parent rapport items on the Parenting Practices instrument. Cronbach's alphas across husbands' and wives' reports and across waves ranged from .76 to .90 (M = .84). Two-month test-retest reliabilities for the mothers' and fathers' reports of rapport have been shown to be .87 and .91, respectively. Since children did not complete the Parenting Practices questionnaire, a rapport scale based on children's reports was not available.

Measures of the Sibling Relationship

Sibling Inventory of Behavior.—This 49-item inventory completed by mothers, fathers, and target children is an expanded version of Schaefer and Edgerton's (1981) 28-item Sibling Inventory of Behavior, reflecting the behavior of the target children toward the target siblings on a variety of dimensions (see Table A1, VI). Twenty-one additional items developed for this study were pooled with the original items; data reduction via factor analysis resulted in six sibling relationship scales: *involvement, empathy, rivalry, avoidance, aggression,* and *teaching.* Cronbach's alphas across parents' and children's reports and across waves ranged from .86 to .93 (M = .91) for the involvement scale, from .64 to .89 (M = .83) for the empathy scale, from .61 to .89 (M = .78) for the rivalry scale, from .75 to .88 (M = .81) for the avoidance scale, from .77 to .90 (M = .86) for the aggression scale, and from .60 to .81 (M = .73) for the teaching scale.

Observational Assessments

Videotapes of 10-min problem-solving interactions between husband and wife, parent and child, and child and sibling as well as mother-father-child triadic situations were made in the home. Only two dyadic problem-solving observations were possible in the one-parent families. In addition, observations were made of a 30-min unstructured segment of the family at dinner. For the husband-wife dyad, topics discussed in the problem-solving interactions were selected from those identified by either spouse as areas of conflict on the Dyadic Adjustment or Child-rearing Issues scales. For the parent-child dyadic and triadic interactions, items were selected from those the participants had identified as frequent topics of disagreement on the Child-rearing Issues scale. Prior to videotaping the child-sibling discussion, both children completed a Sibling Interaction Task scale on which each identified topics of frequent disagreement such as taking things from the other, being bothersome when the sibling was with friends, not performing the proper share of chores, etc. Discussion items were then selected from among those identified as areas of conflict by either one or both of the siblings.

At the start of each problem-solving segment, participating family members were given a slip of paper with two topics listed and were told that the topics were reported to be frequent sources of disagreement between spouses, parents and children, or siblings. They were instructed to discuss one or both topics and to try to come to some resolution. The investigator then left the room and returned after 10 min. No specific instructions were given at the start of the dinner-table interactions.

Each family videotape was rated by a single coder who first rated each problem-solving and dinner-table segment separately. Within segments, each family member's behavior toward all other family members was rated separately; thus, for example, in a mother-child observation, the mother's behavior toward the child was rated separately from the child's behavior toward her. Ratings were global assessments based on both the intensity and the frequency of behaviors. After viewing and coding each segment separately, overall ratings based on a re-review of a family member's behavior toward all other family members across all situations were made. These cross-situational ratings were used in this report.

The Family Interaction Coding System, which was developed for this study, includes 14 five-point rating scales used to assess various aspects of the processes of family interactions. Nine of these indexed spouses', parents', children's, and siblings' hostility/rejection, warmth/involvement, dominance/power, assertiveness, coercion, communication skills, self-disclosure, mood, and transactional conflict. Two additional scales reflected the degree of parental influence and monitoring, and three others reflected the degree to which the children and their siblings were prosocial, antisocial, and shy or withdrawn during interactions. In addition, four scales reflecting parenting and two reflecting the family environment were coded but are not used in this *Monograph.* These scales were based on Baumrind's (1967) parenting typologies and Olson's (Olson, Portner, & Bell, 1982) circumplex model. Across all observational rating scales, each point was defined by specific behaviors that described both the frequency and the intensity of the types of behaviors the given rating would indicate. An example of one of the observational codes, hostility/rejection, can be found in Appendix B.

Thirty-seven percent of the tapes within each wave of assessment were randomly selected to be scored by a second coder. Intercoder reliabilities were calculated for each score awarded to each family member at both the segment and the overall cross-situational levels. Moreover, reliabilities were assessed in three ways: percentage agreement, correlations, and weighted kappas. Weighted kappas were used as they are viewed as more appropriate for rating scales than unweighted kappas (Cohen, 1968). The mean percentage agreement for the factors derived through data reduction and based on the overall ratings used in analyses reported in this *Monograph* was 82 (range = 73–89). The mean Spearman correlation was 70 (range = 50–82). Only two correlations fell below .60, and both were significant at the .001 level. The mean weighted kappa was 77 (range = 61–86).

Data reduction was conducted separately on the process scores of each family member's behavior toward all other members (See App. Table A2). For adults' behavior toward their spouses and children, two factors were identified through the data reduction of the nine observational process scales: positivity, which included warmth/involvement, assertiveness, communication, self-disclosure, and mood; and negativity, which included hostility/rejection, coercion, and transactional conflict. Positivity and negativity factors for children's behavior toward their parents and siblings paralleled those identified for adults, except that mood did not load on either factor. Cronbach's alphas across ratings and across waves ranged from .56 to .86 (M = .75) for the positivity dimension and from .66 to .94 (M = .82) for the negativity dimension. Twenty-three of the 24 (95.8%) positivity dimension alphas and 100% of the negativity dimension alphas were above .60.

A third factor, parental control, was also identified for parents' behavior toward children. This factor included dominance/power, parental influence, and monitoring. Cronbach alphas across ratings of mothers and fathers and across waves ranged from .65 to .79 (M = .72).[3] Spouse-to-spouse, child-to-sibling, sibling-to-child, and child-to-parent dominance/power did not load on any factors.

Finally, single-item scales measuring target children's prosocial, antisocial, and shy-withdrawn behaviors toward mothers, fathers, and siblings were used as observational assessments of children's social adjustment.

[3] Factor scores for parental control are not presented in Chap. V as separate monitoring and control composites were created for this chapter.

PRELIMINARY ANALYSES AND DATA REDUCTION

The first stage of analysis was an attempt to construct cross-assessment dimensions reflecting marital, parent-child, and sibling relationships as well as children's adjustment and to improve the psychometric properties of the subscales of each family process dimension by shifting items grouped by statistical data reduction techniques. However, not surprisingly, it was found that family members' reports of relationships and adjustment sometimes differed from observers' ratings. Consequently, data reduction was conducted separately on questionnaire and on observational data and separately for each assessment wave. Since, as noted above, not all measures of relationships and adjustment were completed by all respondents, data reduction was also conducted separately on wives', husbands', mothers', fathers', children's, and teachers' reports and on observation-based scores of wives, husbands, mothers, fathers, and children. With the exception of the one factor that assesses parental rapport with the child, all factors were derived from single measures.

Prior to statistical analyses, all individual items were rescaled in the same direction to remedy variability in scaling. All scores were converted to *Z* scores by means of the CONDESCRIPTIVE subprogram of SPSS (Nie, Hull, Jenkins, Steinbrenner, & Bent, 1975). Data reduction was conducted on these standardized scores; however, raw means and scale ranges are shown in the tables to permit comparison of results presented here with those reported by other investigators.

Owing to the complexity of the assessment battery and our concern to derive process dimensions marked by internal cohesiveness as well as among-dimension distinctiveness, three different methods of statistical analysis were used; each is described below.

The first method used to investigate the appropriateness of proposed dimensions employed image analysis with Procrustes rotation of the extracted factors. The standardized items believed to tap the domains in question were analyzed using the FACTOR procedure available through SAS (SAS Institute, 1985). A target matrix was established composed of ones, zeros, and negative ones. In each case, the pattern of loadings of the target matrix was based on the a priori factor structure; nonzero elements represented the proposed manifestations of each factor, and negative elements indicated that the variable was assumed to load negatively on that factor.

The factors extracted from the data set by means of image analysis were rotated to this target matrix. The adequacy of the factor structure was based on an examination of the factor-loading matrix. The fit of the data to the target matrix was judged to be acceptable when items had factor loadings at or above .35 on their proposed factors and below .35 on all other factors. The alignment of items in the target matrix was modified on the basis of the results of each run. Loading patterns and conceptual issues were used to determine when variables should be moved between factors and/or dropped from subsequent analyses.

The second method used to establish major dimensions employed maximum likelihood estimation and promax rotation in untargeted factor analyses. The untargeted factor techniques allowed the items to align themselves according to relations present in the data, and we believed that possible errors in the conceptualization of dimensions would be brought into focus through this method.

In contrast to the previous method, in these analyses the number of factors was not limited to the number of a priori dimensions, and solutions with varying numbers of factors were examined. The decision concerning the appropriate number in the given data set was based on the largest number of factors obtainable for which all eigenvalues were greater than or equal to one. This solution was chosen as the starting point for examining the alignment of items in the factor pattern matrix.

Items were deleted from the data set on the basis of both loadings and the interpretability of the emerging factors. Variables whose highest loadings were above .35 on factors in which they did not fit conceptually were deleted; this reduced data set was then refactored, and the resulting factor pattern matrix was again examined for interpretability. This procedure of deleting variables and refactoring was repeated until the highest loadings above .35 of each item resulted in an interpretable factor solution. This provisionally chosen solution was then examined for variables that failed to achieve salient loadings on any factor; such items were deleted, and the reduced set was refactored to establish the appropriate number of factors. These steps were repeated until an acceptable factor pattern was achieved.

In the last stage of data reduction, the internal reliability of each provisionally established factor was tested following a progression of steps outlined by Patterson and Bank (1986, 1987) and using the SPSS subprogram RELIABILITY. The standardized item alpha was used to assess the internal consistency of each factor along with the item total correlations. In keeping with the criteria chosen by Patterson and Bank, the values of alpha coefficients had to be .60 or greater and those of item total correlations .20 or better.

These procedures were repeated for all proposed dimensions at every wave in order to identify factors that were consistent over time. In addition, we wished to identify factors that were consistent over different raters using identical measures. Thus, the factors listed in Table A1 are the best compromise between the information from data reduction and the desirability of maintaining comparability over raters and over time. As indicated in the previous description of measures, the standardized Cronbach's alphas for the final factors were high at all three waves.

OVERVIEW OF ANALYSES

Analyses were conducted within waves in order to assess adjustment and family relationships at each time point and across waves in order to assess both individuals' adjustment over time and changes in family relationships related to target children's entry into adolescence together with the concurrent stresses associated with family transition into a married state.

Composite Variables

Two sets of composite variable scores were created from the measures listed in Table A1; one was used for within-wave analyses and the other for across-wave analyses. Descriptions of each composite's variables are presented in Appendix Table A2.

Within-Wave Composite Variables

The standard *Z* scores for the scales included in a composite were summed and divided by the number of available scales; average composite scores were created because the number of scores available varied by family type (residential fathers' and spousal reports were unavailable for divorced families).

Across-Wave Composite Scores

Each within-wave standardized composite had a mean of 0 and a standard deviation of 1.0. However, because these means and standard deviations represented the distribution of scores within time points, across-wave mean comparisons utilizing these values would not give an accurate picture of changes. To correct for this problem, across-wave composite scores were created for Waves 2 and 3 by standardizing according to the means and standard deviations obtained at Wave 1 for each scale. Thus, these Wave 2 and Wave 3 composite scores indicated the degree to which each differed from the Wave 1 score.

Analyses and Related Issues

Within-Wave Analyses

Analyses of variance (ANOVAs) were conducted on each within-wave composite variable using the SPSS-ANOVA program to assess effects due to family type and children's gender as well as to their interaction; because of unequal sample sizes, unique sums of squares were used in all analyses.

In addition, multiple analyses of variance (MANOVAs) were conducted on subgroupings of the scales that composed the composites, with data from each respondent analyzed separately. Appendix Table A3 lists all the dependent variables in each MANOVA and ANOVA.

Presentation of the MANOVAs includes discussions of univariate results when the initial multivariate main effects or interactions proved significant or when considering univariate contrasts shed light on the validity of a priori hypotheses. In addition, some planned comparisons of family-type differences within children's gender, and of children's-gender differences within family types, were undertaken on the basis of previous research findings. These planned comparisons were made post hoc even in the absence of significant multivariate effects. The results of post hoc analyses are italicized in the tables and should be interpreted with caution. The hypotheses that led to all univariate and planned comparisons are outlined at the beginning of each chapter.

Across-Wave Analyses

These also were conducted at both the composite and the scale levels. The across-wave analyses were conducted in two phases. First, across-wave autocorrelations of composites and scales were run using the SPSS PEARSON CORR program; these provided an assessment of behavior stability within groups. Second, repeated-measures analyses were conducted on both composites and scales to test wave effects and thus to assess short-term changes (between Wave 1 and Wave 2) and long-term changes (between Wave 1 and Wave 3). In all repeated-measures analyses, family type and child gender served as between-subjects factors, while wave (time) served as the within-subjects factor.

Sample Sizes and Results

In order to capitalize on the larger samples available in the early waves, within-wave analyses were conducted using the full sample available for the given time; across-wave analyses were restricted to subjects who participated at both time periods in question. Thus, within-wave and across-wave means and standard deviations differ slightly. To conserve space, only within-wave means and standard deviations of composites are given in the tables; across-wave scale statistics are included in the text at points where significant effects are discussed.

Parenting Typologies

Parenting typologies were developed through cluster analyses. Using the K-MEANS program of BMDP (Dixon & Brown, 1979), a series of cluster analyses were run on the positivity/warmth, control, monitoring, and negativity/conflict composites. Mothers' and fathers' data within each wave were clustered separately, and the degree to which within-wave parenting classification shifted over time was examined.

A series of chi squares was then conducted to examine, within waves, the association between family-type × child-gender groups and the parenting typologies. We attempted to repeat the chi square analyses including wave as an independent variable so as to test possible family-type differences in how much parenting classifications changed over time, but problems of sample size made it impossible. Therefore, two cluster analyses were conducted within each wave, one in which mothers' data were clustered and one in which fathers' data were clustered.

Relations among Family Subsystems and Children's Adjustment

Subsequent to analyses of differences within each family subsystem and in children's adjustment, the question of how these interrelated was examined in Chapter VI. First, Pearson correlations between the composite dimensions of children's adjustment and of parenting were calculated, and significant differences among these were examined as a function of family type and child gender (correlations were calculated within as well as across values). Second, the relations between parenting typologies identified in Chapter V were examined through a series of ANOVAs and repeated-measures MANOVAs in which the between-group factors were family type and parenting type.

Third, Pearson correlations between the dimensions of children's adjustment and of the marital and sibling relationships were calculated. In addition, correlations among dimensions of positivity and negativity across family subsystems were calculated in order to explore how relationships affected one another. Significant differences between these correlations as a function of family type and children's gender were also examined. In order to determine the relative importance of family relationships for children's adjustment and to identify whether these relations were direct or indirect, path analyses were conducted on the composite scores. Separate path analyses were performed for each family-type × child-gender group.

Finally, the transactions between family relationships and children's adjustment over time were examined, and hypotheses about causal direction were tested. Cross-lagged panel regressions were used for these analyses, in which scores from a previous wave were partialed out of scores at a later wave. This permitted an examination of the extent to which family relationships and children's adjustment affected change in one another over time. To parallel the format of the previous chapters, cross-lagged expressions were conducted first on the scores between Wave 1 and Wave 2 and next on the scores between Wave 1 and Wave 3. Because sample size precluded simultaneous examination of all family subsystems, only two-wave, two-variable models were tested. In addition, the decision was made to focus the examination of differences on transaction effects by family type across children's gender, again because of sample size restrictions.

III. THE ADJUSTMENT OF CHILDREN IN NONDIVORCED, DIVORCED SINGLE-MOTHER, AND REMARRIED FAMILIES

Marjorie S. Lindner, Margaret Stanley Hagan, and Jeanne Cavanaugh Brown

In this chapter, we examine the adjustment of children in nondivorced, divorced, and remarried families as a function of family structure and children's gender. Stability and changes in adjustment as all children moved into adolescence and as those in remarried families became increasingly accustomed to the presence of their stepfather are also examined. On the basis of past research findings (see Chap. I), the following hypotheses were proposed.

First, we expected that children in nondivorced families would be more socially responsible and academically competent and would exhibit fewer behavioral and emotional problems than children in either divorced, one-parent households or stepfamilies (Baumrind, 1989; Bray, 1988; Guidubaldi, 1988; Hetherington et al., 1982, 1985; Zill & Peterson, 1983).

Second, since this study involved early adolescents, we expected both boys and girls in the one-parent households to show more problems in adjustment than children in nondivorced homes. Given the patterns of coercive negativity that often characterize mother-son relationships in divorced mother-custody families (Hetherington, 1988), we expected boys' maladjustment in all three waves to be particularly evident in mothers' reports of externalizing and coercive behaviors and in observers' reports of boys' antisocial behavior toward mothers. We expected both sons and daughters of divorced, unremarried mothers to report a higher frequency of delinquent behavior, related to the inadequate levels of parental monitoring sometimes seen in single-parent homes (Baumrind, 1989), and, for girls in particular, we thought that this elevated level of delinquent behavior would emerge as they moved further into adolescence and developed heterosexual interests (Hetherington, 1972, 1989).

Third, we expected teachers—who have been shown to have negative perceptions of children in one-parent households (Ball, Newman, & Scheuren, 1984)—to report more deviance in the behavior of children in divorced families than in the behavior of those in other family groups.

Fourth, in the months immediately following their mothers' remarriages, we expected stepchildren to exhibit the highest levels of behavioral and emotional problems and the lowest levels of competence of all children in the study. By the third wave, however, 26 months after remarriage, improvements in their adjustment were anticipated.

Fifth, we expected differences between stepchildren and children from nondivorced families to be most marked in disruptive interactions within the family. In light of the difficulties that divorced mothers often have with their sons, we expected remarried mothers to continue to describe their sons' externalizing as more severe than that of their daughters. Conversely, we expected stepfathers to view the behavior of their stepdaughters as more negative than that of their stepsons, as past studies of relationships within stepfamilies involving younger children have found the most sustained adverse relationships occurring between stepfathers and stepdaughters (Brand et al., 1988; Hetherington, 1990; Zill & Peterson, 1983).

Sixth, we expected girls to exhibit more social competence and less externalizing than boys (Baumrind, 1989; Emery, 1982; Hetherington, 1988); predictions about internalizing could not be made since the literature is inconsistent in this regard (Baumrind, 1989; Emery, 1982; Zill & Peterson, 1983).

Finally, with the exception of problems involving sexual activities and substance abuse, we anticipated decreases in behavior problems and increases in competence for all children as they moved further into adolescence (Baumrind, 1991; Hetherington, 1989; Hill, Holmbeck, Marlow, Green, & Lynch, 1985a, 1985b; Steinberg, 1981).

The following overview of findings reveals that these hypotheses were partially supported.

OVERVIEW OF FINDINGS

Five findings were notable in our analyses of children's adjustment in the three family groups.

First, when significant differences in adjustment between children in different family groups were obtained, they were almost invariably in the direction of children in the nondivorced group being perceived as more socially and scholastically competent and as exhibiting fewer problems in adjustment than those in either the remarried or the divorced single-mother households.

Second, in contrast to previous findings with younger children (Hetherington et al., 1985), there were few gender differences in the way that children adjusted to their mothers' divorce or remarriage. Gender differences obtained were primarily attributable to parents' and teachers' tendencies to see girls as better adjusted than boys, regardless of family type.

Third, all respondents across settings concurred that children from divorced single-mother homes were still demonstrating difficulties in adjustment, both at home and at school, 4–6 years after the divorce. In remarried families, difficulties were reported by parents, and to some extent by the observers, but not by teachers or the children themselves.

Fourth, contrary to our hypothesis that stepfathers would describe greater maladjustment for their stepdaughters than for their stepsons, the paucity of significant family type × gender interactions suggested that parents across all family types perceived their sons as less well adjusted than their daughters.

Finally, stepchildren demonstrated less adaptation to the remarriage than we had anticipated. These children did show declines in problem behavior over the course of the study, but these changes were attributable only to sample-wide declines in problem behavior. Thus, children in remarried families continued to demonstrate greater problems in adjustment than children in nondivorced families throughout the 26 months of the study, despite the fact that most respondents indicated improved adjustment for all children on specific assessments from time 1 to time 3.

METHOD

The emphasis in the following discussion will be on integrating and highlighting the most consistent and robust findings across the various measures of children's adjustment. Our aim was to identify patterns of adjustment as children entered adolescence, especially patterns that characterize the adjustment of children who were simultaneously confronted with the normative developmental tasks of adolescence and the nonnormative transition to a stepfamily.

Four dimensions of children's psychosocial adjustment were of interest: disruptive, antisocial, *externalizing* behavior; depressed, withdrawn, *internalizing* behavior; prosocial, responsible, *socially competent* behavior; and *scholastic competence*. These dimensions were assessed through observational, interview, and questionnaire measures from observers, parents, children, and teachers individually and also by multimethod/multirespondent composite indices whenever possible. The instruments and procedures used to assess these dimensions of children's adjustment are described in Chapter II.

Our presentation focuses on a discussion of the differences in children's adjustment within each wave, which is followed by a section on the stability and changes over time in children's adjustment. Two points need to be kept in mind when examining the analyses that follow. First, teachers' reports and observational measures for children in one-parent households were not obtained in the last assessment wave; hence, the absence of a reported effect is not analogous to an absence of differences. Second, because no internally reliable multimethod/multirespondent composite index of internalizing behavior could be derived, no internalizing composite is included in the presentation of the results of the analyses.

Only within-wave analyses for *all* measures are given in the tables. To conserve space, repeated-measures analyses of short-term (Wave 1 to Wave 2) and long-term (Wave 1 to Wave 3) changes are given in the tables only for the multimethod/multirespondent composite indices. Since no composite index of internalizing was available, mothers' and fathers' reports on the internalizing subscale of the Child Behavior Checklist are included in the tables to exemplify changes over time on this dimension.

WITHIN-WAVE DIFFERENCES IN CHILDREN'S ADJUSTMENT

Within-wave differences in children's adjustment were first examined with multivariate and subsequent univariate analyses of the multimethod/multirespondent composite indices of externalizing, social competence, and scholastic competence; these results are presented in Tables 3 and 4. Second, multivariate and subsequent univariate analyses were performed on all available measures of externalizing, internalizing, social competence, and scholastic competence provided by a given set of respondents; these results are presented in Tables 5–10. In both sets of tables, presentation of multivariate F values and their associated significance levels precedes the presentation of the means, standard deviations, main and interaction effects, and univariate contrasts conducted to determine the direction of significant effects and/or to test a priori hypotheses on specific scales.

Gender Differences

On the multimethod/multirespondent composite indices, the only consistent gender difference indicated that girls were seen as more socially competent than boys at all three times of assessment; girls were also seen as more scholastically competent, but only at Wave 2 (see Table 4).

A more complex pattern of results emerged when the responses of mothers, fathers, children, teachers, and observers were examined separately (see Tables 5–10). This was due in part to the frequently noted incon-

TABLE 3

F VALUES AND SIGNIFICANCE LEVELS FOR MULTIVARIATE ANALYSES OF MULTIMETHOD/MULTIRESPONDENT COMPOSITE INDICES OF CHILDREN'S ADJUSTMENT

	Wave 1			Wave 2			Wave 3		
Effect	Family	Children's Gender	Interaction	Family	Children's Gender	Interaction	Family	Children's Gender	Interaction
Multivariate	7.28***	4.26***	.43	7.29***	12.13***	1.05	4.47***	3.67*	.85
Multivariate *df*	(6,388)	(3,194)	(6,388)	(6,356)	(3,178)	(6,356)	(6,312)	(3,156)	(6,312)
Externalizing composite	12.29***	.66	.29	11.63**	1.72	.81	8.49***	1.57	1.20
Social competence composite	19.23***	11.29***	.58	20.91***	31.09***	.52	9.41***	10.80***	1.02
Scholastic competence composite	4.98**	2.63	.06	4.67*	4.65*	1.53	4.18*	.19	1.67
Univariate *df*	(2,196)	(1,196)	(2,196)	(2,180)	(1,180)	(2,180)	(2,158)	(1,158)	(2,158)

NOTE.—Multivariate test is Wilks's lambda.

* $p \leq .05$.

** $p \leq .01$.

*** $p \leq .001$.

TABLE 4

Means (Standard Deviations) for the Multimethod/Multirespondent Composite Indices of Children's Adjustment (Standardized within Waves)

	Nondivorced		Divorced		Remarried		Significant Main Effects and Interactions	Significant Contrasts and Planned Comparisons
	Boys	Girls	Boys	Girls	Boys	Girls		
Multimethod/multirespondent composite:								
Externalizing:								
Wave 1	−.20 (.55)	−.28 (.53)	.24 (.72)	.11 (.52)	.15 (.43)	.17 (.54)	Family type	Div, Rem > Nondiv
Wave 2	−.10 (.67)	−.33 (.49)	.15 (.57)	.17 (.44)	.29 (.50)	.17 (.69)	Family type	Div, Rem > Nondiv
Wave 3	−.09 (.60)	−.30 (.50)	.07 (.66)	.16 (.81)	.37 (.41)	.14 (.48)	Family type	Div, Rem > Nondiv
Social competence:								
Wave 1	.16 (.44)	.29 (.40)	−.24 (.41)	.04 (.42)	−.35 (.53)	−.12 (.48)	Family type, gender	Nondiv > Div, Rem; Girls > Boys
Wave 2	.05 (.50)	.36 (.35)	−.25 (.35)	.05 (.42)	−.51 (.51)	−.06 (.42)	Family type, gender	Nondiv > Div > Rem; Girls > Boys
Wave 3	−.03 (.51)	.37 (.43)	−.13 (.62)	−.01 (.53)	−.37 (.46)	−.12 (.44)	Family type, gender	Nondiv, Div > Rem; Girls > Boys
Scholastic competence:								
Wave 1	.08 (.61)	.28 (.69)	−.23 (.82)	−.11 (.83)	−.23 (.77)	−.04 (.68)	Family type	Nondiv > Div, Rem
Wave 2	.05 (.70)	.29 (.61)	−.17 (.81)	−.18 (.80)	−.41 (.90)	.08 (.68)	Family type, gender	Nondiv > Div, Rem; Girls > Boys
Wave 3	.04 (.77)	.30 (.62)	−.08 (.72)	−.32 (.96)	−.20 (.68)	−.06 (.69)	Family type	Nondiv > Div, Rem

Note.—Nondiv = Nondivorced; Div = Divorced; Rem = Remarried.

TABLE 5

F Values and Significance Levels for Multivariate Analyses of Measures of Children's Adjustment for Each Respondent

Effect	Wave 1			Wave 2			Wave 3		
	Family	Children's Gender	Interaction	Family	Children's Gender	Interaction	Family	Children's Gender	Interaction
Externalizing:[a]									
Mothers' reports:									
Multivariate	7.64***	7.40***	1.13	6.84***	6.24**	1.21	7.70***	10.66***	1.19
Multivariate *df*	(4,390)	(2,195)	(4,390)	(4,342)	(2,171)	(4,342)	(4,310)	(2,155)	(4,310)
Externalizing[b]	12.26***	11.04**	1.57	10.96***	12.03***	2.31	13.79***	21.34***	2.19
Coercion[c]	.02	.04	.52	.56	.74	.67	.24	2.43	1.04
Univariate *df*	(2,196)	(1,196)	(2,196)	(2,172)	(1,172)	(2,172)	(2,156)	(1,156)	(2,156)
Fathers' reports:									
Multivariate	19.62***	7.16***	.23	20.89***	10.62***	.03	15.29***	6.76**	.17
Multivariate *df*	(2,128)	(2,128)	(2,128)	(2,112)	(2,112)	(2,112)	(2,106)	(2,106)	(2,106)
Externalizing	37.28***	9.45**	.34	39.28***	17.27***	.07	30.53***	13.24***	.05
Coercion	2.65	.22	.00	2.10	.02	.01	8.53**	4.65*	.16
Univariate *df*	(1,129)	(1,129)	(1,129)	(1,113)	(1,113)	(1,113)	(1,107)	(1,107)	(1,107)
Children's reports:									
Multivariate	2.12	7.55***	1.16	2.25	8.72***	.57	1.58	5.39**	.68
Multivariate *df*	(4,390)	(2,195)	(4,390)	(4,358)	(2,179)	(4,358)	(4,312)	(2,156)	(4,312)
Coercion	2.65	8.99**	1.53	.46	9.83**	.24	1.40	10.18**	1.32
Delinquency[c]	3.54*	.76	.82	4.42*	1.45	1.14	2.83	.15	.39
Univariate *df*	(2,196)	(1,196)	(2,196)	(2,180)	(1,180)	(2,180)	(2,157)	(1,157)	(2,157)
Internalizing:[d]									
Mothers' reports:									
Multivariate	2.96*	8.33***	.97	4.07**	12.70***	1.05	4.04**	13.73***	1.65
Multivariate *df*	(4,378)	(2,189)	(4,378)	(4,342)	(2,171)	(4,342)	(4,310)	(2,155)	(4,310)
Internalizing[e]	5.71**	11.37***	1.02	7.33***	9.08**	1.53	5.20**	17.63***	1.87
Depression[f]	.60	.34	1.72	.10	5.29*	1.50	2.07	3.00	2.40
Univariate *df*	(2,190)	(1,190)	(2,190)	(2,172)	(1,172)	(2,172)	(2,156)	(1,156)	(2,156)
Fathers' reports:									
Multivariate	10.49***	7.30**	.42	16.49***	7.68***	.81	9.14***	5.68**	.04
Multivariate *df*	(2,121)	(2,121)	(2,121)	(2,112)	(2,112)	(2,112)	(2,106)	(2,106)	(2,106)
Internalizing	19.84***	12.16***	.03	32.96***	13.38***	.25	18.26***	9.40**	.04
Depression	.16	.12	.63	1.79	.04	1.63	1.44	.03	.01
Univariate *df*	(1,122)	(1,122)	(1,122)	(1,113)	(1,113)	(1,113)	(1,107)	(1,107)	(1,107)

TABLE 5 (*Continued*)

Effect	Wave 1			Wave 2			Wave 3		
	Family	Children's Gender	Interaction	Family	Children's Gender	Interaction	Family	Children's Gender	Interaction
Social competence:[g]									
Mothers' reports:									
Multivariate	3.34***	1.18	.68	1.63	2.10	1.49	2.37*	2.37*	1.35
Multivariate *df*	(10,354)	(5,177)	(10,354)	(10,306)	(5,153)	(10,306)	(10.282)	(5,141)	(10,282)
Social competence[h]	6.23**	.21	.89	4.65*	.41	5.54**	5.03**	2.00	.08
Prosocial[i]	.58	1.44	.09	1.78	3.32	.20	.86	.46	.68
Social responsibility[j]	8.71***	1.07	1.01	2.65	6.97**	.74	4.48*	7.94**	2.08
Social agency[j]	1.58	.99	.07	.30	.04	.58	2.25	.15	2.47
Popular[j]	.69	1.64	.97	.16	.62	.67	.09	.00	2.05
Univariate *df*	(2,181)	(1,181)	(2,181)	(2,157)	(1,157)	(2,157)	(2,145)	(1,145)	(2,145)
Fathers' reports:									
Multivariate	9.74***	.94	.33	4.66***	1.12	.55	3.82**	1.88	.32
Multivariate *df*	(5,105)	(5,105)	(5,105)	(5,93)	(5,93)	(5,93)	(5,89)	(5,89)	(5,89)
Social competence	23.07***	2.22	.30	5.67*	.52	1.75	10.54**	2.59	.74
Prosocial	13.32***	3.64	.03	14.83***	5.10*	.21	1.16	7.83**	.21
Social responsibility	27.11***	.00	.01	8.89**	.37	.01	10.65**	.38	.05
Social agency	5.87*	.04	.97	1.04	.01	.79	1.07	.45	.33
Popular	.01	.01	.08	.14	.23	.38	.27	.23	.04
Univariate *df*	(1,109)	(1,109)	(1,109)	(1,97)	(1,97)	(1,97)	(1,93)	(1,93)	(1,93)
Children's reports:									
Multivariate	1.87	4.10**	1.00	1.73	10.15***	1.62	.77	5.19***	.49
Multivariate *df*	(8,386)	(4,193)	(8,386)	(8,348)	(4,174)	(8,348)	(8,302)	(4,151)	(8,302)
Prosocial	.42	12.91***	1.14	4.25*	32.43***	3.48*	.74	17.86***	.10
Social responsibility	2.42	.16	1.17	1.42	3.10	.25	.62	.18	1.14
Social agency	2.31	1.21	.02	.64	1.28	.60	1.41	.07	.84
Popular	.39	1.72	1.64	1.00	.59	.67	.29	.53	.09
Univariate *df*	(2,196)	(1,196)	(2,196)	(2,177)	(1,177)	(2,177)	(2,154)	(1,154)	(2,154)

Teachers' reports:									
Multivariate	3.01*	7.16**	.06	3.21*	15.37***	.29	.76	2.89	.77
Multivariate *df*	(4,318)	(2,159)	(4,318)	(4,220)	(2,110)	(4,220)	(2,59)	(2,59)	(2,59)
Self-worth[k]	5.95**	14.35***	.02	6.42**	31.00***	.09	1.46	3.56	.76
Social competence[k]	3.42*	7.19**	.04	3.21*	11.11**	.35	1.25	5.88*	.01
Univariate *df*	(2,160)	(1,160)	(2,160)	(2,111)	(1,111)	(2,111)	(1,60)	(1,60)	(1,60)
Scholastic competence:[l]									
Mothers' reports:									
Multivariate	2.42*	1.58	.30	3.26*	5.30**	1.65	3.63**	.48	1.23
Multivariate *df*	(4,390)	(2,195)	(4,390)	(4,336)	(2,168)	(4,336)	(4,308)	(2,154)	(4,308)
Scholastic competence[m]	4.87**	.00	.09	5.77**	3.05	3.29*	5.38**	.45	2.23
Cognitive agency[n]	.35	2.84	.49	.17	10.27**	.52	3.85*	.14	.07
Univariate *df*	(2,196)	(1,196)	(2,196)	(2,169)	(1,169)	(2,169)	(2,155)	(1,155)	(2,155)
Fathers' reports:									
Multivariate	6.87**	1.63	.33	3.00	4.09*	2.48	5.83**	5.24**	1.23
Multivariate *df*	(2,115)	(2,115)	(2,115)	(2,100)	(2,100)	(2,100)	(2,97)	(2,97)	(2,97)
Scholastic competence	11.14**	.85	.65	4.34*	6.30*	3.95*	11.29**	.04	.60
Cognitive agency	6.68*	3.12	.03	4.59*	5.90*	.00	.60	8.17**	.85
Univariate *df*	(1,116)	(1,116)	(1,116)	(1,101)	(1,101)	(1,101)	(1,98)	(1,98)	(1,98)

NOTE.—Multivariate test is Wilks's lambda.

[a] Because teachers' and observers' reports of externalizing consisted of single measures, no multivariate analyses could be performed for these respondents.

[b] Externalizing subscale of the Child Behavior Checklist.

[c] Coercion and delinquent subscales of the Behavior Events Inventory (24-Hour Checklist).

[d] Because children's, teachers', and observers' reports of internalizing consisted of single measures, no multivariate analyses could be performed for these respondents.

[e] Internalizing subscale of the Child Behavior Checklist.

[f] Depression subscale of the Behavior Events Inventory (24-Hour Checklist).

[g] Because observers' reports of social competence consisted of a single measure, no multivariate analyses could be performed for these respondents.

[h] Social competence subscale of the Child Behavior Checklist.

[i] Prosocial subscale of the Behavior Events Inventory (24-Hour Checklist).

[j] Social responsibility, social agency, and energetic/attractive/popular subscales of the Child Competence Inventory.

[k] General self-worth and social competence subscales from the Perceived Competence Scale for Children.

[l] Because children's and teachers' reports of scholastic competence consisted of a single measure, no multivariate analyses could be performed. There were no reports of scholastic competence by observers.

[m] Scholastic competence subscale of the Child Behavior Checklist.

[n] Cognitive agency subscale of the Child Competence Inventory.

* $p \leq .05$.

** $p \leq .01$.

*** $p \leq .001$.

TABLE 6

MEANS (STANDARD DEVIATIONS) FOR THE ACHENBACH CHILD BEHAVIOR CHECKLIST SCALES

	Nondivorced		Divorced		Remarried		Significant Main Effects and Interactions[a]	Significant Contrasts and Planned Comparisons[a]
	Boys	Girls	Boys	Girls	Boys	Girls		
Total problems:								
Mothers' reports:[b]								
Wave 1	54.1 (7.5)	52.8 (8.8)	56.6 (10.3)	56.3 (8.8)	62.0 (6.5)	58.0 (7.1)	Family type	Rem > Div > Nondiv
Wave 2	52.3 (9.3)	50.0 (8.7)	55.3 (9.1)	56.4 (9.5)	61.3 (8.1)	55.7 (8.9)	Family type	Div, Rem > Nondiv
Wave 3	52.6 (7.2)	48.3 (9.8)	56.5 (7.0)	56.0 (10.0)	60.9 (7.1)	52.7 (8.5)	Family type, gender	Div, Rem > Nondiv; Boys > Girls
Fathers' reports:[b]								
Wave 1	54.6 (7.3)	50.2 (10.3)			61.3 (7.0)	60.5 (7.6)	Family type	Rem > Nondiv
Wave 2	53.3 (9.6)	48.5 (9.1)			63.8 (7.2)	59.5 (8.3)	Family type, gender	Rem > Nondiv; Boys > Girls
Wave 3	51.4 (9.2)	46.5 (9.0)			59.9 (9.0)	57.6 (10.5)	Family type	Rem > Nondiv
Teachers' reports:[b]								
Wave 1	50.3 (8.9)	49.0 (6.9)	55.4 (13.5)	51.6 (9.5)	51.6 (11.3)	51.8 (8.8)	. . .	
Wave 2	51.4 (9.0)	45.9 (5.5)	56.3 (8.1)	51.9 (8.2)	54.1 (13.7)	48.8 (6.7)	Family type, gender	Div > Nondiv; Boys > Girls
Wave 3	51.2 (10.2)	46.5 (5.9)	. . .	. . .	49.6 (11.9)	51.8 (7.4)	. . .	
Externalizing:								
Mothers' reports:								
Wave 1	53.3 (6.6)	51.5 (6.6)	56.9 (8.7)	54.6 (7.0)	61.4 (6.7)	55.5 (6.1)	Family type, gender	Div, Rem > Nondiv; Boys > Girls
Wave 2	52.1 (8.7)	49.8 (5.7)	56.2 (8.1)	54.3 (7.7)	61.2 (7.1)	53.4 (7.2)	Family type, gender	Div, Rem > Nondiv; Boys > Girls
Wave 3	52.7 (8.0)	48.6 (6.2)	57.1 (6.8)	54.3 (7.3)	61.7 (6.9)	53.0 (6.6)	Family type, gender	Div, Rem > Nondiv; Boys > Girls

Fathers' reports:								
Wave 1	54.6	50.1			61.5	58.4	Family type, gender	Rem > Nondiv; Boys > Girls
	(7.4)	(7.6)			(6.6)	(6.3)		
Wave 2	54.1	48.6			63.2	57.0	Family type, gender	Rem > Nondiv; Boys > Girls
	(8.0)	(6.9)			(7.5)	(6.9)		
Wave 3	53.1	47.3			61.1	55.9	Family type, gender	Rem > Nondiv; Boys > Girls
	(8.8)	(5.8)			(8.3)	(7.6)		
Teachers' reports:[b]								
Wave 1	51.5	50.2	56.1	52.6	52.5	52.7	. . .	
	(7.9)	(5.3)	(12.7)	(7.6)	(9.8)	(8.3)		
Wave 2	52.2	48.1	56.6	52.7	54.7	50.1	Family type, gender	Div > Nondiv; Boys > Girls
	(9.0)	(3.8)	(8.3)	(6.9)	(12.2)	(5.8)		
Wave 3	52.1	48.2	. . .	. . .	50.6	52.7	. . .	
	(11.1)	(4.1)			(9.6)	(6.4)		
Internalizing:								
Mothers' reports:								
Wave 1	54.9	52.2	57.1	54.5	61.6	55.2	Family type, gender	Rem > Nondiv; Boys > Girls
	(8.0)	(8.2)	(9.6)	(6.7)	(7.0)	(7.7)		
Wave 2	53.5	50.4	56.0	54.5	61.6	54.4	Family type, gender	Div, Rem > Nondiv; Boys > Girls
	(9.2)	(8.3)	(8.7)	(8.7)	(7.5)	(7.3)		
Wave 3	53.6	49.8	57.3	54.3	60.1	51.2	Family type, gender	Div, Rem > Nondiv; Boys > Girls
	(7.2)	(8.3)	(7.9)	(8.6)	(7.8)	(7.1)		
Fathers' reports:								
Wave 1	55.5	50.5			61.3	56.8	Family type, gender	Rem > Nondiv; Boys > Girls
	(7.1)	(8.6)			(6.5)	(6.9)		
Wave 2	54.2	49.5			63.5	57.3	Family type, gender	Rem > Nondiv; Boys > Girls
	(9.1)	(7.2)			(6.8)	(7.3)		
Wave 3	52.5	47.8			59.8	54.5	Family type, gender	Rem > Nondiv; Boys > Girls
	(8.6)	(8.1)			(7.5)	(8.9)		
Teachers' reports:[b]								
Wave 1	50.7	51.0	55.5	53.2	51.7	51.2	. . .	
	(9.1)	(7.7)	(11.1)	(10.0)	(9.5)	(7.2)		
Wave 2	52.8	48.9	57.8	52.5	55.9	50.4	Family type, gender	Div > Nondiv; Boys > Girls
	(7.1)	(5.7)	(8.4)	(9.1)	(13.1)	(5.7)		
Wave 3	52.1	48.5	. . .	. . .	52.1	52.8	. . .	
	(6.8)	(5.6)			(10.4)	(5.9)		

TABLE 6 (*Continued*)

	Nondivorced		Divorced		Remarried		Significant Main Effects and Interactions[a]	Significant Contrasts and Planned Comparisons[a]
	Boys	Girls	Boys	Girls	Boys	Girls		
Social competence:								
Mothers' reports:								
Wave 1	53.8 (9.0)	52.8 (10.1)	49.0 (8.9)	48.6 (10.4)	46.2 (8.7)	49.5 (8.4)	Family type	Nondiv > Div, Rem
Wave 2	54.8 (9.5)	50.8 (9.2)	51.1 (8.5)	49.9 (8.4)	43.2 (9.2)	51.2 (8.4)	*Family type*	*Nondiv > Rem*
Wave 3	51.4 (12.6)	54.3 (7.6)	49.2 (7.1)	50.7 (10.1)	45.4 (6.4)	47.9 (10.7)	Family type	Nondiv > Rem
Fathers' reports:								
Wave 1	52.1 (8.5)	55.4 (9.1)			45.0 (7.2)	46.6 (9.6)	Family type	Nondiv > Rem
Wave 2	53.00 (10.8)	51.6 (10.8)			44.5 (8.5)	49.2 (13.4)	Family type	Nondiv > Rem
Wave 3	50.0 (10.5)	54.9 (9.5)			45.3 (6.5)	46.8 (8.2)	Family type	Nondiv > Rem
Scholastic competence:								
Mothers' reports:								
Wave 1	49.2 (7.7)	49.9 (7.8)	45.5 (10.8)	44.8 (10.1)	45.6 (9.6)	45.5 (10.6)	Family type	Nondiv > Div, Rem
Wave 2	50.2 (6.1)	51.8 (4.9)	47.6 (8.7)	45.9 (9.4)	44.6 (9.5)	50.7 (6.1)	Family type	Nondiv > Div, Rem
Wave 3	49.8 (6.7)	51.6 (5.2)	48.6 (6.4)	44.7 (10.0)	47.4 (6.2)	47.1 (8.3)	Family type	Nondiv > Div, Rem
Fathers' reports:								
Wave 1	49.9 (6.6)	52.5 (4.6)			46.0 (11.1)	46.2 (10.6)	Family type	Nondiv > Rem
Wave 2	50.2 (6.1)	51.0 (5.9)			44.1 (12.7)	50.9 (5.3)	*Family type*, gender	*Nondiv > Rem;* Girls > Boys
Wave 3	50.7 (5.9)	51.4 (6.1)			47.1 (6.5)	45.7 (8.8)	Family type	Nondiv > Rem

NOTE.—Rem = Remarried; Nondiv = Nondivorced; Div = Divorced.

[a] Italicized contrasts denote planned comparisons.

[b] Univariate analyses.

TABLE 7

MEAN PERCENTAGES[a] (Standard Deviations) FOR THE BEHAVIOR EVENTS INVENTORY (24-Hour Checklist) SCALES

	Nondivorced		Divorced		Remarried		Significant Main Effects and Interactions[b]	Significant Contrasts and Planned Comparisons[b]
	Boys	Girls	Boys	Girls	Boys	Girls		
Coercive behavior:								
Mothers' reports:								
Wave 1	.53 (.24)	.51 (.23)	.49 (.25)	.55 (.22)	.52 (.24)	.50 (.27)	. . .	
Wave 2	.47 (.19)	.49 (.23)	.46 (.23)	.44 (.18)	.54 (.25)	.45 (.29)	. . .	
Wave 3	.42 (.22)	.40 (.22)	.40 (.27)	.39 (.27)	.50 (.19)	.36 (.21)	. . .	
Fathers' reports:								
Wave 1	.47 (.21)	.49 (.25)			.54 (.24)	.56 (.23)	. . .	
Wave 2	.43 (.25)	.43 (.25)			.51 (.25)	.50 (.27)	. . .	
Wave 3	.40 (.25)	.31 (.23)			.56 (.25)	.43 (.25)	Family type, gender	Rem > Nondiv; Boys > Girls
Children's reports:								
Wave 1	.40 (.20)	.43 (.20)	.45 (.20)	.54 (.20)	.38 (.16)	.52 (.21)	Gender	Girls > Boys
Wave 2	.38 (.24)	.46 (.23)	.39 (.19)	.52 (.18)	.40 (.21)	.49 (.21)	Gender	Girls > Boys
Wave 3	.37 (.19)	.41 (.22)	.38 (.21)	.53 (.26)	.36 (.19)	.49 (.22)	Gender	Girls > Boys
Delinquent behavior:								
Children's reports:								
Wave 1	.08 (.09)	.06 (.08)	.14 (.16)	.10 (.11)	.09 (.11)	.10 (.10)	*Family type*	*Div > Nondiv*
Wave 2	.08 (.09)	.05 (.06)	.10 (.10)	.11 (.12)	.13 (.13)	.10 (.12)	*Family type*	*Div, Rem > Nondiv; Girls (Div > Nondiv)*[c]
Wave 3	.08 (.11)	.07 (.08)	.12 (.16)	.15 (.21)	.10 (.09)	.11 (.15)		*Girls (Div > Nondiv)*[c]

TABLE 7 (*Continued*)

	Nondivorced		Divorced		Remarried		Significant Main Effects and Interactions[b]	Significant Contrasts and Planned Comparisons[b]
	Boys	Girls	Boys	Girls	Boys	Girls		
Depressive behavior:								
Mothers' reports:								
Wave 1	.14	.19	.17	.21	.22	.17	. . .	
	(.15)	(.15)	(.20)	(.18)	(.18)	(.16)		
Wave 2	.09	.18	.10	.20	.15	.14	Gender	Girls > Boys
	(.11)	(.20)	(.18)	(.20)	(.15)	(.18)		
Wave 3	.07	.13	.02	.12	.15	.12	. . .	
	(.11)	(.16)	(.06)	(.18)	(.17)	(.20)		
Fathers' reports:								
Wave 1	.12	.15			.15	.14	. . .	
	(.14)	(.15)			(.16)	(.14)		
Wave 2	.09	.13			.17	.13	. . .	
	(.12)	(.19)			(.19)	(.15)		
Wave 3	.09	.09			.12	.13	. . .	
	(.12)	(.16)			(.15)	(.17)		
Children's reports:[d]								
Wave 1	.24	.28	.18	.26	.21	.32	Gender	Girls > Boys
	(.21)	(.20)	(.17)	(.21)	(.15)	(.20)		
Wave 2	.22	.30	.13	.31	.20	.30	Gender	Girls > Boys
	(.20)	(.19)	(.16)	(.21)	(.19)	(.18)		
Wave 3	.17	.30	.18	.24	.21	.32	Gender	Girls > Boys
	(.17)	(.22)	(.22)	(.22)	(.21)	(.19)		

Prosocial behavior:								
Mothers' reports:								
Wave 1	.77 (.18)	.82 (.18)	.78 (.17)	.81 (.16)	.75 (.20)	.77 (.19)	. . .	
Wave 2	.78 (.22)	.82 (.17)	.71 (.20)	.79 (.16)	.72 (.15)	.75 (.17)	. . .	
Wave 3	.69 (.23)	.78 (.19)	.68 (.22)	.68 (.29)	.72 (.15)	.71 (.23)	. . .	
Fathers' reports:								
Wave 1	.68 (.19)	.77 (.18)			.55 (.23)	.62 (.24)	Family type	Nondiv > Rem
Wave 2	.68 (.21)	.76 (.20)			.49 (.23)	.61 (.25)	Family type, *gender*	Nondiv > Rem; *Girls > Boys*
Wave 3	.59 (.21)	.76 (.23)			.56 (.26)	.68 (.28)	Family type, *gender*	Nondiv > Rem; *Girls > Boys*
Children's reports:								
Wave 1	.70 (.23)	.77 (.20)	.72 (.21)	.78 (.20)	.64 (.24)	.81 (.13)	Gender	Girls > Boys
Wave 2	.76 (.22)	.87 (.15)	.68 (.26)	.81 (.18)	.55 (.29)	.85 (.12)	*Family type,* gender	*Nondiv > Rem;* Girls > Boys
Wave 3	.67 (.26)	.84 (.17)	.70 (.25)	.84 (.21)	.74 (.25)	.88 (.18)	Gender	Girls > Boys

NOTE.—Rem = Remarried; Nondiv = Nondivorced; Div = Divorced.

[a] Percentages of items endorsed were averaged across all visits that composed each wave. Nondivorced and divorced families generally required two visits per wave, remarried families three.

[b] Italicized contrasts denote planned comparisons.

[c] t test, $p \leq .05$.

[d] Univariate analyses.

TABLE 8

MEANS (Standard Deviations) FOR REPORTS ON THE CHILD COMPETENCY INVENTORY SCALES

	NONDIVORCED		DIVORCED		REMARRIED		SIGNIFICANT MAIN EFFECTS AND INTERACTIONS[a]	SIGNIFICANT CONTRASTS AND PLANNED COMPARISONS[a]
	Boys	Girls	Boys	Girls	Boys	Girls		
Social responsibility:								
Mothers' reports:								
Wave 1	4.55 (.77)	4.45 (.73)	3.94 (.75)	4.21 (.77)	3.84 (.95)	4.02 (.87)	Family type	Nondiv > Div, Rem
Wave 2	4.24 (.98)	4.65 (.79)	4.13 (.75)	4.27 (.85)	3.79 (.91)	4.34 (.82)	*Gender*	*Girls > Boys*
Wave 3	4.20 (.95)	4.68 (.70)	4.20 (.93)	4.20 (.77)	3.60 (.69)	4.28 (.77)	Family type, gender	Nondiv > Rem; Girls > Boys
Fathers' reports:								
Wave 1	4.40 (.83)	4.39 (.75)			3.62 (.78)	3.63 (.78)	Family type	Nondiv > Rem
Wave 2	4.29 (.89)	4.42 (.92)			3.77 (.94)	3.86 (.69)	Family type	Nondiv > Rem
Wave 3	4.49 (.83)	4.56 (.76)			3.89 (.91)	4.03 (.79)	Family type	Nondiv > Rem
Children's reports:								
Wave 1	3.09 (.42)	3.18 (.37)	2.97 (.47)	3.07 (.36)	3.04 (.44)	2.93 (.50)	. . .	
Wave 2	2.98 (.35)	3.13 (.33)	2.91 (.33)	3.00 (.34)	2.94 (.54)	3.00 (.39)	. . .	
Wave 3	3.04 (.36)	3.12 (.36)	3.03 (.28)	3.01 (.39)	3.08 (.43)	2.93 (.39)	. . .	
Sociability:								
Mothers' reports:								
Wave 1	4.85 (1.1)	4.62 (.98)	4.87 (1.1)	4.78 (1.1)	5.13 (1.0)	5.00 (.90)	. . .	
Wave 2	4.66 (1.2)	4.87 (1.1)	4.91 (1.0)	4.81 (.91)	5.04 (1.2)	4.81 (.91)	. . .	
Wave 3	4.51 (1.2)	4.93 (.94)	4.81 (1.2)	4.58 (.92)	5.30 (.85)	4.91 (.78)	. . .	

Fathers' reports:								
Wave 1	4.54	4.77			5.21	5.05	Family type	Rem > Nondiv
	(1.2)	(.96)			(.91)	(.94)		
Wave 2	4.59	4.82			5.04	4.85	. . .	
	(1.2)	(1.1)			(1.3)	(1.1)		
Wave 3	4.73	4.71			5.08	4.81	. . .	
	(1.0)	(.92)			(.88)	(1.2)		
Children's reports:								
Wave 1	3.19	3.27	3.09	3.15	3.24	3.29	. . .	
	(.40)	(.41)	(.37)	(.33)	(.40)	(.43)		
Wave 2	3.23	3.21	3.09	3.21	3.18	3.30	. . .	
	(.55)	(.39)	(.35)	(.40)	(.53)	(.39)		
Wave 3	3.23	3.27	3.12	3.24	3.37	3.27	. . .	
	(.42)	(.38)	(.43)	(.38)	(.43)	(.42)		
Energetic/attractive/popular:								
Mothers' reports:								
Wave 1	4.60	5.00	4.88	5.12	4.93	4.84	. . .	
	(1.0)	(.91)	(1.0)	(.88)	(1.2)	(.87)		
Wave 2	4.87	4.57	4.75	4.88	4.95	4.70	. . .	
	(1.1)	(1.0)	(1.1)	(1.1)	(1.4)	(.91)		
Wave 3	4.71	4.70	4.55	5.00	5.02	4.55	. . .	
	(1.1)	(.89)	(1.3)	(.98)	(1.0)	(.96)		
Fathers' reports:								
Wave 1	4.83	4.87			4.87	4.79	. . .	
	(1.1)	(1.0)			(1.0)	(1.2)		
Wave 2	4.68	4.65			4.62	4.87	. . .	
	(1.1)	(1.1)			(1.2)	(1.0)		
Wave 3	4.67	4.60			4.84	4.68	. . .	
	(1.0)	(1.1)			(1.4)	(1.1)		
Children's reports:								
Wave 1	3.11	3.14	3.16	3.13	3.20	2.95	. . .	
	(.42)	(.40)	(.43)	(.47)	(.54)	(.49)		
Wave 2	3.17	3.11	3.00	3.05	3.15	2.99	. . .	
	(.55)	(.37)	(.47)	(.47)	(.59)	(.35)		
Wave 3	3.13	3.08	3.13	3.11	3.22	3.13	. . .	
	(.45)	(.43)	(.44)	(.50)	(.59)	(.39)		

TABLE 8 (*Continued*)

	Nondivorced		Divorced		Remarried		Significant Main Effects and Interactions[a]	Significant Contrasts and Planned Comparisons[a]
	Boys	Girls	Boys	Girls	Boys	Girls		
Cognitive agency:								
Mothers' reports:								
Wave 1	3.06	3.31	2.98	3.10	2.72	3.29	. . .	
	(1.4)	(1.4)	(1.4)	(1.4)	(1.1)	(1.0)		
Wave 2	2.88	3.66	3.07	3.45	2.66	3.56	Gender	Girls > Boys
	(1.7)	(1.2)	(1.4)	(1.0)	(1.4)	(1.4)		
Wave 3	3.33	3.43	3.04	3.00	2.59	2.76	Family type	Nondiv > Rem
	(1.3)	(1.0)	(1.3)	(1.4)	(1.3)	(1.5)		
Fathers' reports:								
Wave 1	3.34	3.70			2.89	3.18	Family type	Nondiv > Rem
	(1.0)	(1.1)			(.93)	(.92)		
Wave 2	3.32	3.87			2.82	3.39	*Family type*, gender	*Nondiv > Rem;* Girls > Boys
	(1.0)	(1.3)			(1.2)	(.80)		
Wave 3	3.28	3.72			2.91	3.75	Gender	Girls > Boys
	(1.1)	(1.0)			(1.2)	(1.0)		
Children's reports:[b]								
Wave 1	3.09	3.16	3.00	3.07	3.15	3.04	. . .	
	(.44)	(.48)	(.49)	(.53)	(.50)	(.46)		
Wave 2	3.06	3.06	2.90	2.94	3.05	3.01	. . .	
	(.54)	(.33)	(.47)	(.53)	(.50)	(.45)		
Wave 3	3.07	3.11	2.99	2.79	3.18	2.90	. . .	
	(.50)	(.45)	(.37)	(.55)	(.48)	(.46)		

NOTE.—Rem = Remarried; Nondiv = Nondivorced; Div = Divorced.

[a] Italicized contrasts denote planned comparisons.

[b] Univariate analyses.

TABLE 9

MEANS (Standard Deviations) FOR TEACHERS' REPORTS OF PERCEIVED CHILD COMPETENCE

	Nondivorced		Divorced		Remarried		Significant Main Effects and Interactions[a]	Significant Contrasts and Planned Comparisons[a]
	Boys	Girls	Boys	Girls	Boys	Girls		
General self-worth:								
Wave 1	3.1 (.7)	3.5 (.5)	2.7 (.8)	3.0 (.6)	2.9 (.8)	3.3 (.7)	Family type, gender	Nondiv > Div; Girls > Boys
Wave 2	3.0 (.8)	3.6 (.4)	2.4 (.8)	3.1 (.6)	2.7 (.7)	3.5 (.5)	Family type, gender	Nondiv > Div; Girls > Boys
Wave 3	3.0 (.8)	3.5 (.4)	. . .	. . .	3.0 (.9)	3.2 (.6)	. . .	
Cognitive competence:[b]								
Wave 1	3.2 (.7)	3.4 (.6)	2.8 (.8)	3.0 (.7)	3.1 (.7)	3.6 (.6)	Family type, gender	Nondiv, Rem > Div; Girls > Boys
Wave 2	3.1 (.6)	3.4 (.4)	2.6 (.8)	3.0 (.7)	3.1 (.6)	3.4 (.5)	Family type, gender	Nondiv, Rem > Div; Girls > Boys
Wave 3	3.0 (.8)	3.3 (.6)	. . .	. . .	3.3 (.5)	3.3 (.5)	. . .	
Social competence:								
Wave 1	3.0 (.6)	3.3 (.5)	2.8 (.7)	3.0 (.7)	2.9 (.6)	3.1 (.6)	Family type, gender	Nondiv > Div; Girls > Boys
Wave 2	3.0 (.8)	3.4 (.4)	2.7 (.7)	2.9 (.6)	2.7 (.7)	3.3 (.4)	Family type, gender	Nondiv > Div; Girls > Boys
Wave 3	3.0 (.8)	3.5 (.3)	. . .	. . .	2.8 (.9)	3.2 (.7)	*Gender*	*Girls > Boys*
Physical competence:[b]								
Wave 1	2.9 (.7)	3.2 (.7)	3.0 (.6)	2.7 (.8)	2.9 (.6)	2.9 (.5)	. . .	
Wave 2	2.9 (.8)	3.3 (.5)	2.7 (.8)	2.7 (.8)	2.9 (.6)	2.9 (.7)	. . .	
Wave 3	2.9 (.8)	3.1 (.7)	. . .	. . .	2.8 (.8)	3.1 (.6)	. . .	

NOTE.—Rem = Remarried; Nondiv = Nondivorced; Div = Divorced.

[a] Italicized contrast denotes planned comparison.

[b] Univariate analyses.

TABLE 10

MEANS (Standard Deviations) FOR OBSERVATIONAL RATINGS OF CHILDREN'S ADJUSTMENT[a]

	Nondivorced		Divorced		Remarried		Significant Main Effects and Interactions	Significant Contrasts and Planned Comparisons
	Boys	Girls	Boys	Girls	Boys	Girls		
Antisocial behavior toward:								
Mothers:								
Wave 1	1.8	1.9	2.4	2.1	2.1	2.2	Family type	Div, Rem > Nondiv
	(.8)	(.7)	(1.0)	(.9)	(.7)	(.7)		
Wave 2	2.2	2.0	2.7	2.6	2.2	2.3	Family type	Div > Rem, Nondiv
	(.9)	(.8)	(.9)	(.9)	(.9)	(.7)		
Wave 3	2.0	2.0	...	...	2.4	2.4	...	
	(.9)	(.8)			(1.0)	(1.0)		
Fathers:								
Wave 1	1.6	1.6			2.0	2.3	Family type	Rem > Nondiv
	(.7)	(.6)			(.9)	(.9)		
Wave 2	2.1	1.8			2.1	2.3	...	
	(1.1)	(.6)			(.8)	(.7)		
Wave 3	1.9	1.8			2.2	2.1	...	
	(1.0)	(.9)			(.9)	(1.0)		
Siblings:								
Wave 1	1.8	2.0	2.4	2.5	2.1	2.3	Family type	Div > Nondiv
	(.5)	(.8)	(.8)	(.7)	(.7)	(.8)		
Wave 2	2.4	2.2	2.7	2.9	2.4	2.7	Family type	Div > Nondiv
	(1.0)	(1.0)	(.8)	(1.0)	(1.0)	(1.0)		
Wave 3	2.3	2.3	...	...	3.2	2.7	Family type	Rem > Nondiv
	(1.1)	(1.0)			(.9)	(1.3)		
Shy/withdrawn behavior toward:								
Mothers:								
Wave 1	3.2	2.9	3.3	3.1	3.0	3.1	...	
	(.8)	(.5)	(.7)	(.7)	(.6)	(.7)		
Wave 2	3.3	3.7	3.6	3.8	3.3	3.4	...	
	(.9)	(1.0)	(.9)	(1.0)	(.7)	(.8)		
Wave 3	3.6	3.9			3.3	3.7	...	
	(.9)	(1.0)			(1.0)	(1.0)		

Fathers:								
Wave 1	2.9 (.6)	3.0 (.6)			2.7 (.7)	3.1 (.7)	Family type × gender	Rem (Girls > Boys)
Wave 2	3.1 (.9)	3.5 (1.0)			2.8 (.9)	3.3 (.9)	Gender	Girls > Boys
Wave 3	3.5 (1.0)	3.8 (1.0)			3.1 (1.0)	3.3 (.9)	Family type	Nondiv > Rem
Siblings:								
Wave 1	3.3 (.6)	3.4 (.7)	3.6 (.6)	3.6 (.6)	3.5 (.5)	3.5 (.6)	. . .	
Wave 2	3.9 (1.0)	4.0 (.9)	4.0 (.7)	3.8 (.8)	3.6 (.7)	3.4 (.5)	Family type	Nondiv, Div > Rem
Wave 3	4.0 (.7)	3.8 (.9)			3.8 (.9)	3.1 (.1)	. . .	
Prosocial behavior toward:								
Mothers:								
Wave 1	3.1 (.9)	2.9 (.9)	2.4 (.8)	2.7 (.9)	2.8 (.6)	2.7 (.7)	Family type	Nondiv > Div
Wave 2	2.8 (.9)	2.9 (.8)	2.4 (.8)	2.8 (.8)	2.4 (.8)	2.6 (.6)	. . .	
Wave 3	3.3 (.6)	3.4 (1.1)	. . .	. . .	2.8 (.8)	2.7 (.9)	Family type	Nondiv > Rem
Fathers:								
Wave 1	2.9 (.9)	2.8 (1.1)			2.6 (.7)	2.3 (1.0)	Family type	Nondiv > Rem
Wave 2	2.1 (1.3)	2.2 (1.4)			1.6 (1.2)	1.6 (1.2)	Family type	Nondiv > Rem
Wave 3	2.4 (1.6)	2.5 (1.7)			1.4 (1.4)	1.8 (1.3)	Family type	Nondiv > Rem
Siblings:								
Wave 1	2.9 (.7)	2.8 (.9)	2.3 (.7)	2.5 (.9)	2.6 (.6)	2.5 (.7)	Family type	Nondiv > Div, Rem
Wave 2	2.4 (.7)	2.6 (1.0)	2.0 (.6)	2.3 (.8)	2.3 (.9)	2.2 (.7)	. . .	
Wave 3	2.8 (.8)	3.1 (1.0)	. . .	. . .	2.2 (1.0)	2.2 (.8)	Family type	Nondiv > Rem

NOTE.—Rem = Remarried; Nondiv = Nondivorced; Div = Divorced.

[a] Because observers' reports included only one measure of children's adjustment for each dimension, only univariate analyses could be performed.

sistency between children's self-reports and the reports of others (Cairns & Cairns, 1984). Gender differences that did emerge indicated that girls were seen as better adjusted than boys by most respondents.

Specifically, both parents' and teachers' ratings on the Child Behavior Checklist revealed that girls were seen as exhibiting fewer behavioral and emotional problems than were boys. Significant differences were obtained for both parents' reports of externalizing and internalizing at all three waves, for mothers' reports of total behavior problems at Wave 3 and fathers' reports at Wave 2, and for teachers' reports of total behavior problems, externalizing, and internalizing at Wave 2 (see Table 6).

Interestingly, this clear consensus between parents' and teachers' reports of differences between boys' and girls' behavior problems on the Child Behavior Checklist was not reflected in children's self-reports on the Behavior Events Inventory (see Table 7).[4] When assessing their own behavior, girls reported having engaged in both more coercive and more depressive behaviors than did boys at all three waves. Minimal support for these higher frequencies of problem behaviors came from mothers, who agreed that girls had been more depressed at Wave 2 (the pubertal apex for most girls in this sample), and from observers (Table 10), who agreed that girls were more shy/withdrawn with their stepfathers at Wave 1 and with stepfathers and biological fathers at Wave 2. Fathers' and daughters' reports were inconsistent with respect to problem behavior, as fathers and stepfathers reported that sons rather than daughters were more coercive in the last wave.

In contrast, girls' reports of greater social competence were consistent with those of their parents and teachers. On the Behavior Events Inventory (Table 7), girls reported having engaged in more prosocial behaviors at all three waves, and fathers and stepfathers agreed with the girls at Waves 2 and 3. Similarly, mothers assigned their daughters higher scores than their sons on the social responsibility factor of the Child Competence Inventory (Table 8) at the latter two waves, and teachers described girls as demonstrating greater social competence at all three waves and as possessing greater general self-worth at Waves 1 and 2 on the Perceived Competence Scale for Children (Table 9). No differences between girls and boys were identified for parents' reports on the Child Behavior Checklist's total social competence scale or the Child Competence Inventory's sociability and energetic/attractive/popular factors, for teachers' reports on the physical competence factor of the Perceived Competence Scale for Children, or for observers' reports of prosocial behavior to parents and siblings.

While we had anticipated that girls would evince fewer behavioral and

[4] While the Behavior Events Inventory is a frequency-based measure, the values presented in Table 7 are the percentages of possible items endorsed, averaged across all 24-hour periods preceding each visit within a wave. Nondivorced and remarried families typically required three visits per wave, divorced families only two.

emotional problems and higher levels of social competence, we also found that girls were seen as more scholastically competent than boys by parents and teachers. Fathers reported greater scholastic competence for their daughters at Wave 2 (Child Behavior Checklist, Table 6) and greater cognitive agency at Waves 2 and 3 (Child Competence Inventory, Table 8). Mothers agreed that their daughters were more cognitively agentic at Wave 2, and teachers described girls as having greater cognitive competence at Waves 1 and 2 (Perceived Competence Scale for Children, Table 9). No differences were seen in children's self-reports of scholastic competence (Table 8).

In summary, there was considerable evidence that girls were perceived by both parents and teachers as more socially and scholastically competent and as exhibiting fewer behavior problems than boys, despite the fact that observers detected few gender differences in boys' and girls' interactions with other family members. Interestingly, girls themselves reported more frequent examples of coercive, depressive, and prosocial behaviors than did boys in the 24 hours preceding each interview, which may reflect a more thoughtful awareness of social behavior on their part.

Family-Type Differences and Interactions

Analyses of Multimethod/Multirespondent Composites

Analyses of multimethod/multirespondent composite indices indicated that, relative to children in nondivorced families, who had not experienced the stresses associated with family transitions, children in both restabilized families with a divorced mother and newly remarried families exhibited fairly persistent problems in adjustment (see Table 4). Compared to children in nondivorced families, children from divorced and remarried families received higher composite scores on externalizing and lower composite scores on scholastic competence at all three waves. Furthermore, children from remarried families received lower scores on the social competence index at all three waves, and children from divorced families received lower scores on this index at Waves 1 and 2. Significant differences between children whose divorced mothers had and had not remarried occurred only on the social competence index at Waves 2 and 3, where children from divorced families were rated as more socially competent than those from remarried households.

Analyses of Individual Scales

When scales were examined individually, it became clear that the magnitude of the reported problem behaviors or deficits varied according to who was assessing the child.

Nondivorced families.—Assessments of children's adjustment in nondivorced families are easily summarized. Family members agreed that these children were consistently more scholastically and socially competent, were more socially responsible, and demonstrated fewer behavior problems than children in either restabilized single-mother families or stepfamilies. Moreover, both observers' ratings of children's prosocial and antisocial behaviors and teachers' ratings of behaviors exhibited in the classroom concurred both with the nondivorced parents' perceptions of their children and with these children's self-perceptions. Specific differences between children who had experienced marital transitions and children from nondivorced families are described in the following two sections.

Divorced, single-mother families versus nondivorced families.—All respondents reported on some measures in some waves that children in restabilized homes with a divorced, unremarried mother were having more problems during adjustment to adolescence than children from nondivorced homes. Divorced mothers' reports of behavior problems on the Child Behavior Checklist indicated that their children were exhibiting higher levels of total behavior problems and externalizing at all three waves and higher levels of internalizing at Waves 2 and 3. These differences did not emerge on the Behavior Events Inventory, which seems less sensitive to family-type differences in deviant behavior than the Child Behavior Checklist. Teachers' reports on the Child Behavior Checklist supported those of the mothers' at Wave 2. (Recall that teachers' reports were unavailable for children in one-parent households at Wave 3.)

Further confirmation of mothers' perceptions was provided by observers' reports of greater levels of antisocial behaviors in the presence of mothers and siblings at Waves 1 and 2 (no observers' reports are available for one-parent households at Wave 3; see Table 10) and by children's endorsement of more delinquent acts in the 24 hours preceding the visits that constituted the Wave 1 and 2 assessments (planned comparisons; see Table 7). Hypothesized differences in the percentage of delinquent acts endorsed by girls in nondivorced and divorced families emerged in Waves 2 and 3 as they moved further into adolescence, but only when the two groups were isolated, using *t* tests. This failure to obtain a significant difference between groups using MANOVA techniques may be attributable to the variation in the frequencies indicated by girls from divorced homes. In Wave 3, the standard deviation for girls from divorced homes was .21, whereas the standard deviation for their peers from nondivorced homes was only .08. Similarly, an examination of raw percentages of delinquent acts (not given in the tables) revealed that 40% of girls from divorced homes had committed no delinquent acts (vs. 36% of girls from nondivorced homes), whereas one girl from a divorced home indicated that she had committed, on average, 80% of the possible acts during the visits constituting the third assessment.

Divorced, unremarried mothers also reported that their children were less scholastically competent than children from nondivorced homes at all three waves (Child Behavior Checklist) and less socially competent (Child Behavior Checklist) and socially responsible (Child Competence Inventory) at Wave 1 (Tables 6 and 8). Observers agreed that children from single-mother homes behaved in a less prosocial manner with mothers and siblings at Wave 1 (Table 10), and teachers perceived these children as less cognitively, socially, and generally competent than children from nondivorced families at Waves 1 and 2 (Perceived Competence Scale for Children, Table 9). (No teachers' reports were available for these children at Wave 3.) Given the consensus among mothers, observers, and teachers, it is interesting to note that children did not perceive themselves as having behaved any less prosocially than their peers in the 24 hours preceding the interviews (Table 7).

Every significant difference obtained between the adjustment measures of children from divorced and nondivorced families was consistent with our overall prediction that children with divorced, unremarried mothers would demonstrate higher levels of behavior problems and lower levels of competence than children from nondivorced families. Hypotheses concerning boys' and girls' specific patterns of adjustment were confirmed to the extent that some girls from single-mother homes did endorse a greater percentage of more delinquent acts relative to girls from nondivorced homes as they moved into adolescence and boys continued to demonstrate interpersonal difficulties with their divorced, single mothers. Again, however, it should be underscored that there was variability in the reports of different respondents among measures and across waves.

Remarried versus nondivorced families.—The appraisal of children's adjustment in stepfamilies varied considerably according to who was rating the children and in which setting their behavior was being evaluated (home or school). The respondents who most consistently perceived children in remarried households as being poorly adjusted were the stepfathers. Across all three waves of the study, stepfathers' responses on the Child Behavior Checklist (Table 5) indicated that they saw their stepchildren as exhibiting more total behavior problems—both externalizing and internalizing—and as being less scholastically and socially competent than did fathers in nondivorced families. Contrary to our predictions based on previous findings with younger children, stepfathers did not see any of these problems in adjustment as being more pronounced for girls. Stepfathers also described their stepchildren as demonstrating less cognitive agency at Waves 1 and 2 and less social responsibility at all waves (Child Competence Inventory, Table 8) and as having performed a greater percentage of coercive acts at Wave 3 and a lesser percentage of prosocial acts during all three assessment periods (Behavior Events Inventory, Table 7). Interestingly, on the Child

Competency Inventory, stepfathers described stepchildren as being *more* sociable than children from nondivorced families at Wave 1.

Stepfathers' reports were supported by those of mothers on most indices. Remarried mothers agreed with their new husbands that their children were exhibiting less social and scholastic competence and more pervasive difficulties on all three behavior problem indices of the Child Behavior Checklist at all three waves (see Table 6). These mothers also saw their children as demonstrating deficits in social responsibility at Waves 1 and 3 and deficits in cognitive agency at Wave 3 on the Child Competence Inventory (Table 8), but they did not perceive their children as any different from children of nondivorced parents with respect to sociability or the behaviors assessed by the Behavior Events Inventory (Table 7). Thus, with respect to family type differences in competence, parental remarriage was more closely related to deficits in social responsibility and scholastic competence than to deficits in sociability and peer popularity.

Parents' reports of increased behavior problems and lower levels of competence were partially supported by the observers' reports of social deficits, particularly in children's interactions with their stepfathers. Observers reported that, in the months immediately following their mothers' remarriages (Wave 1), children were demonstrating higher levels of antisocial behavior to both parents and girls were more aloof and shy/withdrawn in the presence of their new stepfathers. Children were also less prosocial to their stepfathers at all three waves and to their mothers at the last wave. In interactions with their siblings, children were less prosocial at Waves 1 and 3, more antisocial by Wave 3, and less shy/withdrawn at Wave 2.

Contrary to both their parents' perceptions and observers' ratings, children in stepfamilies did not perceive themselves as having many more problems than children in nondivorced homes. Although they did report having performed fewer prosocial and more delinquent acts in the 24 hours preceding the second interview, these were the only significant self-reported differences between the two groups, and these comparisons were planned (Table 7).

Children's self-appraisals were supported by those of their teachers. Contrary to expectations, teachers perceived no differences between children in remarried and nondivorced families at any time during the study (Tables 6 and 9). This absence of perceived differences between groups of children suggests that, despite the problems demonstrated by children from remarried families within the home, there was no detectable generalization of these problems to the school setting, at least in the 26 months following the remarriage.

To summarize, parents agreed that children experiencing the transitions and changes involved in remarriage demonstrated fairly severe behavior problems, deficits in scholastic and social responsibility, and difficulties in their interactions with other family members. The lack of significant family type × gender interactions in these findings suggests that, like the parents in the other family types, remarried parents saw these difficulties as more pronounced for boys than for girls. Parents' reports were partially supported by those of the observers, who agreed that children in stepfamilies were exhibiting difficulties in their interactions with other family members; however, the children perceived themselves as having few such difficulties, and their teachers agreed with this appraisal.

Remarried versus divorced, single-mother families.—Contrary to expectations, but in accordance with the findings of Allison and Furstenberg (1989), very few differences prevailed between children's adjustment in remarried and single-mother families. Those that were obtained varied as a function of the reporter.

Relative to divorced single mothers, mothers who had remarried rated their children as having a greater number of total behavior problems at Wave 1, immediately following the remarriage (Child Behavior Checklist). Observers rated children from single-mother homes as being more antisocial to their mothers and shy/withdrawn with their siblings at Wave 2, and teachers rated children without fathers in the home as being less cognitively competent than those who had recently gained a stepfather, at both available waves. Given teachers' tendency to perceive children from divorced homes as lacking in competence in general, it seems unlikely that their ratings would have changed by Wave 3, although no firm statement can be made since Wave 3 teacher data for this group of children were unavailable. Finally, there were no differences in self-reports of children who had experienced either one or both types of marital transitions (Tables 6 and 7).

Family type and gender differences on the Child Behavior Checklist subscales.—Since the Child Behavior Checklist is the most widely used standardized measure of children's behavior problems, results obtained for this measure were explored in greater detail.

In addition to the summary scales of total behavior problems, externalizing, and internalizing, Achenbach and Edelbrock (1983) also describe several subscales of psychopathology. Of course, somatic complaints and schizoid, aggressive, and delinquent behavior subscales apply to both genders. In addition, boys are assessed on measures of obsessive-compulsive, hostile-withdrawn, immature, hyperactive, and uncommunicative behaviors and girls on measures of anxious-obsessive, depressed-withdrawn, immature-hyperactive, and cruel behaviors.

Although not focal to this study, behaviors assessed by these subscales were examined separately to provide additional descriptive information regarding the degree to which the parents in the three types of families perceived differences in their children's adjustment. The total numbers of significant differences between boys and girls in different family types,

TABLE 11

NUMBER OF SIGNIFICANT DIFFERENCES BETWEEN MEANS OF BOYS AND GIRLS ON THE PSYCHOPATHOLOGY SUBSCALES OF THE CHILD BEHAVIOR CHECKLIST

	MOTHERS' REPORTS		FATHERS' REPORTS	
SIGNIFICANT DIFFERENCES	Boys	Girls	Boys	Girls
Nondivorced < Remarried	19	6	22	19
	(27)	(24)	(27)	(24)
Remarried < Nondivorced	0	0	0	0
	(27)	(24)	(27)	(24)
Nondivorced < Divorced	5	10	...	...
	(27)	(24)		
Divorced < Nondivorced	0	0	...	...
	(27)	(24)		
Divorced < Remarried	3	0	...	...
	(27)	(24)		
Remarried < Divorced	0	2	...	...
	(27)	(24)		

NOTE.—Numbers in parentheses show the number of possible comparisons across all three waves.

collapsed across all three waves, are presented in Table 11. Because collapsing across waves invalidates the assumption of independent observations, inferential statistical tests were not conducted on these totals; they are included purely for descriptive purposes.

In comparisons between nondivorced and remarried parents, mothers' reports showed 19 significant differences for boys and six for girls. Fathers reports' showed 22 significant differences for boys and 19 for girls. In all instances, children in remarried homes were rated as the more disturbed.

Fewer differences were seen when the other two combinations of family types were contrasted. According to mothers, boys from single-mother homes were demonstrating greater difficulties in adjustment than boys from nondivorced homes on five of the psychopathology subscales and girls from single-mother homes on 10 of these. This small number of differences for boys is surprising in light of both the conflictual mother-son relationships cited in many studies of mother-headed families and the differences found in our data on the more molar scales of total behavior problems, externalizing, and internalizing. Comparisons of maternal reports for children from divorced versus remarried families showed only three differences for sons and two for daughters, with boys in the remarried families and girls in divorced households demonstrating the poorer adjustment.

Achenbach and Edelbrock also provide clinical cutoffs for parents' ratings of externalizing ($T \geq 64$ for boys, and $T \geq 63$ for girls), internalizing ($T \geq 64$), and total behavior problems ($T \geq 64$). Scores above these cutoffs can be viewed as indicating abnormally high levels of psychopathology. The

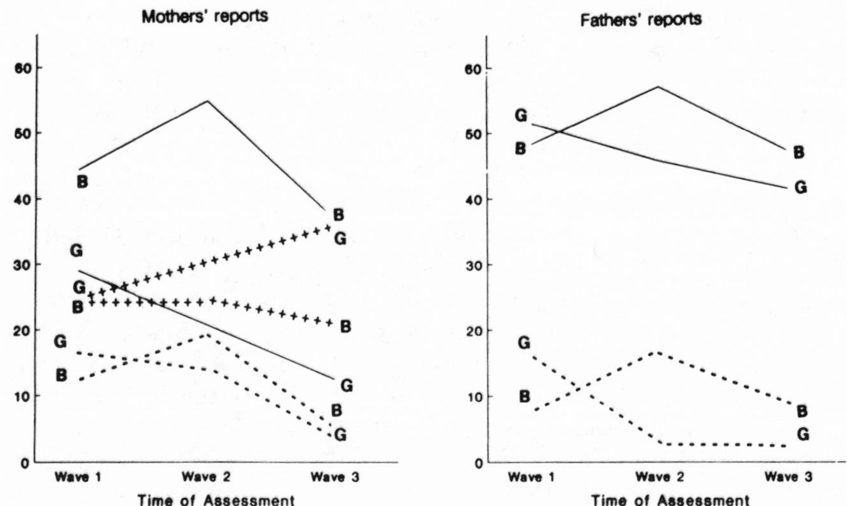

Fig. 1.—Parents' reports of the percentage of children in each family type scoring above the clinical cutoff on the total behavior problems scale. (B = boys; G = girls. Nondivorced: - - - -; Divorced: + + + +; Remarried: ———.)

percentages of children in each family group who scored above the clinical cutoff for total behavior problems at each wave are depicted in Figure 1.

According to maternal reports, 33% of the children in remarried families were functioning at what would be considered high levels of psychopathology at the first two waves; paternal reports put the figure above 43%. This was in sharp contrast to the percentages obtained for children in nondivorced homes—an average of 10% at Waves 1 and 2 and 4% at Wave 3—and to the national norms, which are 10%. The percentage of children in single-mother homes scoring above the clinical cutoff fell between the other two groups.

To identify statistically significant relations between children's psychopathology classifications and family structure, a series of classification × family type chi square analyses were performed for mothers' and fathers' reports of boys and girls (separately) at each of the three waves. When analyses of mothers' reports of the three family groups yielded significant chi square values, reduced matrices were examined as the degrees of freedom allowed.

Results of these analyses indicated that mothers classified larger percentages of boys from remarried homes and girls from divorced homes as showing extreme psychopathology—in comparison to the percentages of children from nondivorced homes. For boys, this relation was evident at all three waves (Yates's corrected chi square values were, respectively, 6.46, *p*

$\leq .05$; 5.91, $p \leq .05$; and 6.50, $p \leq .05$); for girls, it was evident only at the last wave (7.09, $p \leq .01$). This emergence of severe psychopathology for some girls in divorced homes at Wave 3 is in accordance with the elevated mean levels of delinquent acts reported by these girls on the Behavior Events Inventory (see Table 7). Fathers' reports indicated that both stepsons and stepdaughters were more disturbed than their peers from nondivorced homes at all three waves (chi square values for stepsons were, respectively, 11.70, $p \leq .001$; 8.66, $p \leq .01$; and 8.60, $p \leq .01$; and for stepdaughters, respectively, 7.49, $p \leq .01$; 10.80, $p \leq .001$; and 8.43, $p \leq .01$).

Thus, a slightly different picture of the effects of marital transitions emerged when severe behavior problems were considered in light of the full range of behavior problems; gender differences did emerge in the analyses of mothers' reports of children scoring above the clinical cutoff, whereas they had not in the previous analyses.

STABILITY AND CHANGE OVER TIME IN CHILDREN'S ADJUSTMENT

Correlational Analyses of Stability over Time

To analyze within-group stability over time, Pearson correlations were computed for the multimethod/multirespondent composite measures from Waves 1–2, 2–3, and 1–3 (see Table 12). Analyses combining gender (not given in the tables) produced coefficients ranging from .43 to .78, indicating that children's externalizing, social competence, and particularly scholastic competence were quite stable across time.

Analyses performed on boys and girls in each family type separately yielded similar results; exceptions were the nonsignificant correlations between Waves 1 and 3 obtained in remarried families for externalizing for both boys ($r = -.08$) and girls ($r = .03$) and for social competence for girls ($r = .10$). These correlations differed significantly from the pooled correlations of children's same-gender peers in the other two family types, suggesting that these dimensions of children's adjustment in the months immediately following their mothers' remarriages may be unrelated to their adjustment 26 months later. Two nonsignificant correlations were also obtained from Waves 2–3 for children in divorced families—for externalizing in boys ($r = .33$) and for social competence in girls ($r = .30$)—but these correlations did not differ significantly from those of children in nondivorced families.

Correlations for internalizing depended on the reports made by parents on the Child Behavior Checklist. Like externalizing, social competence, and scholastic competence, internalizing appeared to be very stable over time with all but one coefficient falling between .50–.86. The only exception

TABLE 12

ACROSS-TIME CORRELATIONS FOR THE CHILD ADJUSTMENT MULTIMETHOD/MULTIRESPONDENT COMPOSITE INDICES AND FOR PARENTS' REPORTS OF INTERNALIZING

	Composite Externalizing			Composite Scholastic Competence			Composite Social Competence			Mothers' Reports of Internalizing			Fathers' Reports of Internalizing		
	Wave 1	Wave 2	Wave 3	Wave 1	Wave 2	Wave 3	Wave 1	Wave 2	Wave 3	Wave 1	Wave 2	Wave 3	Wave 1	Wave 2	Wave 3
Nondiv boys:															
Wave 1	...			...			...			...			...		
Wave 2	.72***	...		.75***	...		.43**	...		.73***	...		.65***	...	
Wave 3	.63***	.69***	...	.73***	.87***	...	.55***	.65***	...	.65***	.70***	...	.73***	.75***	...
Nondiv girls:															
Wave 1	...			...			...			...			...		
Wave 2	.73***	...		.84***	...		.53***	...		.71***	...		.76***	...	
Wave 3	.59***	.78***	...	.75***	.81***	...	.53***	.54***	...	.79***	.66***	...	.77***	.74***	...
Div boys:															
Wave 1	...			...			...			...					
Wave 2	.59***	...		.78***	...		.50**	...		.66***	...				
Wave 3	.38*	.33	...	.80***	.69***	...	.44*	.43*	...	.62***	.67***	...			
Div girls:															
Wave 1	...			...			...			...					
Wave 2	.48**	...		.71***	...		.47**	...		.64***	...				
Wave 3	.45**	.36*	...	.79***	.74***	...	.52**	.30	...	.65***	.78***	...			
Rem boys:															
Wave 1	...			...			...			...			...		
Wave 2	.50**	...		.78***	...		.67***	...		.49*	...		.77***	...	
Wave 3	−.08	.49*	...	.57**	.46*	...	.56**	.74***	...	.66***	.50*	...	.57**	.86***	...
Rem girls:															
Wave 1	...			...			...			...			...		
Wave 2	.67***	...		.75***	...		.65***	...		.72***	...		.68***	...	
Wave 3	.03	.35*	...	.62***	.75***	...	.10	.44*	...	.32	.51**	...	.63***	.75***	...

NOTE.—Nondiv = Nondivorced; Div = Divorced; Rem = Remarried.

* $p \leq .05$.

** $p \leq .01$.

*** $p \leq .001$.

was $r = .32$ for remarried mothers' reports of their daughters' behavior at Waves 1–3, and this correlation was not significantly different from that of girls in nondivorced families.

These findings suggested that, in general, children's pre- and early adolescent functioning was closely related to their functioning as they moved further into adolescence. However, the experience of maternal remarriage during this normative transition seems to have upset this stability for some of the children.

Repeated-Measures MANOVAs Assessing Changes over Time

Group changes over time were examined using repeated-measures MANOVAs performed on the multimethod/multirespondent composite indices as well as on each respondent's reports on each of the individual measures of children's adjustment. In order to capitalize on the available sample sizes, short-term change was examined from Wave 1 to Wave 2 and long-term change from Wave 1 to Wave 3. Means, standard deviations, and significant differences obtained in the analyses of the multimethod/multirespondent composites and of mothers' and fathers' reports of internalizing are presented in Tables 13 and 14. (Wave 1 means vary slightly across the two tables since the *N*'s involve subjects available at Waves 1 and 2 in the former and Waves 1 and 3 in the latter instance.)

Few changes over time were suggested by the repeated-measures analyses of the composite indices; those that were evident were attributable to changes across the sample rather than changes by boys or girls or by children within a particular family type.

From time 1 to time 2, main effects for wave indicated that children were increasing in externalizing, $F(1,182) = 4.86$, $p \leq .05$, and decreasing in socially competent behavior, $F(1,182) = 7.00$, $p \leq .01$. Interestingly, these changes were not reflected in the Waves 1–3 analyses. This increasing difficulty in adjustment from Wave 1 to Wave 2, followed by an apparent improvement or at least a return to previous (Wave 1) status by Wave 3, is in agreement with other research findings indicating an increase in adjustment problems and difficulties in family relationships in very early adolescence as children move into the pubertal apex and a decline thereafter (Hill et al., 1985a, 1985b; Steinberg, 1981). However, it should be noted that the relatively greater improvement in adjustment predicted for children whom we had expected to become increasingly accustomed to the presence of a stepfather in the home did not occur in the 26 months of the study. No changes over time were seen in the repeated-measures analyses of scholastic competence, and shifts in internalizing are discussed with changes in the other single scales.

TABLE 13

MEANS (Standard Deviations) FOR REPEATED-MEASURES ANALYSES OF SHORT-TERM CHANGES (Wave 1 to Wave 2) IN CHILDREN'S ADJUSTMENT

	Nondivorced		Divorced		Remarried		Significant Main Effects and Interactions	Significant Contrasts
	Boys	Girls	Boys	Girls	Boys	Girls		
Multimethod/multirespondent composite:								
Externalizing:								
Wave 1	−.22 (.53)	−.28 (.51)	.26 (.70)	.08 (.56)	.10 (.45)	.14 (.56)	Wave	1 < 2
Wave 2	−.08 (.72)	−.32 (.56)	.31 (.60)	.25 (.53)	.22 (.62)	.21 (.67)	Family type	Div, Rem > Nondiv
Social competence:								
Wave 1	.14 (.46)	.30 (.45)	−.30 (.45)	.03 (.48)	−.25 (.48)	−.08 (.51)	Wave	1 > 2
Wave 2	.00 (.54)	.31 (.39)	−.36 (.43)	−.03 (.48)	−.53 (.56)	−.10 (.47)	Family type	Nondiv > Div, Rem
Scholastic competence:								
Wave 1	.09 (.61)	.33 (.63)	−.20 (.86)	−.03 (.78)	−.33 (.78)	.06 (.64)	Family type	Nondiv > Div, Rem
Wave 2	.10 (.68)	.34 (.60)	−.13 (.75)	.12 (.75)	−.34 (.86)	.12 (.64)	Gender	Girls > Boys
Internalizing:								
Mothers' reports on the CBC:								
Wave 1	55.28 (8.09)	51.92 (8.14)	56.52 (9.62)	53.85 (6.60)	59.85 (6.12)	55.96 (7.40)	Family type	Rem > Nondiv
Wave 2	53.47 (9.16)	50.44 (8.31)	56.00 (8.68)	54.55 (8.67)	61.60 (7.53)	54.42 (7.29)	Gender	Boys > Girls
Fathers' reports on the CBC:								
Wave 1	55.51 (7.24)	50.31 (8.60)			61.33 (6.04)	56.67 (6.82)	Family type	Rem > Nondiv
Wave 2	54.19 (9.13)	49.49 (7.23)			63.48 (6.82)	57.29 (7.25)	Gender	Boys > Girls

NOTE.—Nondiv = Nondivorced; Div = Divorced; Rem = Remarried; CBC = Child Behavior Checklist.

TABLE 14

MEANS (STANDARD DEVIATIONS) FOR REPEATED-MEASURES ANALYSES OF LONG-TERM CHANGES (WAVE 1 TO WAVE 3) IN CHILDREN'S ADJUSTMENT

	Nondivorced		Divorced		Remarried		Significant Main Effects and Interactions	Significant Contrasts
	Boys	Girls	Boys	Girls	Boys	Girls		
Multimethod/multirespondent composite:								
Externalizing:								
Wave 1	−.25 (.54)	−.26 (.53)	.24 (.73)	.10 (.57)	.10 (.44)	.09 (.47)	Family type	Div, Rem > Nondiv
Wave 3	−.22 (.70)	−.38 (.63)	−.11 (.72)	.00 (.91)	.34 (.53)	.11 (.67)		
Social competence:								
Wave 1	.12 (.47)	.30 (.46)	−.25 (.47)	.03 (.49)	−.24 (.46)	−.04 (.49)	Family type	Nondiv > Div, Rem
Wave 3	.14 (.56)	.60 (.63)	−.15 (.64)	−.03 (.57)	−.23 (.57)	−.06 (.51)	Gender	Girls > Boys
Scholastic competence:								
Wave 1	.08 (.63)	.30 (.63)	−.20 (.73)	−.07 (.80)	−.19 (.78)	.06 (.65)	Family type	Nondiv > Div, Rem
Wave 3	.08 (.72)	.32 (.58)	−.09 (.68)	−.29 (.89)	−.14 (.63)	.00 (.61)		
Internalizing:								
Mothers' reports on the CBC:								
Wave 1	54.71 (8.04)	51.81 (8.30)	56.92 (9.89)	53.39 (6.87)	60.11 (6.42)	54.42 (7.02)		
Wave 3	53.60 (7.15)	49.75 (8.30)	57.33 (7.92)	54.25 (8.62)	60.05 (7.80)	51.17 (7.06)		
Fathers' reports on the CBC:								
Wave 1	55.31 (7.34)	50.52 (8.78)			61.42 (6.26)	56.13 (7.89)	Wave	1 > 3
Wave 3	52.49 (8.56)	47.79 (8.15)			59.79 (7.53)	54.46 (8.93)	Family type, gender	Rem > Nondiv; Boys > Girls

NOTE.—Nondiv = Nondivorced; Div = Divorced; Rem = Remarried; CBC = Child Behavior Checklist.

Results of analyses of change on individual measures showed some discrepancies across measures and informants (only those for internalizing are presented in the tables). For example, on the Child Behavior Checklist, mothers reported declines in total behavior problems from Wave 1 to Wave 3, particularly for children in nondivorced and remarried families (for wave, $F[1,156] = 6.60, p \leq .05$, and for the wave $\times$ family type interaction, $F[2,156] = 3.42, p \leq .05$). On the Behavior Events Inventory, mothers reported both short- and long-term declines in the percentages of coercive behaviors for all children (short term: wave, $F[1,180] = 4.61, p \leq .05$; long term: wave, $F[1,158] = 26.53, p \leq .001$). Similar declines in depressive behaviors (short term: wave, $F[1,174] = 5.41, p \leq .05$; long term: wave, $F[1,152] = 18.42, p \leq .001$) were modified by a wave $\times$ family type interaction, $F(2,152) = 3.21, p \leq .05$. Analyses performed to determine the direction of this interaction indicated that remarried mothers did not perceive the same decline in their children's depressive behavior over the 26 months of the study as was perceived by the other mothers.

In seeming contradiction, mothers also perceived their children as becoming less prosocial from Wave 1 to Wave 3. This is suggested by declines in the percentages of prosocial acts reported on the Behavior Events Inventory (wave, $F[1,157] = 13.64, p \leq .001$) and ratings of peer involvement on the Child Competence Inventory (wave, $F[1,143] = 9.42, p \leq .01$).

Unlike mothers, who reported decreases in both maladaptive and adaptive behaviors, both nondivorced fathers and stepfathers reported decreases in the former but increases in the latter. On the Child Behavior Checklist, fathers indicated that their children were demonstrating fewer total behavior problems, less externalizing, and less internalizing from Wave 1 to Wave 3 (total behavior problems: wave, $F[1,107] = 17.35, p \leq .001$; externalizing: wave, $F[1,107] = 10.27, p \leq .01$; and internalizing: wave, $F[1,107] = 12.81$, $p \leq .001$; see also Table 13), with some indication that declines in internalizing were occurring earlier (from Wave 1 to Wave 2) for children in nondivorced families than for those who had recently experienced their mothers' remarriages (wave $\times$ family type interaction, $F[1,113] = 4.70, p \leq .05$; see also Table 12). On the Behavior Events Inventory, fathers indicated a drop in the percentages of coercive behaviors from both Wave 1 to Wave 2 (wave, $F[1,118] = 4.28, p \leq .05$) and Wave 1 to Wave 3, particularly for daughters (wave, $F[1,107] = 14.54, p \leq .001$; wave $\times$ gender interaction, $F[1,107] = 5.08, p \leq .05$). Fathers' reports on the Child Competence Inventory indicated that children from both nondivorced and remarried families were also more socially responsible at Wave 3 than at Wave 1 (wave, $F[1,192] = 6.29, p \leq .05$).

Fewer changes over time were reported by children and teachers. Children in nondivorced families and girls in all families did report a greater percentage of prosocial acts at Wave 2 than at Wave 1 on the Behavior Events Inventory (wave × family type interaction, $F[2,180] = 3.07$, $p \leq .05$; wave × gender interaction, $F[1,180] = 3.96$, $p \leq .05$), but teachers failed to identify any changes in children's adjustment over time.

Unlike parents, who tended to note improvements in adjustment, and children and teachers, who reported little change over time, observers tended to see children as increasingly less well adjusted over the course of the study. Their ratings indicated that all children demonstrated short-term increases in antisocial behavior toward their fathers or stepfathers (wave, $F[1,95] = 8.49$, $p \leq .001$) and both short- and long-term increases in antisocial behavior toward their mothers and siblings (toward mothers: Wave 1 to Wave 2, $F[1,153] = 17.05$, $p \leq .001$; Wave 1 to Wave 3, $F[1,87] = 4.50$, $p \leq .05$; toward siblings: Wave 1 to Wave 2, $F[1,109] = 18.83$, $p \leq .001$; Wave 1 to Wave 3, $F[1,59] = 18.09$, $p \leq .001$). This increase in antisocial behavior was accompanied by a general decrease from Wave 1 to Wave 2 in prosocial behavior toward siblings and fathers by both boys and girls and toward mothers by their sons (toward siblings: wave, $F[1,109] = 13.96$, $p \leq .001$; toward fathers: wave, $F[1,95] = 7.48$, $p \leq .01$; and toward mothers: wave × gender interaction, $F[1,153] = 4.92$, $p \leq .05$).

Observers also reported short-term increases in withdrawal from mothers, particularly by daughters, and from siblings (from mothers: wave, $F[1,152] = 28.13$, $p \leq .001$; wave × gender interaction, $F[1,152] = 4.91$, $p \leq .05$; from siblings: wave, $F[1,109] = 7.79$, $p \leq .01$). This increase extended to both parents by Wave 3 (from mothers: wave, $F[1,85] = 18.60$, $p \leq .001$; from fathers: wave, $F[1,87] = 10.92$, $p \leq .01$) but disappeared in analyses of the sibling relationship for children in divorced and remarried families (wave × family type interaction, $F[1,59] = 6.46$, $p \leq .05$).

In summary, correlational analyses indicated that there was considerable individual stability across time in measures of adjustment. In addition, the repeated-measures analyses of composite measures indicated some short-term deterioration in adjustment from Wave 1 to Wave 2 but little long-term change from Wave 1 to Wave 3 as children moved further into adolescence. Some changes were detected in analyses of the individual scales, however, suggesting differences in the perceptions of different informants on different measures, despite adequate Cronbach's alphas for the multimethod/multirespondent composite measures (see Chap. II). Mothers tended to see both prosocial and maladaptive behaviors as declining, fathers and stepfathers saw adaptive behaviors increasing and maladaptive behaviors declining, children and teachers reported few changes over time, and observers saw short-term decreases in prosocial behaviors and both short- and long-term increases in deviant behaviors. In a few instances, the patterns of changes were moderated by children's family type and gender.

SUMMARY AND CONCLUSIONS

Children who had experienced their parents' marital transitions demonstrated greater difficulties in adjustment than children who had been spared such experiences, as all children approached and entered adolescence. The differences between children in remarried and nondivorced families were both more marked and more frequent than those between children in single-mother and nondivorced families, although some discrepancies occurred across informants, measures, and waves.

Children from single-mother homes were exhibiting difficulties in adjustment even 4–6 years after the divorce, at the time of these assessments. These difficulties manifested themselves in higher levels of behavior problems, such as externalizing and internalizing, and in deficiencies in scholastic, social, and general competence and were most often noted by mothers and observers.

The greater adverse effects of divorce on boys relative to girls reported in studies of younger children were not obtained in this study. The analysis of the multimethod/multirespondent composite measures of externalizing indicated that elevated levels of acting-out antisocial behavior were present for both boys and girls in divorced families. This provides some support for findings of the reemergence in adolescence of behavior problems for girls in divorced families (Baumrind, 1989; Hetherington, 1990; and Udry, 1987).

Reports concerning children's adjustment in stepfamilies varied as a function of the respondent. Stepfathers perceived their stepchildren as demonstrating higher levels of problem behavior and lower levels of scholastic and social competence than did nondivorced fathers. Remarried mothers agreed with their recent husbands on most indices, although they were less inclined to report that increases in problem behaviors were accompanied by deficits in competence and prosocial behavior. Observers' reports provided inconsistent support for the accuracy of parents' perceptions, and teachers and the children themselves reported very few differences between stepchildren and their peers. This suggests that the problems in adjustment, so evident in the home setting, had not generalized to the school setting in the 26 months following remarriage.

Contrary to expectations, analyses of stability and change did not indicate that the behavior profiles of children in remarried and nondivorced families had begun to converge over time. Changes in adjustment that did occur were attributable to sample-wide fluctuations in functioning as all children entered adolescence rather than to a growing adaptation to the remarriage and a concomitant decline in problem behavior by stepchildren.

The few family type × gender interactions and the high levels of problem behaviors demonstrated by both adolescent boys and adolescent girls in divorced and remarried families contrast markedly with the findings of studies of younger children indicating that the problems associated with divorce are more severe and sustained for boys and that those accompanying remarriage are more severe for girls. The findings of this study suggest a continuation of problem behavior in boys and a reemergence of adaptive difficulties for girls in divorced families when they enter adolescence or when a custodial mother remarries. In addition, for both boys and girls, adolescence seems to be an especially difficult period in which to have a stepfather enter the household. This is evidenced by the fact that, across all three waves, children in stepfamilies showed significantly more behavior problems and less social and scholastic competence than children from nondivorced households. In contrast to studies of younger children, in which boys in particular have been found to adapt well to and benefit from the presence of a stepfather two years after their mothers' remarriage (Hetherington et al., 1985), our results indicated that early adolescents showed little sign of such coping 26 months after remarriage.

Finally, an important precautionary note must be mentioned. Despite the large differences in group means of children who had and those who had not experienced their parents' marital transitions, it was clear from the variability in the responses of children from both single-mother and remarried families that some of these children were functioning quite well. This suggests that, while marital transitions may place children at risk for adjustment problems, the emergence of problems is not inevitable and is likely to be related to other factors than just family status.

IV. THE MARITAL RELATIONSHIP IN REMARRIED FAMILIES

James E. Deal, Margaret Stanley Hagan, and Edward R. Anderson

Much of the early research on family members' adjustment to remarriage focused on the establishment of the stepparent-stepchild relationship, changes in the custodial parent-child relationship, and children's adjustment. In recent years, emphasis on a systems perspective in family research has underscored the importance of also understanding the marital relationship in stepfamilies. Owing in part to measurement and methodological differences across studies (these were noted in Chap. I), findings concerning the similarities and differences between first and second marriages have been inconsistent (Albrecht et al., 1983).

In this chapter, the marital relationships in newly remarried families were compared with the corresponding relationships in nondivorced families on several dimensions, namely, the husbands' and wives' reports of depression, marital satisfaction, the degree to which housekeeping and child-rearing roles were shared, and the positivity and negativity spouses directed toward each other during observed marital interactions. As previous research has found that conflict over child-rearing issues is common among remarried couples (Walker & Messinger, 1979), comparisons of the frequency of such disagreements were also made.

HYPOTHESES

On the basis of previous research, the following hypotheses were proposed.

First, because the nondivorced spouses have a longer shared family history, the congruence between husbands' and wives' perceptions of their relationships and behaviors toward one another was expected to be greater in nondivorced families than in the newly forming remarried families.

Second, in the early months following remarriage, remarried spouses were expected to experience a "honeymoon" period characterized by higher self-reported marital satisfaction, higher observed positivity, and lower observed negativity during interactions than were characteristic of nondivorced spouses (Hetherington, 1988). Moreover, it was expected that remarried spouses would perceive their marriages as more egalitarian with respect to the performance of child-rearing and housekeeping roles (Centers et al., 1971; Furstenberg, 1979, 1982; Giles-Sims, 1984, 1987; Weingarten, 1980).

Third, as the new marital relationship stabilized over time, remarried couples were expected to resemble nondivorced couples more closely in terms of marital satisfaction, role sharing, and patterns of observed interactions. However, it was also expected that remarried husbands and wives would evince greater depression as they became increasingly exposed to the challenges and stresses involved in the establishment of a new stepfamily.

Fourth, on the basis of Gottman and Levenson's work (1988; Levenson & Gottman, 1985), it was predicted that conflict and negativity would be more consistently associated with marital satisfaction than positivity and that these two factors would have more adverse effects on marital satisfaction for males than for females.

Finally, because remarried spouses were establishing or modifying parent-child relationships while simultaneously establishing their marital bond, conflict over child-rearing issues was expected to play a more prominent role in their relationship than in that of nondivorced couples, particularly as the children entered adolescence (Walker & Messinger, 1979). Conflict over child rearing was expected to increase over time and have an increasing effect on marital satisfaction and on depression in spouses in the remarried families. Although spouses' depression was expected to influence marital satisfaction, no gender differences in this relation could be predicted owing to the inconsistency of previous findings in this area (Cowan et al., 1989; Cox et al., 1989).

OVERVIEW OF FINDINGS

Throughout our comparison of marital relationships in nondivorced and remarried families, one finding consistently emerged: the two groups were much more alike than they were different. In fact, with the exception of self-reported marital satisfaction and depression, few consistent differences were found. Instead, in congruence of perceptions and behaviors, in changes over time, and in relations among specific dimensions of the relationship, an impressive degree of similarity in the marital relationship in first and second marriages was found.

METHOD

Several dimensions of the marital relationship were of interest: marital satisfaction and conflict, husbands' and wives' roles within the family, spouses' positive and negative behavior toward each other, and depression. These dimensions were assessed using interview measures from husbands and wives as well as observational reports of the spouses' behavior toward each other; detailed description of the specific measures and scales was presented in Chap. II. For each scale, comparisons were made between spouses in remarried families and those in nondivorced families as well as between husbands and wives. For this chapter only, gender of the target child was not included as a factor in the analyses as it did not seem directly relevant to the specific aspects of the marital relationship examined here; furthermore, most of these families contained more than one child, often including sons and daughters.

WITHIN-WAVE ASSESSMENTS OF THE MARITAL RELATIONSHIP

The congruence between husbands' and wives' reports and behaviors.—In order to test the hypothesis that the nondivorced husbands and wives held more congruent perceptions of their marital relationships and demonstrated more similarity in their behaviors toward one another than did their newly remarried counterparts, correlations between spouses' scores were computed and the significance of the differences in correlations subsequently tested using Fisher's r to Z transformation. Results of these analyses are presented in Table 15. Significance criteria varied across groups and across waves owing to differences in sample sizes.

Within both nondivorced and remarried families, husbands' and wives' reports of marital satisfaction were positively related at each assessment. Correlations between the observed positivity and the observed negativity in spousal interactions were also consistently positive within both types of families, with the exception of Wave 2 for remarried families. Thus, when one partner acted in a positive or, conversely, negative manner toward the spouse, the other spouse tended to behave similarly. The only other instances of nonsignificant within-pair agreement occurred in the remarried families; spouses seemed to differ in their perceptions of conflict over both adolescent issues and daily routines at Wave 3. Finally, correlations between husbands' and wives' perceptions of role responsibilities were also significant and positive in both family types.

Tests of the differences between correlations yielded only two significant differences. First, nondivorced spouses were more similar in their observed positivity at Wave 2 than were remarried spouses, $Z = 2.6, p \leq .05$.

TABLE 15

Correlations between Nondivorced and Remarried Husbands' and Wives' Reports and Behaviors

	Nondivorced	Remarried
Dyadic Adjustment scale:		
Marital satisfaction:		
Wave 1	.48***	.70***
Wave 2	.42***	.68***
Wave 3	.39***	.65***
Observational ratings:		
Positivity to spouse:		
Wave 1	.68***	.63***
Wave 2	.57***	.11
Wave 3	.52***	.48***
Negativity to spouse:		
Wave 1	.79***	.80***
Wave 2	.81***	.77***
Wave 3	.86***	.80***
Conflict over child-rearing issues:		
Adolescent issues:		
Wave 1	.67***	.54***
Wave 2	.40**	.44***
Wave 3	.52***	.24
Children's adherence to daily routines:		
Wave 1	.45***	.64***
Wave 2	.25*	.31**
Wave 3	.48***	.23
Housekeeping and child-rearing roles:		
Housekeeping:		
Wave 1	.65***	.50***
Wave 2	.61***	.69***
Wave 3	.43**	.72***
Child rearing:		
Wave 1	.36***	.56***
Wave 2	.30**	.55***
Wave 3	.60***	.46**

* $p \leq .05$.
** $p \leq .01$.
*** $p \leq .001$.

Second, spouses in remarried families were more similar in their reports of responsibility for housekeeping roles, $Z = 2.0$, $p \leq .05$. Contrary to expectations, husbands and wives within both nondivorced and remarried families were remarkably congruent in their reports about the quality of their relationship and in their behaviors toward each other. Nevertheless, it could be that the processes underlying consistency may differ. Among nondivorced spouses, consistency may reflect the maturity and stability of their relationships or simply a tendency of couples with similar views to remain together. For remarried couples, it may reflect a search for commonalities in the relationship and the degree to which the pair discussed aspects of their new marriage.

Differences between nondivorced and remarried spouses.—Because the correlational results may have masked significant group differences between nondivorced and remarried spouses, MANOVAs were conducted on three dimensions of the marital relationship at each wave: positivity (marital satisfaction, observed positivity), negativity (conflict over adolescent issues, conflict over daily routines, and observed negativity), and roles (housekeeping, child rearing). All MANOVAs were run with family type as the between-subjects factor and spouse as the repeated factor. The results of the MANOVAs are presented in Table 16.

Univariate contrasts were examined when the multivariate F values indicated a significant effect or when our hypotheses suggested particular planned comparisons. Results of these analyses are presented in Table 17, which also includes results of a separate ANOVA conducted on the measure of depression.

Marital satisfaction, affective relations, and conflict.—Remarried couples reported greater marital satisfaction than nondivorced couples across all three waves (planned comparison at Wave 3). In contrast to previous research involving younger children (Glenn, 1981; Hetherington, 1990), remarried wives' reports of marital satisfaction were not any lower than those of their husbands. This may be a reflection of the situation in which the wives in this sample found themselves. Remarriage after an extended period as a single mother, with the child approaching adolescence, may have made the marital relationship more attractive and important to the mother.

Interestingly, the greater marital satisfaction of remarried couples was rarely reflected in self- or observer-reported behavior. Despite findings that child-rearing issues are the most frequent sources of conflict for remarried couples (Walker & Messinger, 1979), no family-type effects emerged on our scales of observed negativity, conflict over adolescent issues, or conflict over daily routines. With respect to positivity, remarried husbands were more positive toward their wives than were nondivorced husbands, but only at Wave 1, and no differences prevailed between wives. However, across both family types, wives were observed to be more positive than husbands in their dyadic interactions at all three waves, and they reported less marital conflict over adolescent issues at Wave 1 and over target children's adherence to daily routines at Wave 2 (planned comparison) than their husbands.

It should be noted that, although all the marital satisfaction means for the nondivorced and remarried groups are above the Dyadic Adjustment scale's clinical cutoff, they are still below the level that Spanier (1976) refers to as normative. This lower than average marital satisfaction may be a reflection of these families' position in the family life cycle. Research in this area shows a moderate decline in marital satisfaction (Martin, 1987) and an

TABLE 16

F Values and Significance Levels for Multivariate Analyses of Measures of the Marital Relationship

Effect	Wave 1			Wave 2			Wave 3		
	Family	Spouse	Interaction	Family	Spouse	Interaction	Family	Spouse	Interaction
Positivity:									
Multivariate	11.14***	4.70**	2.63	6.38**	4.92**	.71	2.50	5.30**	.61
Multivariate *df*	(2,126)	(2,126)	(2,126)	(2,99)	(2,99)	(2,99)	(2,90)	(2,90)	(2,90)
Marital satisfaction	22.39***	1.57	.24	12.88***	.04	.14	4.69*	1.36	.75
Observed positivity	1.33	7.19**	4.82*	1.00	9.86**	1.26	.60	10.09**	.35
Univariate *df*	(1,127)	(1,127)	(1,127)	(1,100)	(1,100)	(1,100)	(1,91)	(1,91)	(1,91)
Negativity:									
Multivariate	.26	2.70*	1.27	.81	2.30	1.43	.92	1.40	1.02
Multivariate *df*	(3,125)	(3,125)	(3,125)	(3,98)	(3,98)	(3,98)	(3,84)	(3,84)	(3,84)
Conflict over adolescent issues	.09	6.12**	.02	.19	2.72	.02	1.94	.07	.50
Conflict over children's adherence to daily routines	.01	.77	.78	.53	4.84*	1.03	.28	1.27	.08
Observed negativity	.55	1.75	3.19	.01	1.41	3.07	.22	2.62	1.55
Univariate *df*	(1,127)	(1,127)	(1,127)	(1,100)	(1,100)	(1,100)	(1,86)	(1,86)	(1,86)
Housekeeping and child-rearing roles:									
Multivariate	8.44**	5.14**	.08	3.31*	4.42**	.78	3.95*	9.72***	.27
Multivariate *df*	(2,98)	(2,98)	(2,98)	(2,87)	(2,87)	(2,87)	(2,74)	(2,74)	(2,74)
Housekeeping	9.75**	6.54**	.09	6.29**	8.93**	1.27	4.38*	18.08***	.74
Child rearing	.17	5.12*	.05	.02	1.07	.02	.78	.49	.49
Univariate *df*	(1,99)	(1,99)	(1,99)	(1,88)	(1,88)	(1,88)	(1,75)	(1,75)	(1,75)

Note.—Multivariate test is Wilks's lambda.

* $p \leq .05$.

** $p \leq .01$.

*** $p \leq .001$.

increase in parenting stress and conflict as parents move into middle age and their children move into adolescence (Steinberg, 1988). In addition, the life-span literature indicates that adults in this age range often experience a major identity crisis. Given a combination of life stressors, there is every reason to suspect that this time period should be stressful for nondivorced as well as for remarried families (Stolberg & Anker, 1983) and that it is this stress that may be reflected in the lower levels of marital satisfaction in both family groups.

Roles.—Reports of responsibility for housekeeping revealed significant family and spouse effects at all three waves. Follow-up analyses revealed that spouses in stepfamilies were more likely to report more shared responsibilities than their nondivorced counterparts. The spouse effect was due to a tendency for mothers to report more sole responsibility than did fathers. It should be noted, however, that both husbands and wives in both family types tended to report that the mother had more responsibility for housekeeping. For reports of child-rearing responsibilities, in contrast, only a spouse effect was found and only at Wave 1. Again, mothers reported more sole responsibility than did fathers.

Depression.—Analyses of spouses' depression scores yielded a finding consistent at all three waves: while no differences prevailed between husbands and wives, the means of remarried spouses were significantly higher than those of the nondivorced spouses. It must be emphasized, however, that the mean level of depression reported for all groups at all time points was low and few of our spouses scored above the clinical cutoff for depression. Thus, it is best to view this as dysphoria rather than clinical depression. However, variations in this dysphoria were often found to be associated with marital relations and parenting and with negativity and externalizing in children in both nondivorced and remarried families as well as with job satisfaction in nondivorced families (for a discussion of these findings, see Hetherington, Lindner, Miller, & Clingempeel, 1991).

Conclusion.—In summary, with the exception of marital satisfaction and depression, few differences were found at any time in nondivorced and remarried husbands' and wives' reports of their marital relationship or in their observed behaviors. There was some evidence to suggest that married spouses experienced a honeymoon period following their remarriage in that both husbands and wives in this group reported more satisfaction with their marriages than nondivorced spouses reported. Furthermore, these higher levels of satisfaction were still evident 26 months after marriage, despite the fact that conflict and negativity tended to be no less frequent in the remarried couples' than in the nondivorced couples' relationships and that remarried spouses reported being more dysphoric than their nondivorced counterparts at all three waves.

TABLE 17

MEANS (Standard Deviations) FOR MEASURES OF MARITAL ADJUSTMENT

	Nondivorced		Remarried		Significant Main Effects and Interactions[a]	Significant Contrasts and Planned Comparisons[a]
	Wives	Husbands	Wives	Husbands		
Dyadic Adjustment scale:						
Marital satisfaction:						
Wave 1	108.7 (10.2)	107.1 (12.1)	117.3 (12.9)	116.7 (13.5)	Family type	Rem > Nondiv
Wave 2	105.5 (14.1)	106.2 (11.8)	113.9 (13.0)	113.6 (11.9)	Family type	Rem > Nondiv
Wave 3	107.3 (11.6)	104.8 (10.3)	111.0 (14.9)	110.8 (13.7)	*Family type*	*Rem > Nondiv*
Observational measures:						
Positivity to spouse:						
Wave 1	3.4 (.5)	3.2 (.5)	3.4 (.6)	3.4 (.6)	Spouse, Family type × spouse	Rem Husbands > Nondiv Husbands; Wives > Husbands
Wave 2	3.4 (.5)	3.1 (.5)	3.4 (.5)	3.3 (.6)	Spouse	Wives > Husbands
Wave 3	3.4 (.5)	3.3 (.5)	3.5 (.5)	3.3 (.6)	Spouse	Wives > Husbands
Negativity to spouse:						
Wave 1	1.5 (.5)	1.6 (.6)	1.7 (.6)	1.7 (.7)	...	
Wave 2	1.5 (.5)	1.6 (.6)	1.6 (.5)	1.5 (.5)	...	
Wave 3	1.6 (.7)	1.6 (.7)	1.7 (.6)	1.6 (.6)	...	
Conflict over child rearing:						
Conflict over adolescent issues:						
Wave 1	9.5 (4.1)	10.3 (4.2)	9.3 (4.0)	10.0 (3.6)	Spouse	Husband > Wives
Wave 2	10.1 (3.8)	10.7 (3.7)	9.9 (2.9)	10.4 (3.3)	...	
Wave 3	10.3 (3.1)	10.6 (3.3)	9.8 (2.3)	9.6 (2.5)	...	

Conflict over children's adherence to daily routines:						
Wave 1	15.8	17.0	16.6	16.5	. . .	
	(7.9)	(7.8)	(8.0)	(8.7)		
Wave 2	15.1	17.8	16.9	17.8	*Spouse*	*Husbands > Wives*
	(6.2)	(8.6)	(7.5)	(7.9)		
Wave 3	15.9	16.6	15.1	16.3	. . .	
	(6.6)	(6.9)	(4.8)	(7.2)		
Child-rearing and housekeeping roles:						
Housekeeping:						
Wave 1	1.8	2.0	2.2	2.4	Spouse, family type	Husbands > Wives; Rem > Nondiv
	(.6)	(.6)	(.7)	(.7)		
Wave 2	1.9	2.1	2.2	2.5	Spouse, family type	Husbands > Wives; Rem > Nondiv
	(.7)	(.5)	(.9)	(.9)		
Wave 3	1.8	2.1	2.1	2.5	Spouse, family type	Husbands > Wives; Rem > Nondiv
	(.6)	(.6)	(.8)	(.9)		
Child rearing:						
Wave 1	2.3	2.4	2.2	2.4	Spouse	Husbands > Wives
	(.6)	(.6)	(.8)	(.7)		
Wave 2	2.3	2.4	2.3	2.4	. . .	
	(.6)	(.5)	(.9)	(.6)		
Wave 3	2.4	2.3	2.3	2.3	. . .	
	(.6)	(.6)	(.7)	(.7)		
Beck Depression Inventory:						
Depression:[b]						
Wave 1	1.6	1.8	2.7	2.3	Family type	Rem > Nondiv
	(2.1)	(2.7)	(2.9)	(2.9)		
Wave 2	1.7	1.7	3.9	3.0	Family type	Rem > Nondiv
	(2.2)	(2.8)	(4.6)	(3.1)		
Wave 3	1.7	1.6	2.4	3.0	Family type	Rem > Nondiv
	(2.1)	(2.6)	(2.6)	(3.7)		

NOTE.—Nondiv = Nondivorced; Rem = Remarried.

[a] Italicized contrasts denote planned comparisons.

[b] Univariate analyses.

STABILITY AND CHANGES OVER TIME IN THE MARITAL RELATIONSHIP

Correlational analyses of the marital relationship.—The stability of spouses' perceptions and behaviors toward each other was examined by computing correlations for each marital relationship measure across all time points; these are presented in Table 18.

For the most part, husbands' and wives' perceptions and behaviors proved quite stable across time. For nondivorced spouses, the only dimension of the marital relationship lacking stability was observed positivity, where husbands' data yielded nonsignificant correlations from time 1 to time 3 and wives' data from time 1 to time 3 and from time 2 to time 3. Given the many years that nondivorced couples have had to develop stable patterns of perceptions and behaviors, such general stability is not surprising.

The perceptions and behaviors of remarried spouses also proved to be fairly consistent, with a lack of stability emerging most often in the observational data. For remarried wives, nonsignificant correlations were obtained for observed positivity, observed negativity, conflict over adolescent issues, and conflict over daily routines from Wave 1 to Wave 3 and for depression from Wave 2 to Wave 3. For remarried husbands, lack of stability was seen in observed positivity from Wave 2 to Wave 3, in observed negativity from Wave 1 to Wave 3 and from Wave 2 to Wave 3, and also in reports of conflict over daily routines from time 1 to time 3. It should be noted, however, that, despite the stronger association obtained for nondivorced spouses, few significant differences were found between the correlations of the two sets of wives and the two sets of husbands, and those that were found formed no consistent pattern (all differences were tested using Fisher's Z transformation).

Of additional interest is the fact that, for husbands and wives in both family types, correlations from time 1 to time 2 indicated stability across all dimensions of the marital relationship; changes in the relationship did not appear until Wave 3 as children moved further into adolescence. This suggests that, while spouses' behaviors and perceptions tended to remain stable, some changes in their relationship did occur as they adjusted to their children's entry into adolescence. However, this process did not seem to differ as a function of family type.

Repeated-measures ANOVAs.—To test the hypothesis that marital relationships in remarried families would increasingly come to resemble those in nondivorced families, repeated-measures ANOVAs were conducted between spouses' perceptions and behaviors at Waves 1 and 2 (short-term change and adjustment) and at Waves 1 and 3 (long-term change and adjustment). Results of these analyses, which included family type as the between-subjects factor and spouse and time as within-subjects factors, are presented in Tables 19 and 20; across-wave means differ from within-wave means owing to differences in the number of subjects involved in the two analyses.

Overall, there was little short- or long-term change in marital relationships, and what change was present tended to be modified by interactions with family type or gender of the spouse.

Only two significant short-term changes were found. The first was a decline in remarried husbands' and wives' marital satisfaction from time 1 to time 2, $F(1,120) = 7.20$, $p \leq .01$). The second was a spouse × wave interaction for reports of child-rearing roles, $F(1,107) = 4.46$, $p \leq .04$, with mothers reporting slightly more shared responsibilities over time and fathers slightly less (although follow-up tests indicated that these trends were not significant). Long-term changes included a significant decline in marital satisfaction occurring for remarried but not nondivorced spouses, $F(1,109) = 12.11$, $p \leq .001$. In contrast, effects for observed positivity were due to within-wave differences, with nondivorced husbands demonstrating less positivity than either their wives or their remarried peers at Wave 1 and husbands in both types of families demonstrating less positivity than their wives at Wave 3, $F(1,87) = 4.30$, $p \leq .05$. No significant time effects were found for reports of dysphoria, observed negativity, self-reported conflict, or role responsibility.

Relations among dimensions: Determinants of marital satisfaction.—It has been hypothesized that negativity and marital conflict are better predictors of later marital satisfaction than is positivity (Levenson & Gottman, 1985). To test this hypothesis for remarried families and for nondivorced families, the correlations between family conflict (single item), observed negativity and observed positivity at Wave 1, and marital satisfaction at Waves 2 and 3 were compared, as were correlations between the former variables at Wave 2 and marital satisfaction at Wave 3. These correlations are presented in Table 21.

Contrary to expectations, spouses' positivity was found to be significantly related to later marital satisfaction for nondivorced wives but not for remarried spouses and only at Wave 2 for nondivorced husbands. Also contrary to Levenson and Gottman's (1985) finding, there was little evidence that conflict or negative interactions played a more significant role in marital dissatisfaction for men than for women. For both nondivorced and remarried husbands and wives, perceptions of family conflict at Wave 1 were negatively related to marital satisfaction at the later waves (with the exception of remarried wives at Wave 3). Moreover, for both remarried and nondivorced wives, but not for their husbands, the negativity initially displayed by their spouses during interactions predicted lower levels of marital satisfaction at Waves 2 and 3. These results offer little support for Levenson

TABLE 18

ACROSS-TIME CORRELATIONS FOR MEASURES OF THE MARITAL RELATIONSHIP

	Marital Satisfaction			Observed Positivity			Observed Negativity			Conflict over Adolescent Issues		
	Wave 1	Wave 2	Wave 3	Wave 1	Wave 2	Wave 3	Wave 1	Wave 2	Wave 3	Wave 1	Wave 2	Wave 3
Nondiv wives:												
Wave 1	. . .			. . .			. . .			. . .		
Wave 2	.61***	. . .		.50***	. . .		.45***	. . .		.42***	. . .	
Wave 3	.72***	.82***	. . .	.11	.11	. . .	.47***	.35**	. . .	.39***	.67**	. . .
Nondiv husbands:												
Wave 1	. . .			. . .			. . .			. . .		
Wave 2	.59***	. . .		.51**	. . .		.44***	. . .		.51***	. . .	
Wave 3	.55***	.85***	. . .	.17	.41***	. . .	.56***	.34**	. . .	.56***	.66***	. . .
Rem wives:												
Wave 1	. . .			. . .			. . .			. . .		
Wave 2	.47***	. . .		.41**	. . .		.48***	. . .		.61**	. . .	
Wave 3	.57***	.78***	. . .	.04	.30*	. . .	−.02	.32*	. . .	.17	.34**	. . .
Rem husbands:												
Wave 1	. . .			. . .			. . .			. . .		
Wave 2	.64***	. . .		.57***	. . .		.46***	. . .		.54***	. . .	
Wave 3	.65***	.82***	. . .	.27*	.27	. . .	.21	.27	. . .	.16	.48***	. . .

Nondiv wives:												
Wave 1	. . .			. . .			. . .			. . .		
Wave 2	.42***	. . .		.71***	. . .		.58***	. . .		.39***	. . .	
Wave 3	.35**	.72***	. . .	.60***	.62***	. . .	.62***	.50***	. . .	.54***	.55***	. . .
Nondiv husbands:												
Wave 1	. . .			. . .			. . .			. . .		
Wave 2	.42***	. . .		.34**	. . .		.53***	. . .		.63***	. . .	
Wave 3	.31**	.50***	. . .	.26**	.69***	. . .	.52***	.40***	. . .	.65***	.83***	. . .
Rem wives:												
Wave 1	. . .			. . .			. . .			. . .		
Wave 2	.50***	. . .		.71***	. . .		.49***	. . .		.46**	. . .	
Wave 3	.18	.26*	. . .	.50**	.54***	. . .	.51***	.66***	. . .	.30*	.17	. . .
Rem husbands:												
Wave 1	. . .			. . .			. . .			. . .		
Wave 2	.43***	. . .		.48***	. . .		.61***	. . .		.53***	. . .	
Wave 3	.28*	.60***	. . .	.28*	.60***	. . .	.46**	.56***	. . .	.74***	.69***	. . .

NOTE.—Nondiv = Nondivorced; Rem = Remarried.
* $p \leq .05$.
** $p \leq .01$.
*** $p \leq .001$.

TABLE 19

MEANS (Standard Deviations) FOR REPEATED-MEASURES ANALYSES OF SHORT-TERM CHANGES (Wave 1 to Wave 2) IN THE MARITAL RELATIONSHIP

	NONDIVORCED		REMARRIED		SIGNIFICANT MAIN EFFECTS AND INTERACTIONS	SIGNIFICANT CONTRASTS
	Wives	Husbands	Wives	Husbands		
Dyadic Adjustment scale:						
Marital satisfaction:						
Wave 1	108.12	107.72	118.93	119.24	Family type	Rem Wives (1 > 2);
	(10.1)	(11.4)	(10.4)	(11.7)	× wave	Rem Husbands (1 > 2)
Wave 2	105.67	106.17	113.59	113.12		
	(14.1)	(11.8)	(13.0)	(11.7)		
Observational measures of the marital relationship:						
Positivity:						
Wave 1	3.36	3.18	3.43	3.40	. . .	
	(.5)	(.5)	(.5)	(.6)		
Wave 2	3.37	3.13	3.39	3.28		
	(.5)	(.5)	(.5)	(.6)		
Negativity:						
Wave 1	1.5	1.5	1.6	1.6	. . .	
	(.5)	(.5)	(.5)	(.5)		
Wave 2	1.5	1.6	1.6	1.6		
	(.5)	(.6)	(.5)	(.6)		

Conflict over child-rearing issues:						
Adolescent issues:						
Wave 1	9.7	10.4	9.6	9.9	. . .	
	(4.4)	(4.5)	(4.1)	(3.4)		
Wave 2	10.1	10.7	9.9	10.5		
	(3.8)	(3.7)	(2.9)	(3.3)		
Children's adherence to daily routines:						
Wave 1	15.1	17.6	16.4	16.3	. . .	
	(6.9)	(8.3)	(7.5)	(8.6)		
Wave 2	15.2	17.9	16.9	17.7		
	(6.2)	(8.8)	(7.6)	(8.0)		
Housekeeping and child-rearing roles:						
Housekeeping:						
Wave 1	1.8	2.0	2.2	2.4	. . .	
	(.6)	(.6)	(.7)	(.7)		
Wave 2	2.0	2.1	2.2	2.5		
	(.7)	(.6)	(.9)	(.9)		
Child rearing:						
Wave 1	2.3	2.5	2.2	2.4	Spouse × wave	No significant contrasts
	(.6)	(.6)	(.8)	(.7)		
Wave 2	2.3	2.4	2.3	2.3		
	(.6)	(.5)	(.8)	(.6)		
Beck Depression Inventory:						
Depression:						
Wave 1	1.6	1.9	2.7	2.8	. . .	
	(2.1)	(2.8)	(2.8)	(3.2)		
Wave 2	1.7	1.8	3.9	3.6		
	(2.2)	(2.8)	(4.6)	(3.1)		

NOTE.—Rem = Remarried.

TABLE 20

MEANS (Standard Deviations) FOR REPEATED-MEASURES ANALYSES OF LONG-TERM CHANGE FROM WAVE 1 TO WAVE 3

	NONDIVORCED		REMARRIED		SIGNIFICANT MAIN EFFECTS AND INTERACTIONS	SIGNIFICANT CONTRASTS
	Wives	Husbands	Wives	Husbands		
Dyadic Adjustment scale:						
Marital satisfaction:						
Wave 1	108.2 (9.2)	106.0 (12.5)	116.5 (4.5)	116.1 (12.6)	Family type × wave	Rem Wives (1 > 3); Rem Husbands (1 > 3)
Wave 3	107.5 (11.2)	105.0 (9.9)	110.3 (14.8)	110.1 (13.7)		
Observational measures of the marital relationship:						
Positivity:						
Wave 1	3.4 (.5)	3.2 (.5)	3.5 (.5)	3.5 (.7)	Family type × spouse × wave	1 [Nondiv (Wives > Husbands)]; 1 [Husbands (Rem > Nondiv)]
Wave 3	3.4 (.5)	3.3 (.5)	3.6 (.5)	3.3 (.6)		
Negativity:						
Wave 1	1.5 (.5)	1.6 (.5)	1.7 (.6)	1.6 (.7)	...	
Wave 3	1.6 (.7)	1.6 (.7)	1.7 (.7)	1.6 (.6)		
Conflict over child-rearing issues:						
Adolescent issues:						
Wave 1	9.3 (4.2)	10.4 (4.5)	8.7 (1.7)	9.7 (3.2)	...	
Wave 3	10.3 (3.2)	10.6 (3.3)	9.9 (2.3)	9.6 (2.5)		

Children's adherence to daily routines:					
Wave 1	14.7	16.6	15.9	16.0	. . .
	(6.0)	(7.4)	(7.6)	(8.1)	
Wave 3	15.9	16.7	15.1	16.5	
	(6.6)	(7.0)	(4.7)	(7.3)	
Housekeeping and child-rearing roles:					
Housekeeping:					
Wave 1	1.8	2.0	2.2	2.3	. . .
	(.6)	(.6)	(.7)	(.6)	
Wave 3	1.8	2.1	2.3	2.5	
	(.6)	(.6)	(.8)	(.9)	
Child rearing:					
Wave 1	2.4	2.5	2.3	2.3	. . .
	(.6)	(.6)	(.8)	(.8)	
Wave 3	2.4	2.3	2.3	2.3	
	(.6)	(.6)	(.7)	(.7)	
Beck Depression Inventory:					
Depression:					
Wave 1	1.6	1.7	1.9	2.4	. . .
	(2.1)	(2.6)	(2.0)	(3.1)	
Wave 3	1.7	1.6	2.4	3.0	
	(2.1)	(2.6)	(2.6)	(3.7)	

NOTE.—Nondiv = Nondivorced; Rem = Remarried.

TABLE 21

IDENTIFYING POTENTIAL PREDICTORS OF SUBSEQUENT MARITAL SATISFACTION

	Wave 1 Predicting Marital Satisfaction at Wave 2	Wave 1 Predicting Marital Satisfaction at Wave 3	Wave 2 Predicting Marital Satisfaction at Wave 3
Nondivorced wives:			
Family conflict	−.48*** (73)	−.34** (68)	−.55*** (67)
Husbands' observed positivity to wives	.26* (71)	.27* (66)	.38** (55)
Husbands' observed negativity to wives	−.36** (71)	−.38** (66)	−.12 (55)
Nondivorced husbands:			
Family conflict	−.42*** (73)	−.43*** (68)	−.52*** (63)
Wives' observed positivity to husbands	.17 (71)	.27* (66)	.13 (55)
Wives' observed negativity to husbands	−.11 (71)	−.12 (66)	−.03 (55)
Remarried wives:			
Family conflict	−.40** (48)	.23 (43)	−.41** (42)
Husbands' observed positivity to wives	.10 (47)	.05 (42)	.12 (38)
Husbands' observed negativity to wives	−.35** (47)	−.34* (42)	−.10 (38)
Remarried husbands:			
Family conflict	−.30** (49)	−.48*** (43)	−.49*** (41)
Wives' observed positivity to husbands	−.03 (47)	−.08 (41)	.04 (37)
Wives' observed negativity to husbands	−.23 (47)	−.21 (41)	−.31 (37)

NOTE.—Numbers in parentheses refer to sample size for that correlation.
* $p \leq .05$.
** $p \leq .01$.
*** $p \leq .001$.

and Gottman's model of gender differences in factors leading to marital satisfaction. Instead, they suggest that, while both husbands and wives are attuned to their own perceptions of conflict, only wives are sensitive to their husbands' actual negative behaviors toward them. The nature and strength of these relations were highly similar for both family types.

Correlations between dysphoria and marital satisfaction are presented in Table 22. In all waves and for both remarried and first-married husbands and wives, there was a fairly consistent tendency for contemporaneous dysphoria to be negatively associated with marital satisfaction; the few instances of nonsignificant correlations followed no pattern. To assess the degree to which dysphoria predicted later marital satisfaction, correlations between (*a*) Wave 1 dysphoria and marital satisfaction at Waves 2 and 3 and (*b*) Wave 2 dysphoria and Wave 3 marital satisfaction were computed.

Earlier studies (Cowan et al., in press; Cox et al., 1989) have found moderately strong longitudinal relations between depression and later marital satisfaction for wives during the transition to parenthood. Although not entirely consistent, our results showed the same general finding for both husbands and wives in remarried and nondivorced families when short-term relations were considered. That is, with the exception of nondivorced wives from Wave 1 to Wave 2 and remarried wives from Wave 2 to Wave 3, dysphoria was a moderate, short-term negative predictor of marital satisfaction. Long-term prediction (i.e., from Wave 1 to Wave 3), however, was found only for remarried husbands.

SUMMARY AND DISCUSSION

Our results suggest that remarried spouses may experience a honeymoon period during which both husbands and wives report higher marital satisfaction than longer-married nondivorced spouses. In this sample, however, the honeymoon period was found only in self-reports of marital satisfaction. On all other dimensions, nondivorced and remarried spouses looked more similar than different. Couples in both family types reported infrequent spousal conflict and demonstrated similar interactional styles. With the decline in marital satisfaction of the remarried spouses, couples from the two family groups came to look even more similar. Thus, no evidence was found to support Bray's (1988) earlier reports of less positivity, poorer communication, and more coercive behaviors between newly remarried couples.

It is interesting to note the stability of marital satisfaction in the nondivorced families. Despite the potential stress associated with children's entrance into adolescence, there was little evidence that the spouses' contentment with their marriage was being adversely affected. Instead, there was

TABLE 22

Concurrent and Longitudinal Correlations between Depression and Marital Satisfaction

	Concurrent		
	Wave 1	Wave 2	Wave 3
Nondivorced wives	−.19 (74)	−.31** (72)	−.35** (68)
Nondivorced husbands	−.45*** (75)	−.50*** (72)	−.33** (68)
Remarried wives	−.32** (58)	−.25 (44)	−.47** (42)
Remarried husbands	−.23 (58)	−.46** (45)	−.38** (43)
	Longitudinal		
	Depression at Wave 1 Predicting Marital Satisfaction at Wave 2	Depression at Wave 1 Predicting Marital Satisfaction at Wave 3	Depression at Wave 2 Predicting Marital Satisfaction at Wave 3
Nondivorced wives	−.11 (72)	−.07 (67)	−.31** (68)
Nondivorced husbands	−.24* (73)	−.22 (68)	−.37* (68)
Remarried wives	−.28* (49)	−.22 (44)	−.10 (39)
Remarried husbands	−.29* (49)	−.39* (43)	−.33* (43)

Note.—Numbers in parentheses refer to sample size for that correlation.

* $p \leq .05$.

** $p \leq .01$.

*** $p \leq .001$.

considerable stability in marital satisfaction in this group. However, as noted previously, according to Spanier's (1976) criteria, this "stabilization" lies in the low-satisfied range. The drop in satisfaction for remarried couples may reflect the normative stresses of this period as well as those peculiar to stepfamily formation. While such couples may be able to deal with children's transition into adolescence as long as the marital relationship is new and exciting, early optimism may subsequently yield to the realities of the problems that they confront—those of dealing with difficult, resistant children and with the complexities of the extended stepfamily. If this is the case, then it is interesting to note that the repeated-measures analyses failed to show the accompanying increase in dysphoria suggested by the literature linking the quality of the marital relationship in remarried couples with personal well-being (Spanier & Furstenberg, 1987).

There is evidence in the literature to suggest that the model of functioning generally used with nondivorced families may not be appropriate for remarried families with children from a previous marriage (Brand & Clingempeel, 1987; Crosbie-Burnett, 1984). The nondivorced model is basically a "top-down" model: the marital subsystem is presumed to be the one that organizes and "drives" the other subsystems in the family. Disturbances in this subsystem affect parent-child relationships, parenting quality, and children's adjustment.

The marital subsystem in a remarried family, however, may be operating from a position of less strength than the same subsystem in a nondivorced family. In the remarried family, the new stepfather is often, at least initially, in a position of greater marginality than either the mother or her biological children (Hobart, 1987, 1988). As a result of this and of the mother-child bond first developed in the biological family and strengthened in the single-parent family, it is important for the stepfather to establish a positive relationship with his new wife's children (Hetherington, 1989; Hobart, 1987). Such a relationship may be necessary not only to cement the new husband-wife bond but also to prevent the husband-wife relationship from being seen as threatening to the preexisting mother-child relationship (Brand & Clingempeel, 1987). In the remarried family, the relations among the marital relationship, the parent-child relationship, and children's adjustment may differ significantly from those found in nondivorced families (Brand et al., 1988; Bray, Berger, Mann, Silverblatt, & Gershenhorn, 1987; Hetherington, 1990). It may thus be that the primary difference between first marriages and remarriages lies not in the quality of the marital relationship but in the relative importance of the marital relationship within the whole family system. Analyses of the relations among family subsystems in nondivorced and remarried families are presented in Chapter VII.

V. PARENT-CHILD RELATIONSHIPS IN NONDIVORCED, DIVORCED SINGLE-MOTHER, AND REMARRIED FAMILIES

Margaret Stanley Hagan, E. Ann Hollier, Thomas G. O'Connor, and Marlene Eisenberg

Previous research findings have indicated that, at least in the early stages of marital transitions, parent-child relationships are disrupted and parents are less authoritative in both divorced and remarried families than in nondivorced families. Late preadolescent and early adolescent children who are concurrently experiencing the changes and challenges associated with the transition to adolescence may be more vulnerable to the effects of parental divorce and/or remarriage (Anderson, Hetherington, & Clingempeel, 1989; Hetherington, 1990; Hetherington et al., 1985; Hetherington et al., 1989; Lewis & Wallerstein, 1987; Wallerstein & Kelly, 1980). As children enter adolescence, families show a pattern of increased conflict between mothers and children that declines as children move through the pubertal apex (Steinberg, 1987a, 1988). This is accompanied by increasing parental distancing as adolescents grow older and more independent (Steinberg, 1988). In divorced families, mothers and early adolescent sons sustain their preadolescent levels of high conflict, and increasing conflict emerges between divorced mothers and their daughters even though they previously may have had relatively harmonious relationships (Hetherington, 1988). Recent evidence suggests that disruptions in family relationships may also occur in both new and more established stepfamilies when children move into adolescence (Bray, 1990; Hetherington, 1989).

In this chapter, we examine patterns of parent-child relationships in nondivorced, single-mother, and stepfather families as well as changes in these relationships as children moved into adolescence. Several hypotheses based on previous research guided our multilevel analyses.

First, we hypothesized that parent-child relationships in divorced and remarried families would generally be more negative and conflictual and less authoritative than in nondivorced families but that the nature of the differences would depend on children's gender, family type, and time of assessment.

Second, we expected that, following remarriage, mother-child relationships initially would become more negative and conflictual but that this conflict would decrease over time. However, because of parental preoccupation and involvement in the new marital relationship, we expected that monitoring and control by both remarried mothers and stepfathers would remain low (Hetherington, 1988; Patterson, 1989; Wallerstein et al., 1988).

Third, although we predicted that a disengaged parenting style would be more common in stepfathers than in nondivorced fathers, we expected that stepfathers would assume more parental responsibilities and grow closer to their stepchildren over time (Bray, 1988; Bray, Berger, Mann, et al., 1987; Bray, Gershenhorn, & Bennett, 1987; Hetherington, 1989; Hetherington et al., 1985; Patterson, 1989; Wallerstein et al., 1988).

Fourth, since it is especially difficult for children to adjust to a remarriage during early adolescence, we predicted that, in contrast to the relationship between children and fathers in nondivorced families, children in remarried families would continue to be less positive and more negative toward their stepfathers over the course of the 26 months of the study (Brand et al., 1988; Bray, Berger, Silverblatt, & Hollier, 1987; Hetherington, 1989).

Fifth, we expected mothers and sons in restabilized divorced households to exhibit enduring conflict and negativity (Hetherington, 1989; Hetherington et al., 1985; Wallerstein & Kelly, 1980).

Sixth, we hypothesized that divorced mothers and their daughters, but not their sons, would exhibit a warm, close relationship initially. However, as their daughters moved further into adolescence, we believed that single mothers, in comparison to nondivorced and remarried mothers, would not only exhibit higher levels of conflictual and negative behaviors but also make more attempts to monitor and control their daughters as these girls exhibited more acting-out behavior. Thus, the degree of conflict between divorced mothers and their sons and daughters was expected to be similar in later waves and to be higher than that found in nondivorced or remarried families (Hetherington, 1972, 1989; Kalter, 1977; Wallerstein, 1982).

Finally, we expected that, as children moved further into early adolescence, there would be more distancing between parents and children in all families. This distancing would be reflected in decreased levels of warmth, conflict, monitoring, and control on the part of the parent and decreased positivity as well as increased negativity on the part of the child (Steinberg, 1988). However, we also predicted that conflict would be higher between mothers and sons and that mothers would monitor daughters' behavior more closely than that of sons (Steinberg, 1988).

OVERVIEW OF FINDINGS

We obtained several major findings related to the characteristics of the parent-child relationships in the three family types and of their changes over time.

First, there was evidence to support our hypothesis that, over time, mother-child relationships in remarried families became more similar to those in nondivorced families.

Second, mother-child relationships in divorced families differed significantly from those in both nondivorced and remarried families at all three time points. Compared to other families, there was greater conflict between divorced mothers and both sons and daughters as the children moved further into adolescence.

Third, all mothers except divorced mothers of daughters appeared to be disengaging somewhat and declining in conflictual and negative behavior as their children moved further into adolescence.

Fourth, at all three waves, stepfathers were less likely to be authoritative than were nondivorced fathers, and, even 26 months after the remarriage, children were behaving less positively and more adversely toward their stepfathers.

METHOD

The emphasis in this chapter will be on integrating the most consistent findings as well as highlighting findings that address the hypotheses. The parenting dimensions considered included positivity/warmth, negativity/conflict, monitoring, and control. These dimensions are important factors that have been linked both theoretically and in previous empirical research to children's adjustment (Baumrind, 1991; Hetherington, 1989; Maccoby & Martin, 1983; Patterson, 1982). The positivity and negativity that children directed toward their parents during observed interactions were also examined and, in conjunction with parental positivity and negativity, provided measures of the affective nature of the parent-child relationships. Using the techniques described in Chapter II, four multimethod composite indices of parents' behaviors were created: positivity/warmth, negativity/conflict, monitoring, and control. Separate sets of composite scores were created to assess the mothers' and the fathers' parenting. Both within-wave and across-wave analyses were conducted on these composite scores and on the individual scales used to create the composites as well as on children's observed positivity and negativity. The results of both within- and across-wave analyses conducted at the composite level are given in the tables; however, to conserve space, only the within-wave results of analyses conducted at the scale level are presented in the tables.

In order to gain an understanding of the parenting styles that involve configurations of child-rearing behavior characteristic of mothers and fathers in each family type, parenting typologies were developed using the cluster-analytic procedures described in Chapter II and using the four composite indices of parenting: positivity/warmth, negativity/conflict, monitoring, and control. For these analyses, solutions for two through five clusters were performed using the K-MEANS program of the BMDP statistical package. In every case, the three-cluster solution was determined to provide the best fit according to the criteria of significant differences among clusters on all parenting composites: low within-cluster correlations among parenting composites and no graphic overlap of cases across clusters. Because of the obvious lack of residential fathers' data for divorced families, separate cluster solutions were identified for mothers and for fathers. In addition, cluster solutions were replicated at each wave.

The chapter is organized into three main sections. A discussion of children's gender and family-type differences in parent-child relationships within each of the three waves is presented first, followed by a discussion of the stability and changes in parent-child relationships over time. A description of the parenting typologies characteristic of mothers and fathers in each family type at each wave is presented last.

WITHIN-WAVE DIFFERENCES IN PARENT-CHILD RELATIONSHIPS

The multivariate analyses of multimethod/multirespondent composites of mothers' parenting are presented in Table 23 and the means and standard deviations for these analyses in Table 24. The within-wave multivariate analyses for each respondent's report of mothers' parenting are found in Table 25, followed in Table 26 by the means and standard deviations for these analyses. Parallel data for fathers are presented in Tables 27–30. Within-wave means and standard deviations for children's observed positivity and negativity toward mothers are contained in Table 31 and toward fathers in Table 32.

Gender Differences

Many studies have reported differences in the behavior shown by parents to young sons and daughters, especially by fathers, but few differences

TABLE 23

F VALUES AND SIGNIFICANCE LEVELS FOR MULTIMETHOD/MULTIRESPONDENT COMPOSITES OF MOTHERS' PARENTING

	WAVE 1			WAVE 2			WAVE 3		
	Family	Children's Gender	Interaction	Family	Children's Gender	Interaction	Family	Children's Gender	Interaction
Multivariate	2.77**	1.91	2.59**	3.20**	2.41	1.09	3.67***	1.06	.74
Multivariate *df*	(8,386)	(4,193)	(8,386)	(8,348)	(4,174)	(8,348)	(8,308)	(4,154)	(8,308)
Positivity/warmth	.19	1.67	1.11	1.12	6.59*	1.89	3.07*	.27	.24
Negativity/conflict	3.57*	.14	4.77**	3.61*	3.23	1.66	7.88***	1.31	.29
Monitoring	4.27*	7.64**	3.33*	7.23***	3.21	.12	3.29*	3.94*	1.63
Control	.33	1.17	4.12**	3.59*	.02	.52	2.61	.51	1.60
Univariate *df*	(2,196)	(1,196)	(2,196)	(2,177)	(1,177)	(2,177)	(2,157)	(1,157)	(2,157)

NOTE.—Multivariate test is Wilks's lambda.

* $p \leq .05$.

** $p \leq .01$.

*** $p \leq .001$.

have been consistently found in the relationships of parents with their adolescent offspring (Huston, 1983; Steinberg, 1987b, 1988). Similarly, few main effects for gender were obtained in the current study. When found, gender differences were, with one exception, in the direction of greater positivity, monitoring, and control and less negativity within parent-daughter than within parent-son relationships. Only in one instance—in Wave 2 children's reports of mothers' control of behaviors related to character development (i.e., choice of friends, etc.)—was this pattern reversed in that boys reported higher levels of maternal control than did girls. As can be seen in Tables 25 and 26, the few gender effects in mother-child relationships were found inconsistently across waves and reporters. Tables 29 and 30 show that gender differences in fathers' and stepfathers' relationships with their children were also inconsistent across waves and respondents; however, the differences that did arise suggested warmer relationships with daughters than with sons. At the level of composite measures presented in Table 27, gender differences were found only in positivity at Wave 3; however, as can be seen in Table 30, different respondents varied in their perceptions of the nature of these differences. Fathers, stepfathers, and children agreed that all fathers were more affectionately expressive toward girls than toward boys at Wave 1. In subsequent waves, as the children moved further into adolescence, the fathers and stepfathers no longer saw themselves as more expressive toward daughters, but husbands and wives agreed that the male parents had more rapport with daughters or stepdaughters than with sons or stepsons at Wave 3, and daughters reported that fathers were more affectionate. Fathers and stepfathers also reported a correspondingly greater frequency of conflict with boys. Gender-differentiated aspects of parent-child relationships that were functions of the interaction of children's gender and family type are addressed in the sections that follow; however, it will be seen that few such interactions were obtained.

Family Differences in Parent-Child Relationships

At all three waves, both mother-child and father-child relationships in nondivorced families were characterized by moderate positivity and low negativity. Nondivorced parents also exhibited moderate to high levels of monitoring and control. At least at the multimethod/multirespondent composite level, differences between parent-child relationships in nondivorced families and the other two family types were almost uniformly in the direction of higher positivity, monitoring, and control and lower negativity in the relationships in nondivorced families (see Tables 24 and 28). The only exceptions to this were in the Wave 3 parenting of nondivorced versus

TABLE 24

MEANS (Standard Deviations) FOR THE MULTIMETHOD/MULTIRESPONDENT COMPOSITE INDICES OF MOTHERS' PARENTING (Standardized within Waves)

	Nondivorced		Divorced		Remarried		Significant Main Effects and Interactions	Significant Contrasts and Planned Comparisons[a]
	Boys	Girls	Boys	Girls	Boys	Girls		
Positivity/warmth:								
Wave 1	−.01 (.51)	−.04 (.55)	−.10 (.46)	.13 (.47)	−.03 (.59)	.07 (.55)	. . .	. . .
Wave 2	.01 (.67)	.01 (.54)	−.11 (.55)	.16 (.36)	−.29 (.45)	.06 (.51)	. . .	. . .
Wave 3	−.01 (.58)	−.04 (.54)	.13 (.62)	.26 (.64)	−.10 (.67)	−.06 (.51)	Family type	Div > Nondiv, Rem
Negativity/conflict:								
Wave 1	−.04 (.63)	−.23 (.44)	.20 (.62)	−.03 (.46)	−.10 (.40)	.22 (.69)	Family type, family type × gender	Div, Rem > Nondiv; Boys (Div > Nondiv, Rem); Girls (Rem > Nondiv); Rem (Girls > Boys)
Wave 2	.05 (.73)	−.29 (.51)	.13 (.51)	.17 (.66)	.05 (.42)	−.14 (.62)	Family type	Div > Nondiv, Rem
Wave 3	−.05 (.69)	−.25 (.36)	.33 (.76)	.30 (.90)	.03 (.46)	−.09 (.49)	Family type	Div > Nondiv, Rem

Monitoring:								
Wave 1	.14	.10	−.21	.25	−.31	−.05	Family type, family type × gender	Nondiv > Div, Rem; Div (Girls > Boys); Boys (Nondiv > Div, Rem); Girls (Div > Rem)
	(.58)	(.66)	(.49)	(.60)	(.60)	(.53)		
Wave 2	.04	.15	.05	.22	−.38	−.17	Family type	Nondiv, Div > Rem
	(.48)	(.53)	(.57)	(.50)	(.80)	(.76)		
Wave 3	−.05	.09	−.04	.40	−.15	−.15	Family type	Div > Rem; *Girls (Div > Nondiv, Rem)*[b]
	(.57)	(.56)	(.71)	(.63)	(.61)	(.61)		
Control:								
Wave 1	.12	−.06	−.19	.11	−.06	.05	Family type × gender	Div (Girls > Boys); Boys (Nondiv > Div)
	(.52)	(.51)	(.58)	(.50)	(.47)	(.46)		
Wave 2	.12	.03	.09	.03	−.24	−.13	Family type	Nondiv, Div > Rem
	(.55)	(.52)	(.44)	(.42)	(.69)	(.70)		
Wave 3	.02	.01	.01	.32	−.06	−.15	. . .	*Girls (Div > Nondiv, Rem)*[b]
	(.48)	(.58)	(.64)	(.67)	(.68)	(.47)		

NOTE.—Nondiv = Nondivorced; Div = Divorced; Rem = Remarried.

[a] Italicized contrasts denote planned comparisons.

[b] t test, $p \leq .05$.

TABLE 25

F Values and Significance Levels for Multivariate Analyses of Mothers' Parenting

	Wave 1			Wave 2			Wave 3		
	Family	Children's Gender	Interaction	Family	Children's Gender	Interaction	Family	Children's Gender	Interaction
Positivity/warmth:									
Mothers' reports:									
Multivariate	1.79	.53	.77	.44	.86	.76	.42	.17	.54
Multivariate *df*	(6,388)	(3,194)	(6,388)	(6,348)	(3,174)	(6,348)	(6,310)	(3,155)	(6,310)
Expressive affection	2.87	.24	1.28	.94	.73	.89	.32	.06	1.35
Instrumental affection	4.19*	.12	.53	.60	.36	.03	.86	.13	.32
Rapport	.16	.81	.34	.29	2.59	1.65	.08	.08	.01
Univariate *df*	(2,196)	(1,196)	(2,196)	(2,176)	(1,176)	(2,176)	(2,157)	(1,157)	(2,157)
Children's reports:									
Multivariate	1.83	2.64	.58	2.89*	2.19	.84	4.70**	1.11	.84
Multivariate *df*	(4,390)	(2,195)	(4,390)	(4,352)	(2,176)	(4,352)	(4,310)	(2,155)	(4,310)
Expressive affection	2.44	5.30*	.99	.32	4.09*	.10	3.54*	2.23	.78
Instrumental affection	3.43*	2.22	.45	5.00**	.35	.84	9.47***	.47	.20
Univariate *df*	(2,196)	(1,196)	(2,196)	(2,177)	(1,177)	(2,177)	(2,156)	(1,156)	(2,156)
Negativity/conflict:									
Mothers' reports:									
Multivariate	.95	.60	.87	1.04	2.28	1.37	2.14	2.68*	1.15
Multivariate *df*	(8,386)	(4,193)	(8,386)	(8,346)	(4,173)	(8,346)	(8,306)	(4,153)	(8,306)
Daily routines	2.57	1.01	.87	1.36	7.96**	.89	4.13	10.08**	.41
Adolescent issues	1.01	.06	.89	2.07	.25	1.54	1.19	.58	.61
Use of negative sanctions	1.50	.11	1.69	1.47	1.52	1.45	2.89	4.30*	.44
Nagging communication	1.04	.67	2.53	.04	.89	2.92	.10	3.41*	2.18
Univariate *df*	(2,196)	(1,196)	(2,196)	(2,176)	(1,176)	(2,176)	(2,156)	(1,156)	(2,156)

Children's reports:									
Multivariate	1.43	.25	1.47	1.07	1.85	.70	3.53***	.32	.93
Multivariate *df*	(8,384)	(4,192)	(8,384)	(8,348)	(4,174)	(8,348)	(8,306)	(4,153)	(8,306)
Daily routines	.13	.06	2.93	1.19	.61	.97	11.70***	1.07	.41
Adolescent issues	.04	.00	1.87	2.03	.67	.56	7.61***	.84	1.07
Use of negative sanctions	1.81	.55	2.75	3.42*	.37	.67	11.75***	.59	.24
Nagging communication	.16	.51	4.39*	1.54	2.04	1.06	7.71***	1.04	.07
Univariate *df*	(2,195)	(1,195)	(2,195)	(2,177)	(1,177)	(2,177)	(2,156)	(1,156)	(2,156)
Monitoring:									
Mothers' reports:									
Multivariate	2.97*	1.80	1.20	2.37	.34	1.93	2.56*	2.39	2.84
Multivariate *df*	(4,390)	(2,195)	(4,390)	(4,340)	(2,170)	(4,340)	(4,312)	(2,156)	(4,312)
Character development	4.33*	.96	1.35	3.69*	.00	.01	4.61*	.20	.46
Deviant behavior	5.51**	3.53	1.96	3.57*	.43	2.71	3.65*	3.79*	4.86**
Univariate *df*	(2,196)	(1,196)	(2,196)	(2,171)	(1,171)	(2,171)	(2,157)	(1,157)	(2,157)
Children's reports:									
Multivariate	1.71	2.20	1.68	3.47**	1.05	.86	.04	.43	.73
Multivariate *df*	(4,390)	(2,195)	(4,390)	(4,352)	(2,176)	(4,352)	(4,310)	(2,155)	(4,310)
Character development	2.60	2.44	2.72	.65	1.88	1.47	.06	.03	.14
Deviant behavior	2.97	4.31*	2.80	5.68**	1.48	.16	.07	.69	1.07
Univariate *df*	(2,196)	(1,196)	(2,196)	(2,177)	(1,177)	(2,177)	(2,156)	(1,156)	(2,156)
Spouses' reports:									
Multivariate	1.54	.51	.21	8.51***	.25	1.43	2.89	.69	.00
Multivariate *df*	(2,128)	(2,128)	(2,128)	(2,111)	(2,111)	(2,111)	(2,106)	(2,106)	(2,106)
Character development	3.01	.46	.05	17.18***	.01	1.39	5.80*	.70	.00
Deviant behavior	.83	1.03	.10	9.74**	.27	.01	2.50	1.40	.00
Univariate *df*	(1,129)	(1,129)	(1,129)	(1,112)	(1,112)	(1,112)	(1,107)	(1,107)	(1,107)
Control:									
Mothers' reports:									
Multivariate	2.66*	2.85	2.12	3.74**	8.01***	.54	1.90	.44	1.28
Multivariate *df*	(4,390)	(2,195)	(4,390)	(4,340)	(2,170)	(4,340)	(4,312)	(2,156)	(4,312)
Character development	5.19**	.05	1.58	6.41**	.45	.53	2.16	.07	.14
Deviant behavior	1.79	3.27	2.94	5.29**	5.88*	.17	2.49	.70	1.34
Univariate *df*	(2,196)	(1,196)	(2,196)	(2,171)	(1,171)	(2,171)	(2,157)	(1,157)	(2,157)

TABLE 25 (*Continued*)

	Wave 1			Wave 2			Wave 3		
	Family	Children's Gender	Interaction	Family	Children's Gender	Interaction	Family	Children's Gender	Interaction
Children's reports:									
Multivariate	1.68	1.43	.60	.12	4.20*	.14	.75	2.02	2.10
Multivariate *df*	(4,388)	(2,194)	(4,388)	(4,352)	(2,176)	(4,352)	(4,310)	(2,155)	(4,310)
Character development	3.29*	2.58	.83	.03	7.21**	.27	1.50	1.37	1.68
Deviant behavior	1.07	.33	.10	.14	.91	.13	.42	.52	3.52*
Univariate *df*	(2,195)	(1,195)	(2,195)	(2,177)	(1,177)	(2,177)	(2,156)	(1,156)	(2,156)
Spouses' reports:									
Multivariate	2.68	.83	1.99	5.92**	.29	1.28	3.89*	.92	1.29
Multivariate *df*	(2,128)	(2,128)	(2,128)	(2,111)	(2,111)	(2,111)	(2,105)	(2,105)	(2,105)
Character development	1.18	.44	3.53	6.32*	.05	2.50	2.77**	.32	1.48
Deviant behavior	.88	.21	.38	11.89***	.39	1.06	4.48*	.28	2.58
Univariate *df*	(1,129)	(1,129)	(1,129)	(1,112)	(1,112)	(1,112)	(1,106)	(1,106)	(1,106)
Observers' ratings:									
Multivariate	4.03**	.31	2.74*	4.23**	.07	1.28	1.36	.72	1.94
Multivariate *df*	(4,380)	(2,190)	(4,380)	(4,314)	(2,157)	(4,314)	(2,90)	(2,90)	(2,90)
Dominance/power	5.09**	.63	2.43	1.94	.00	.12	.11	.75	.02
Parental influence	5.91**	.08	5.15**	6.43**	.10	2.00	2.30	.04	2.89
Univariate *df*	(2,191)	(1,191)	(1,191)	(2,158)	(1,158)	(2,158)	(1,91)	(1,91)	(1,91)

NOTE.—Multivariate test is Wilks's lambda.

* $p \leq .05$.

** $p \leq .01$.

*** $p \leq .001$.

TABLE 26

MEANS (Standard Deviations) FOR SCALES INCLUDED IN THE COMPOSITE INDICES OF MOTHERS' PARENTING

	Nondivorced		Divorced		Remarried		Significant Main Effects and Interactions[a]	Significant Contrasts and Planned Comparisons[a]
	Boys	Girls	Boys	Girls	Boys	Girls		
Scales included in the positivity/warmth composites:								
Expressive affection:								
Mothers' self-reports:								
Wave 1	32.5 (7.7)	30.9 (6.5)	33.4 (6.4)	35.0 (6.2)	30.9 (6.9)	32.5 (7.9)		
Wave 2	31.9 (8.0)	31.0 (6.7)	29.3 (6.4)	31.5 (6.0)	29.0 (5.0)	30.4 (8.1)	...	
Wave 3	29.9 (7.6)	27.3 (6.7)	28.8 (6.4)	29.8 (6.8)	27.8 (5.8)	28.7 (6.9)	...	
Children's reports of mothers:								
Wave 1	24.7 (7.5)	25.2 (8.4)	25.5 (7.4)	28.6 (7.5)	25.7 (8.5)	30.1 (9.3)	*Gender*	*Girls > Boys*
Wave 2	24.4 (8.7)	27.6 (8.5)	25.8 (8.5)	27.8 (6.1)	24.5 (9.5)	26.8 (7.9)	*Gender*	*Girls > Boys*
Wave 3	22.9 (8.9)	26.9 (7.4)	28.5 (6.9)	29.1 (8.3)	25.4 (9.2)	26.7 (7.6)	Family type	Div > Nondiv
Instrumental affection:								
Mothers' self-reports:								
Wave 1	17.2 (3.4)	16.9 (4.5)	19.3 (6.1)	19.1 (4.9)	17.2 (3.0)	18.4 (4.3)	*Family type*	*Div > Nondiv*
Wave 2	17.1 (4.0)	17.3 (4.3)	16.9 (4.1)	17.1 (2.8)	16.1 (2.8)	16.7 (3.5)	...	
Wave 3	15.8 (3.7)	15.4 (3.4)	16.1 (3.6)	16.8 (4.9)	16.0 (2.7)	16.4 (4.0)	...	
Children's reports of mothers:								
Wave 1	15.2 (4.6)	15.4 (4.9)	16.1 (5.0)	18.0 (6.7)	17.0 (6.7)	18.5 (6.7)	*Family type*	*Div, Rem > Nondiv*
Wave 2	15.1 (5.0)	14.5 (3.6)	16.8 (6.1)	18.6 (5.1)	15.8 (6.5)	16.2 (6.3)	Family type	Div > Nondiv
Wave 3	13.8 (4.8)	13.7 (4.4)	17.5 (5.9)	18.6 (6.0)	14.6 (6.2)	15.5 (5.4)	Family type	Div > Nondiv, Rem

TABLE 26 (*Continued*)

	Nondivorced		Divorced		Remarried		Significant Main Effects and Interactions[a]	Significant Contrasts and Planned Comparisons[a]
	Boys	Girls	Boys	Girls	Boys	Girls		
Rapport:								
Mothers' self-reports:								
Wave 1	25.4 (2.7)	24.8 (2.4)	25.6 (2.5)	25.0 (3.1)	25.3 (2.9)	25.5 (2.5)	. . .	
Wave 2	25.5 (3.1)	25.2 (2.5)	24.9 (3.2)	25.8 (2.8)	34.2 (2.9)	25.7 (2.3)	. . .	
Wave 3	25.1 (3.0)	25.2 (2.7)	25.3 (3.5)	25.5 (3.9)	25.2 (3.3)	25.3 (2.8)	. . .	
Fathers' reports of mothers:[b]								
Wave 1	26.4 (2.9)	25.9 (3.3)			25.5 (3.0)	26.5 (3.2)	. . .	
Wave 2	26.9 (2.1)	26.5 (2.4)			24.9 (3.2)	26.3 (3.0)	Family type	Nondiv > Rem
Wave 3	27.2 (2.7)	26.8 (2.7)			26.1 (2.5)	26.1 (3.8)	. . .	
Mothers' positivity:								
Observers' ratings:[b]								
Wave 1	3.4 (.5)	3.4 (.4)	3.2 (.4)	3.4 (.4)	3.5 (.9)	3.2 (.5)	. . .	
Wave 2	3.3 (.6)	3.4 (.4)	3.2 (.5)	3.4 (.4)	3.1 (.4)	3.4 (.5)	Gender	Girls > Boys
Wave 3	3.5 (.4)	3.4 (.6)	. . .	. . .	3.3 (.8)	3.3 (.4)	. . .	
Scales included in the negativity composite:								
Conflict over daily routines:								
Mothers' reports:								
Wave 1	24.8 (7.2)	22.4 (6.5)	26.8 (8.4)	24.9 (8.0)	26.0 (7.3)	27.0 (9.1)	. . .	
Wave 2	24.3 (7.4)	20.6 (5.9)	25.1 (7.6)	24.0 (8.9)	25.7 (7.2)	21.1 (6.5)	*Gender*	*Boys > Girls*
Wave 3	21.6 (7.9)	18.1 (5.1)	24.1 (8.6)	22.1 (6.5)	22.2 (5.3)	17.8 (4.1)	Gender	Boys > Girls

Children's reports of mothers:								
Wave 1	22.2	21.4	22.5	19.8	19.6	24.1	. . .	
	(9.0)	(8.3)	(7.7)	(7.4)	(8.1)	(10.7)		
Wave 2	20.3	17.9	20.5	21.8	20.6	19.0	. . .	
	(7.9)	(6.1)	(7.8)	(8.9)	(8.2)	(7.6)		
Wave 3	17.1	17.0	22.8	24.2	16.1	18.8	Family type	Div > Nondiv, Rem
	(6.4)	(5.1)	(8.9)	(10.4)	(8.0)	(7.6)		
Conflict over adolescent issues:								
Mothers' reports:								
Wave 1	11.5	11.1	12.6	12.1	11.1	12.4	. . .	
	(3.8)	(4.2)	(4.7)	(4.8)	(2.8)	(4.8)		
Wave 2	12.3	10.4	12.6	13.1	11.8	12.2	. . .	
	(5.4)	(2.9)	(4.1)	(5.0)	(3.6)	(4.2)		
Wave 3	11.6	10.3	11.9	12.1	12.0	11.6	. . .	
	(4.8)	(2.5)	(3.9)	(4.6)	(2.9)	(3.4)		
Children's reports of mothers:								
Wave 1	13.8	13.0	14.0	12.8	12.1	14.2	. . .	
	(6.1)	(4.3)	(5.0)	(4.3)	(4.3)	(6.9)		
Wave 2	13.0	11.3	13.8	13.9	12.9	12.6	. . .	
	(4.6)	(3.8)	(4.7)	(6.5)	(4.2)	(5.8)		
Wave 3	11.7	11.1	14.1	16.5	12.1	12.6	Family type	Div > Nondiv, Rem
	(4.1)	(3.3)	(6.6)	(7.9)	(5.0)	(5.4)		
Use of negative sanctions:								
Mothers' self-reports:								
Wave 1	22.8	20.2	23.2	23.5	22.3	23.7	. . .	
	(6.4)	(5.6)	(6.7)	(6.0)	(5.1)	(9.5)		
Wave 2	21.5	18.7	21.3	22.0	20.6	19.4	. . .	
	(6.6)	(5.2)	(6.0)	(6.8)	(5.3)	(5.3)		
Wave 3	19.7	16.5	20.8	19.4	17.9	16.5	Gender	Boys > Girls
	(6.8)	(4.5)	(7.7)	(7.2)	(3.0)	(3.8)		
Children's reports of mothers:								
Wave 1	19.5	17.8	21.1	20.8	17.5	21.8	. . .	
	(8.0)	(5.9)	(8.2)	(6.8)	(6.0)	(8.6)		
Wave 2	17.4	16.5	19.1	20.4	17.0	18.4	*Family type*	*Div > Nondiv*
	(6.5)	(6.1)	(5.9)	(7.2)	(6.3)	(6.1)		
Wave 3	15.7	15.6	22.1	23.2	16.3	18.3	Family type	Div > Nondiv, Rem
	(5.4)	(4.6)	(10.8)	(11.2)	(7.4)	(7.5)		

TABLE 26 (*Continued*)

	Nondivorced		Divorced		Remarried		Significant Main Effects and Interactions[a]	Significant Contrasts and Planned Comparisons[a]
	Boys	Girls	Boys	Girls	Boys	Girls		
Nagging communication:								
Mothers' self-reports:								
Wave 1	19.1	16.5	19.2	18.3	18.3	19.9	. . .	
	(6.0)	(4.4)	(4.9)	(4.4)	(4.7)	(7.6)		
Wave 2	18.3	15.4	16.8	17.3	16.7	17.1	. . .	
	(5.2)	(3.8)	(4.9)	(5.2)	(3.5)	(4.7)		
Wave 3	17.6	14.2	17.0	15.1	15.2	16.0	Gender	Boys > Girls
	(5.8)	(4.7)	(5.9)	(4.9)	(2.6)	(4.8)		
Children's reports of mothers:								
Wave 1	14.9	14.0	15.2	13.8	12.1	15.9	. . .	
	(5.3)	(5.2)	(5.5)	(4.4)	(4.7)	(7.3)		
Wave 2	12.4	13.2	12.7	15.3	12.5	12.3	. . .	
	(4.7)	(5.3)	(4.1)	(5.2)	(6.7)	(5.1)		
Wave 3	11.4	12.8	15.8	16.6	12.9	13.5	Family type	Div > Nondiv, Rem
	(4.4)	(4.3)	(6.8)	(7.7)	(5.8)	(5.6)		
Mothers' negativity:								
Observers' ratings:[b]								
Wave 1	1.6	1.6	2.0	1.8	1.9	2.0	Family type	Div, Rem > Nondiv
	(.6)	(.5)	(.6)	(.5)	(.6)	(.7)		
Wave 2	1.9	1.6	2.0	1.8	2.0	1.7	Gender	Boys > Girls
	(.6)	(.5)	(.7)	(.5)	(.5)	(.6)		
Wave 3	1.8	1.8	. . .	. . .	2.3	1.8	. . .	
	(.6)	(.7)			(.9)	(.8)		
Scales used in the monitoring composite:								
Monitoring character development:								
Mothers' self-reports:								
Wave 1	17.6	17.5	17.7	18.5	17.2	17.3	Family type	Div > Rem
	(1.9)	(1.7)	(1.5)	(1.4)	(1.8)	(1.7)		
Wave 2	17.3	17.2	17.7	17.7	16.8	16.8	*Family type*	*Div > Rem*
	(1.5)	(1.7)	(1.9)	(1.6)	(1.4)	(1.7)		
Wave 3	16.9	16.8	17.4	17.9	16.6	16.6	Family type	Div > Nondiv, Rem
	(1.5)	(1.7)	(1.7)	(2.4)	(2.1)	(1.7)		

Children's reports of mothers:								
Wave 1	17.4	16.8	15.8	16.6	15.7	17.1	. . .	
	(2.2)	(2.2)	(2.5)	(2.6)	(3.4)	(2.0)		
Wave 2	16.2	16.9	16.9	16.6	15.6	16.8	. . .	
	(2.2)	(2.0)	(1.5)	(2.1)	(4.3)	(2.4)		
Wave 3	16.6	16.9	16.9	16.9	17.0	16.8	. . .	
	(2.4)	(2.3)	(2.3)	(2.4)	(2.6)	(1.9)		
Fathers' reports of mothers:								
Wave 1	17.9	18.2	. . .	. . .	17.3	17.7	. . .	
	(1.6)	(1.9)			(2.1)	(2.0)		
Wave 2	17.7	17.7	. . .	. . .	15.4	16.4	Family type	Nondiv > Rem
	(1.8)	(2.0)			(2.6)	(2.9)		
Wave 3	17.5	17.9	. . .	. . .	16.6	17.0	*Family type*	*Nondiv > Rem*
	(2.0)	(1.5)			(1.6)	(2.6)		
Monitoring deviant behavior:								
Mothers' self-reports:								
Wave 1	13.1	13.3	13.2	14.1	12.9	12.9	Family type	Div > Nondiv, Rem
	(1.7)	(1.2)	(1.3)	(1.0)	(1.5)	(1.5)		
Wave 2	13.0	13.1	13.1	13.9	13.1	12.6	*Family type*	*Div > Nondiv, Rem*
	(1.2)	(1.4)	(1.5)	(1.1)	(1.3)	(1.5)		
Wave 3	12.7	12.7	12.5	14.0	12.6	12.5	Family type, family type × gender	Div > Nondiv, Rem; Girls (Div > Nondiv, Rem); Div (Girls > Boys)
	(1.5)	(1.5)	(1.9)	(1.1)	(1.5)	(1.3)		
Children's reports of mothers:								
Wave 1	13.0	12.6	11.3	12.4	11.3	12.8	. . .	
	(1.8)	(2.6)	(2.3)	(2.7)	(3.2)	(2.1)		
Wave 2	12.1	12.6	12.1	12.3	10.4	11.2	Family type	Nondiv > Div, Rem
	(2.3)	(2.3)	(2.2)	(2.3)	(3.7)	(3.1)		
Wave 3	11.5	12.1	11.5	12.5	12.2	11.7	. . .	
	(2.5)	(2.7)	(2.7)	(2.6)	(2.2)	(2.7)		

TABLE 26 (*Continued*)

	Nondivorced		Divorced		Remarried		Significant Main Effects and Interactions[a]	Significant Contrasts and Planned Comparisons[a]
	Boys	Girls	Boys	Girls	Boys	Girls		
Fathers' reports of mothers:								
Wave 1	13.4 (1.8)	13.8 (1.3)	. . .	. . .	13.3 (1.4)	13.5 (1.6)	. . .	
Wave 2	13.2 (1.5)	13.5 (1.8)	. . .	. . .	12.0 (2.2)	12.3 (2.6)	Family type	Nondiv > Rem
Wave 3	13.1 (1.6)	13.6 (1.4)	. . .	. . .	12.6 (1.7)	13.1 (2.3)	. . .	
Monitoring:								
Observers' ratings:[b]								
Wave 1	4.5 (.5)	4.3 (.6)	3.9 (.8)	4.2 (.8)	3.9 (.6)	4.1 (.6)	Family type	Nondiv > Div, Rem
Wave 2	3.9 (.7)	4.2 (.7)	3.7 (.8)	4.0 (.6)	3.8 (.9)	4.0 (.8)	Gender	Girls > Boys
Wave 3	4.2 (.8)	4.4 (.8)	. . .	. . .	4.1 (.7)	4.0 (.7)	. . .	
Scales included in the control composite:								
Control of behaviors related to character development:								
Mothers' self-reports:								
Wave 1	15.3 (2.7)	14.5 (2.7)	15.8 (2.6)	16.7 (2.1)	15.1 (2.8)	15.3 (2.8)	Family type	Div > Nondiv, Rem
Wave 2	15.3 (2.2)	14.8 (2.5)	16.5 (2.5)	16.0 (2.2)	14.6 (2.7)	14.9 (2.4)	Family type	Div > Nondiv, Rem
Wave 3	15.2 (2.4)	15.0 (2.9)	15.8 (3.0)	15.9 (2.5)	14.6 (2.1)	14.9 (2.4)	. . .	

Children's reports of mothers:								
Wave 1	12.5 (4.4)	11.0 (3.8)	11.2 (2.8)	9.9 (3.5)	10.0 (4.2)	10.2 (4.1)	*Family type*	*Nondiv > Rem*
Wave 2	11.9 (3.1)	10.7 (3.7)	12.5 (3.7)	10.4 (3.5)	11.9 (4.5)	10.7 (4.0)	Gender	Boys > Girls
Wave 3	10.4 (4.0)	10.6 (3.6)	11.5 (3.4)	11.6 (4.0)	12.7 (4.1)	10.3 (3.9)	. . .	
Fathers' reports of mothers:								
Wave 1	16.4 (2.6)	16.0 (2.9)	. . .	. . .	15.0 (3.1)	16.4 (2.5)	. . .	
Wave 2	15.6 (2.9)	15.8 (3.0)	. . .	. . .	13.3 (3.1)	15.3 (3.2)	Family type	Nondiv > Rem
Wave 3	16.2 (2.4)	15.8 (2.3)	. . .	. . .	14.0 (2.6)	15.0 (3.9)	Family type	Nondiv > Rem
Control of deviant behavior:								
Mothers' self-reports:								
Wave 1	12.3 (2.0)	12.4 (1.9)	12.3 (2.3)	13.7 (1.4)	12.6 (1.6)	12.5 (2.1)	. . .	
Wave 2	12.0 (2.0)	12.5 (2.2)	12.8 (1.8)	13.7 (1.2)	11.9 (2.3)	12.7 (1.9)	Family type, gender	Div > Nondiv, Rem; Girls > Boys
Wave 3	12.1 (1.9)	12.1 (2.4)	12.4 (1.6)	13.4 (1.3)	12.3 (1.9)	12.3 (1.6)	. . .	
Children's reports of mothers:								
Wave 1	10.8 (3.3)	10.3 (3.3)	10.2 (2.4)	10.1 (3.3)	9.8 (3.6)	9.7 (3.4)	. . .	
Wave 2	10.8 (2.5)	10.6 (3.5)	11.0 (2.5)	10.3 (2.9)	10.6 (3.0)	10.3 (2.7)	. . .	
Wave 3	10.5 (2.6)	10.8 (2.5)	10.2 (2.0)	11.8 (2.3)	11.5 (2.8)	10.4 (2.4)	*Family type × gender*	*Div (Girls > Boys)*
Fathers' reports of mothers:								
Wave 1	12.4 (2.5)	12.6 (2.4)	. . .	. . .	12.5 (2.0)	13.2 (2.1)	. . .	
Wave 2	12.5 (1.9)	12.9 (2.1)	. . .	. . .	10.5 (3.0)	11.8 (2.5)	Family type	Nondiv > Rem
Wave 3	12.5 (2.4)	12.8 (2.1)	. . .	. . .	10.7 (2.6)	12.5 (2.5)	Family type	Nondiv > Rem

TABLE 26 (*Continued*)

	Nondivorced		Divorced		Remarried		Significant Main Effects and Interactions[a]	Significant Contrasts and Planned Comparisons[a]
	Boys	Girls	Boys	Girls	Boys	Girls		
Mothers' dominance/power:								
Observers' ratings:								
Wave 1	4.0	3.9	3.8	3.9	4.0	4.0	Family type	Nondiv, Rem > Div
	(.3)	(.3)	(.4)	(.3)	(.0)	(.3)		
Wave 2	3.9	3.8	3.8	3.8	3.7	3.7	. . .	
	(.4)	(.4)	(.4)	(.4)	(.5)	(.6)		
Wave 3	3.9	3.8	. . .	. . .	3.9	3.7	. . .	
	(.4)	(.5)			(.5)	(.4)		
Mothers' parental influence:								
Observers' ratings:								
Wave 1	3.9	3.7	3.3	3.7	3.8	3.7	Family type, family type × gender	Nondiv, Rem > Div; Boys (Nondiv, Rem > Div); Nondiv (Boys > Girls); Div (Girls > Boys)
	(.5)	(.5)	(.7)	(.5)	(.6)	(.5)		
Wave 2	3.9	3.6	3.3	3.4	3.5	3.6	Family type	Nondiv > Div, Rem
	(.7)	(.5)	(.6)	(.7)	(.5)	(.6)		
Wave 3	3.8	3.8	. . .	. . .	3.8	3.3	. . .	
	(.7)	(.6)			(.8)	(.7)		

Note.—Nondiv = Nondivorced; Div = Divorced; Rem = Remarried. Observational data were not available for divorced families at Wave 3.

[a] Italicized contrasts denote planned comparisons.

[b] Univariate analyses.

TABLE 27

F Values and Significance Levels for Multimethod/Multirespondent Composites of Fathers' Parenting

	Wave 1			Wave 2			Wave 3		
	Family	Children's Gender	Interaction	Family	Children's Gender	Interaction	Family	Children's Gender	Interaction
Multivariate	8.01**	.62	2.04	7.50***	.95	.66	7.90***	2.49*	.40
Multivariate *df*	(4,126)	(4,126)	(4,126)	(4,113)	(4,113)	(4,113)	(4,104)	(4,104)	(4,104)
Positivity/warmth	3.13	.88	.60	17.78***	2.09	.64	20.84***	6.70*	.42
Negativity/conflict	.59	.01	3.86	1.45	2.44	1.42	1.56	1.88	.81
Monitoring	18.82***	2.33	5.08*	11.51***	1.08	.16	9.68**	1.10	.72
Control	21.65***	.80	6.30*	19.47***	.10	.86	12.67***	.29	1.27
Univariate *df*	(1,129)	(1,129)	(1,129)	(1,116)	(1,116)	(1,116)	(1,107)	(1,107)	(1,107)

* $p \leq .05$.
** $p \leq .01$.
*** $p \leq .001$.

TABLE 28

MEANS (Standard Deviations) FOR THE COMPOSITE INDICES OF FATHERS' PARENTING

	Nondivorced		Remarried		Significant Main Effects and Interactions	Significant Contrasts
	Boys	Girls	Boys	Girls		
Positivity/warmth:						
Wave 1	.07 (.55)	.09 (.54)	−.19 (.61)	−.02 (.68)	. . .	
Wave 2	.16 (.55)	.23 (.47)	−.38 (.62)	−.14 (.69)	Family type	Nondiv > Rem
Wave 3	.10 (.58)	.31 (.55)	−.48 (.67)	−.12 (.47)	Family type; gender	Nondiv > Rem; Girls > Boys
Negativity/conflict:						
Wave 1	.06 (.64)	−.14 (.42)	−.06 (.52)	.13 (.69)	. . .	
Wave 2	.10 (.75)	−.21 (.40)	.10 (.64)	.06 (.57)	. . .	
Wave 3	.08 (.68)	−.19 (.42)	.12 (.72)	.07 (.58)	. . .	
Monitoring:						
Wave 1	.22 (.62)	.15 (.42)	−.45 (.64)	−.06 (.67)	Family type, family type × gender	Nondiv > Rem; Boys (Nondiv > Rem); Rem (Girls > Boys)
Wave 2	.13 (.56)	.20 (.54)	−.33 (.82)	−.16 (.72)	Family type	Nondiv > Rem
Wave 3	.13 (.53)	.16 (.68)	−.35 (.74)	−.12 (.56)	Family type	Nondiv > Rem
Control:						
Wave 1	.28 (.49)	.12 (.42)	−.44 (.69)	−.09 (.69)	Family type, family type × gender	Nondiv > Rem; Boys (Nondiv > Rem); Rem (Girls > Boys)
Wave 2	.24 (.48)	.17 (.52)	−.38 (.86)	−.24 (.67)	Family type	Nondiv > Rem
Wave 3	.20 (.44)	.13 (.49)	−.34 (.80)	−.15 (.68)	Family type	Nondiv > Rem

NOTE.—Nondiv = Nondivorced; Rem = Remarried.

TABLE 29

F VALUES AND SIGNIFICANCE LEVELS FOR MULTIVARIATE ANALYSES OF FATHERS' PARENTING

	WAVE 1			WAVE 2			WAVE 3		
	Family	Children's Gender	Interaction	Family	Children's Gender	Interaction	Family	Children's Gender	Interaction
Positivity/warmth:									
Fathers' reports:									
Multivariate	6.23*	2.67	2.57	14.81***	3.35	1.08	10.73***	3.77*	.85
Multivariate *df*	(3,114)	(3,114)	(3,114)	(3,114)	(3,114)	(3,114)	(3,105)	(3,105)	(3,105)
Expressive affection	12.59***	4.02*	.74	17.86***	2.51	.42	15.94***	.96	.76
Instrumental affection	12.04***	.62	.21	3.32	.02	1.81	3.46	.12	1.26
Rapport	9.85**	2.67	.91	41.88***	10.75**	2.17	30.06***	10.70**	2.17
Univariate *df*	(1,116)	(1,116)	(1,116)	(1,116)	(1,116)	(1,116)	(1,107)	(1,107)	(1,107)
Children's reports:									
Multivariate	1.26	3.34*	1.01	11.19***	3.61*	.45	6.63**	3.18*	.84
Multivariate *df*	(2,128)	(2,128)	(2,128)	(2,115)	(2,115)	(2,115)	(2,106)	(2,106)	(2,106)
Expressive affection	.30	3.99*	1.99	22.46***	3.46	.00	12.93***	5.80*	.22
Instrumental affection	.71	.01	.48	7.28**	.13	.60	4.58*	.10	1.68
Univariate *df*	(1,129)	(1,129)	(1,129)	(1,116)	(1,116)	(1,116)	(1,107)	(1,107)	(1,107)
Negativity/conflict:									
Fathers' reports:									
Multivariate	.74	1.21	1.43	1.71	3.52**	.54	.17	2.68*	.78
Multivariate *df*	(4,126)	(4,126)	(4,126)	(4,112)	(4,112)	(4,112)	(4,102)	(4,102)	(4,102)
Daily routines	.01	2.26	1.10	.15	7.45**	.76	.01	8.83**	.00
Adolescent issues	.91	3.53	5.12*	.67	4.87*	1.32	.05	6.72*	.61
Use of negative sanctions	.78	2.30	1.01	.57	3.25	1.23	.01	5.21*	.85
Nagging communication	.97	.46	.00	3.34	.01	1.87	.26	3.39	.03
Univariate *df*	(1,129)	(1,129)	(1,129)	(1,115)	(1,115)	(1,115)	(1,105)	(1,105)	(1,105)

TABLE 29 (*Continued*)

	Wave 1			Wave 2			Wave 3		
	Family	Children's Gender	Interaction	Family	Children's Gender	Interaction	Family	Children's Gender	Interaction
Children's reports:									
Multivariate	.85	.70	1.98	.79	.17	2.68*	3.52**	.13	.44
Multivariate *df*	(4,125)	(4,125)	(4,125)	(4,113)	(4,113)	(4,113)	(4,103)	(4,103)	(4,103)
Daily routines	.08	2.58	3.33	.53	.32	.91	1.00	.37	1.12
Adolescent issues	.04	1.08	2.62	.03	.00	2.43	1.34	.36	.56
Use of negative sanctions	.67	1.97	7.72**	.42	.06	.83	2.59	.14	.94
Nagging communication	.01	.66	2.90	.53	.01	1.58	1.65	.20	.04
Univariate *df*	(1,128)	(1,128)	(1,128)	(1,116)	(1,116)	(1,116)	(1,106)	(1,106)	(1,106)
Monitoring:									
Fathers' reports:									
Multivariate	6.52**	5.04	.52	5.51**	1.47	.99	3.02	1.93	1.65
Multivariate *df*	(2,128)	(2,128)	(2,128)	(2,111)	(2,111)	(2,111)	(2,106)	(2,106)	(2,106)
Character development	11.90***	4.86*	.99	9.71**	2.22	1.60	5.49*	3.89	2.10
Deviant behavior	9.00**	10.05**	.64	8.28**	.07	.09	4.81*	1.98	3.26
Univariate *df*	(1,129)	(1,129)	(1,129)	(1,112)	(1,112)	(1,112)	(1,107)	(1,107)	(1,107)
Children's reports:									
Multivariate	5.09**	.61	5.67**	5.88**	.84	.79	1.32	.26	1.65
Multivariate *df*	(2,127)	(2,127)	(2,127)	(2,115)	(2,115)	(2,115)	(2,106)	(2,106)	(2,106)
Character development	3.96*	.11	11.31**	1.03	.95	1.12	.67	.00	.27
Deviant behavior	10.25**	.41	5.31*	9.67**	.00	.05	2.58	.29	1.01
Univariate *df*	(1,128)	(1,128)	(1,128)	(1,116)	(1,116)	(1,116)	(1,107)	(1,107)	(1,107)
Spouses' reports:									
Multivariate	3.19*	.17	2.22	2.35	.52	.42	2.90	.42	.57
Multivariate *df*	(2,128)	(2,128)	(2,128)	(2,112)	(2,112)	(2,112)	(2,106)	(2,106)	(2,106)
Character development	3.00	.05	1.63	4.06*	.05	.79	5.57*	.72	1.14
Deviant behavior	6.23*	.26	.00	4.11*	.28	.24	4.79*	.19	.78
Univariate *df*	(1,129)	(1,129)	(1,129)	(1,113)	(1,113)	(1,113)	(1,107)	(1,107)	(1,107)

Control:									
Fathers' reports:									
Multivariate	8.59***	3.71*	1.74	15.43***	1.28	3.04	9.67***	.96	4.87**
Multivariate *df*	(2,128)	(2,128)	(2,128)	(2,111)	(2,111)	(2,111)	(2,106)	(2,106)	(2,106)
Character development	16.76***	.94	3.09	30.84***	1.58	5.03*	18.38***	.64	9.13**
Deviant behavior	7.23**	5.65*	3.14	20.13***	2.57	.91	17.30***	1.68	7.23*
Univariate *df*	(1,129)	(1,129)	(1,129)	(1,112)	(1,112)	(1,112)	(1,107)	(1,107)	(1,107)
Children's reports:									
Multivariate	2.13	1.36	2.90	1.85	1.66	.27	.16	.52	.93
Multivariate *df*	(2,127)	(2,127)	(2,127)	(2,115)	(2,115)	(2,115)	(2,106)	(2,106)	(2,106)
Character development	3.32	.65	2.57	1.93	1.71	.40	.29	.00	1.06
Deviant behavior	4.00*	.16	5.80*	3.71	.01	.22	.22	.54	.00
Univariate *df*	(1,128)	(1,128)	(1,128)	(1,116)	(1,116)	(1,116)	(1,107)	(1,107)	(1,107)
Spouses' reports:									
Multivariate	4.97**	1.72	2.36	4.95**	1.77	1.22	2.47	2.33	.82
Multivariate *df*	(2,128)	(2,128)	(2,128)	(2,112)	(2,112)	(2,112)	(2,105)	(2,105)	(2,105)
Character development	6.53*	.56	3.19	5.31*	.39	2.02	3.20	.05	1.46
Deviant behavior	10.00**	.25	.35	9.93**	2.59	2.32	4.96*	.92	1.60
Univariate *df*	(1,129)	(1,129)	(1,129)	(1,113)	(1,113)	(1,113)	(1,106)	(1,106)	(1,106)
Observers' ratings:									
Multivariate	5.94**	1.10	.84	1.98	.27	1.43	5.14**	.56	3.03
Multivariate *df*	(2,123)	(2,123)	(2,123)	(2,97)	(2,97)	(2,97)	(2,90)	(2,90)	(2,90)
Dominance/power	8.76**	.01	.02	2.04	.46	.01	8.39*	.96	5.96*
Parental influence	8.08**	1.96	1.53	3.96*	.05	1.78	7.39*	.02	2.62
Univariate *df*	(1,124)	(1,124)	(1,124)	(1,98)	(1,98)	(1,98)	(1,91)	(1,91)	(1,91)

NOTE.—Multivariate test is Wilks's lambda.

* $p \leq .05$.

** $p \leq .01$.

*** $p \leq .001$.

TABLE 30

MEANS (Standard Deviations) FOR SCALES INCLUDED IN THE COMPOSITE INDICES OF FATHERS' PARENTING

	NONDIVORCED		REMARRIED		SIGNIFICANT MAIN EFFECTS AND INTERACTIONS[a]	SIGNIFICANT CONTRASTS AND PLANNED COMPARISONS[a]
	Boys	Girls	Boys	Girls		
Scales included in the positivity/warmth composites:						
Expressive affection:						
Fathers' self-reports:						
Wave 1	27.5 (6.1)	30.2 (7.5)	23.7 (6.5)	25.6 (6.8)	Family type, gender	Nondiv > Rem; Girls > Boys
Wave 2	26.2 (8.1)	27.4 (6.8)	19.6 (5.4)	22.6 (7.7)	Family type	Nondiv > Rem
Wave 3	25.4 (8.0)	25.5 (6.6)	18.9 (5.7)	21.4 (6.1)	Family type	Nondiv > Rem
Children's reports of fathers:						
Wave 1	23.2 (7.8)	24.1 (9.4)	20.2 (8.4)	25.4 (9.1)	Gender	Girls > Boys
Wave 2	23.9 (9.0)	26.8 (7.9)	16.2 (8.7)	19.3 (8.7)	Family type	Nondiv > Rem
Wave 3	22.4 (8.7)	25.4 (8.3)	16.1 (6.4)	20.5 (7.1)	Family type, gender	Nondiv > Rem; Girls > Boys
Instrumental affection:						
Fathers' self-reports:						
Wave 1	17.0 (4.3)	15.5 (3.6)	13.6 (4.2)	14.0 (4.2)	Family type	Nondiv > Rem
Wave 2	16.1 (5.2)	14.9 (3.4)	13.5 (3.8)	14.5 (4.5)	...	
Wave 3	15.4 (4.3)	14.8 (4.0)	13.1 (4.1)	14.2 (3.7)	...	
Children's reports of fathers:						
Wave 1	15.1 (5.0)	14.3 (5.3)	15.3 (7.0)	15.9 (6.9)	...	
Wave 2	15.4 (6.0)	14.3 (3.9)	12.2 (4.1)	12.6 (5.1)	Family type	Nondiv > Rem
Wave 3	14.5 (4.3)	13.7 (4.0)	11.6 (4.2)	13.0 (4.9)	Family type	Nondiv > Rem

Rapport:						
Fathers' self-reports:						
Wave 1	24.7 (3.1)	24.6 (2.7)	22.0 (3.3)	23.8 (3.8)	Family type	Nondiv > Rem
Wave 2	24.4 (3.3)	25.2 (2.6)	19.5 (3.5)	22.1 (3.9)	Family type, gender	Nondiv > Rem; Girls > Boys
Wave 3	24.2 (2.9)	25.4 (2.7)	19.8 (3.6)	22.8 (3.9)	Family type, gender	Nondiv > Rem; Girls > Boys
Mothers' reports of fathers:[b]						
Wave 1	24.2 (3.7)	23.5 (2.8)	22.4 (4.3)	23.7 (3.8)	. . .	
Wave 2	24.4 (3.4)	24.9 (2.4)	20.6 (4.0)	22.5 (3.7)	Family type	Nondiv > Rem
Wave 3	23.9 (3.8)	25.1 (3.7)	20.9 (3.7)	23.5 (3.6)	Family type, gender	Nondiv > Rem; Girls > Boys
Fathers' positivity:						
Observers' ratings:[b]						
Wave 1	3.2 (.5)	3.3 (.5)	3.3 (.6)	3.3 (.6)	. . .	
Wave 2	3.1 (.5)	3.2 (.5)	3.1 (.7)	3.2 (.7)	. . .	
Wave 3	3.2 (.5)	3.5 (.6)	3.1 (.9)	3.2 (.5)	. . .	
Scales included in the negativity composite:						
Conflict over daily routines:						
Fathers' reports:						
Wave 1	25.6 (10.0)	21.7 (7.8)	23.9 (9.9)	23.2 (6.9)	. . .	
Wave 2	24.1 (9.7)	18.3 (5.1)	25.4 (10.9)	22.0 (8.7)	Gender	Boys > Girls
Wave 3	21.8 (8.2)	18.1 (5.1)	21.7 (7.7)	18.0 (3.9)	Gender	Boys > Girls

TABLE 30 (*Continued*)

	Nondivorced		Remarried		Significant Main Effects and Interactions[a]	Significant Contrasts and Planned Comparisons[a]
	Boys	Girls	Boys	Girls		
Children's reports of fathers:						
Wave 1	18.0	17.7	15.7	20.8	...	
	(7.4)	(7.5)	(7.7)	(11.0)		
Wave 2	16.7	14.7	16.4	16.9	...	
	(7.2)	(4.5)	(9.4)	(7.8)		
Wave 3	15.0	14.4	14.9	17.0	...	
	(5.8)	(4.9)	(7.4)	(8.3)		
Conflict over adolescent issues:						
Fathers' reports:						
Wave 1	12.6	10.1	11.8	12.0	Family type × gender	Girls (Rem > Nondiv); Nondiv (Boys > Girls)
	(4.4)	(2.3)	(3.4)	(3.4)		
Wave 2	13.1	10.4	12.5	11.7	Gender	Boys > Girls
	(5.8)	(3.4)	(4.1)	(3.2)		
Wave 3	12.6	10.1	12.2	10.8	Gender	Boys > Girls
	(5.2)	(2.4)	(4.7)	(2.1)		
Children's reports of fathers:						
Wave 1	12.2	11.7	11.0	13.3	...	
	(4.7)	(3.8)	(4.8)	(6.7)		
Wave 2	12.2	10.7	10.9	12.4	...	
	(5.3)	(3.5)	(4.4)	(6.7)		
Wave 3	10.6	10.5	10.9	12.1	...	
	(4.3)	(3.1)	(5.6)	(5.1)		
Use of negative sanctions:						
Fathers' self-reports:						
Wave 1	20.0	18.2	20.7	19.4	...	
	(5.9)	(4.5)	(7.3)	(6.1)		
Wave 2	19.7	16.4	19.1	18.3	...	
	(7.1)	(4.3)	(7.1)	(6.1)		
Wave 3	18.4	15.2	17.6	16.3	...	
	(6.7)	(3.6)	(4.2)	(4.1)		

Children's reports of fathers:						
Wave 1	17.5	15.8	13.2	18.2	. . .	
	(7.7)	(5.1)	(4.3)	(8.7)		
Wave 2	15.6	14.2	15.3	16.1	. . .	
	(5.4)	(5.4)	(8.2)	(7.9)		
Wave 3	14.0	13.3	14.7	16.2	. . .	
	(4.6)	(3.0)	(8.6)	(7.4)		
Nagging communication:						
Fathers' self-reports:						
Wave 1	15.7	15.1	16.6	16.0	. . .	
	(4.5)	(3.4)	(6.4)	(5.2)		
Wave 2	14.6	13.4	15.0	16.1	. . .	
	(5.0)	(3.3)	(5.0)	(4.6)		
Wave 3	14.7	13.2	15.3	13.5	. . .	
	(4.8)	(3.5)	(5.3)	(4.2)		
Children's reports of fathers:						
Wave 1	12.8	11.8	11.1	13.7	. . .	
	(5.4)	(4.6)	(5.8)	(7.6)		
Wave 2	11.2	12.3	11.7	10.5	. . .	
	(4.6)	(4.2)	(6.4)	(4.8)		
Wave 3	11.4	11.7	10.1	10.7	. . .	
	(5.0)	(4.0)	(5.9)	(4.2)		
Fathers' negativity:						
Observers' ratings:[b]						
Wave 1	1.6	1.6	1.7	1.7	. . .	
	(.5)	(.5)	(.5)	(.6)		
Wave 2	1.7	1.5	1.7	1.7	. . .	
	(.7)	(.4)	(.5)	(.6)		
Wave 3	1.7	1.6	2.0	1.8	. . .	
	(.7)	(.7)	(1.1)	(.6)		
Scales used in the monitoring composite:						
Monitoring character development:						
Fathers' self-reports:						
Wave 1	16.7	17.1	15.0	16.2	*Family type, gender*	*Nondiv > Rem; Girls > Boys*
	(2.0)	(1.7)	(2.6)	(2.3)		
Wave 2	16.7	16.8	14.8	16.0	Family type	Nondiv > Rem
	(1.7)	(2.0)	(3.3)	(2.2)		
Wave 3	16.2	16.4	14.6	16.0	*Family type*	*Nondiv > Rem*
	(1.7)	(2.0)	(2.4)	(2.7)		

TABLE 30 (*Continued*)

	Nondivorced		Remarried		Significant Main Effects and Interactions[a]	Significant Contrasts and Planned Comparisons[a]
	Boys	Girls	Boys	Girls		
Children's reports of fathers:						
Wave 1	16.7 (2.9)	14.9 (3.7)	13.5 (3.6)	15.7 (3.5)	Family type, family type × gender	Nondiv > Rem; Boys (Nondiv > Rem); Nondiv (Boys > Girls); Rem (Girls > Boys)
Wave 2	15.0 (3.1)	15.0 (3.0)	13.7 (4.6)	15.0 (2.8)	. . .	
Wave 3	15.1 (3.5)	14.8 (3.8)	14.3 (3.1)	14.6 (2.6)	. . .	
Mothers' reports of fathers:						
Wave 1	15.7 (2.6)	15.2 (2.3)	14.3 (2.9)	15.0 (3.0)	. . .	
Wave 2	15.4 (2.4)	15.7 (2.3)	14.9 (2.6)	14.3 (2.7)	*Family type*	*Nondiv > Rem*
Wave 3	15.2 (2.3)	15.1 (2.4)	13.6 (3.0)	14.5 (2.2)	*Family type*	*Nondiv > Rem*
Monitoring deviant behavior:						
Fathers' self-reports:						
Wave 1	12.4 (2.3)	13.3 (1.3)	11.0 (2.6)	12.5 (2.1)	Family type, *gender*	Nondiv > Rem; *Girls > Boys*
Wave 2	12.7 (1.5)	12.7 (2.1)	11.4 (2.8)	11.6 (2.3)	Family type	Nondiv > Rem
Wave 3	12.5 (1.2)	12.4 (2.2)	11.1 (2.3)	12.3 (2.0)	*Family type*	*Nondiv > Rem*

Children's reports of fathers:						
Wave 1	12.6 (2.0)	11.1 (2.8)	9.8 (3.5)	10.6 (3.5)	Family type, family type × gender	Nondiv > Rem; Boys (Nondiv > Rem); Nondiv (Boys > Girls)
Wave 2	11.6 (2.4)	11.5 (3.0)	9.7 (3.6)	9.9 (3.1)	Family type	Nondiv > Rem
Wave 3	11.1 (2.3)	11.4 (3.0)	10.8 (3.0)	10.0 (2.7)	. . .	
Mothers' reports of fathers:						
Wave 1	12.1 (2.4)	12.3 (1.6)	11.1 (1.9)	11.3 (2.6)	Family type	Nondiv > Rem
Wave 2	12.0 (2.0)	12.4 (1.8)	11.4 (2.5)	11.4 (2.4)	*Family type*	*Nondiv > Rem*
Wave 3	11.8 (2.1)	11.6 (2.3)	10.5 (2.5)	11.0 (2.0)	*Family type*	*Nondiv > Rem*
Monitoring:						
Observers' ratings:[b]						
Wave 1	3.8 (.7)	3.9 (.7)	3.4 (.6)	3.6 (.9)	Family type	Nondiv > Rem
Wave 2	3.4 (.8)	3.8 (.9)	3.3 (.7)	3.4 (.8)	. . .	
Wave 3	3.7 (1.0)	4.0 (.9)	3.6 (1.2)	3.4 (.6)	. . .	
Scales included in the control composite:						
Control of behaviors related to character development:						
Fathers' self-reports:						
Wave 1	15.1 (3.0)	14.7 (2.8)	11.7 (3.7)	13.3 (3.9)	Family type	Nondiv > Rem
Wave 2	15.2 (2.5)	14.6 (3.4)	10.4 (3.4)	12.6 (3.9)	Family type	Nondiv > Rem
Wave 3	15.4 (2.7)	14.0 (3.0)	10.9 (3.3)	13.3 (3.8)	Family type, family type × gender	Nondiv > Rem; Boys (Nondiv > Rem); Rem (Girls > Boys)

TABLE 30 (*Continued*)

	Nondivorced		Remarried		Significant Main Effects and Interactions[a]	Significant Contrasts and Planned Comparisons[a]
	Boys	Girls	Boys	Girls		
Children's reports of fathers:						
Wave 1	12.2 (4.5)	10.3 (4.2)	9.4 (4.9)	10.1 (5.1)	. . .	
Wave 2	12.0 (3.4)	10.5 (3.6)	10.4 (5.6)	9.9 (4.6)	. . .	
Wave 3	10.8 (4.0)	9.9 (3.9)	10.4 (5.1)	11.2 (4.1)	. . .	
Mothers' reports of fathers:						
Wave 1	14.8 (3.0)	13.3 (3.2)	12.3 (3.7)	12.9 (3.7)	Family type	Nondiv > Rem
Wave 2	14.3 (2.7)	13.8 (2.8)	12.1 (3.7)	13.3 (3.3)	Family type	Nondiv > Rem
Wave 3	14.3 (3.1)	13.3 (3.2)	12.3 (3.6)	13.0 (3.4)	. . .	
Control of deviant behavior:						
Fathers' self-reports:						
Wave 1	11.7 (2.6)	12.0 (2.7)	9.5 (3.3)	11.6 (2.9)	Family type, gender	Nondiv > Rem; Girls > Boys
Wave 2	11.9 (2.2)	12.3 (2.3)	9.1 (3.4)	10.4 (3.3)	Family type	Nondiv > Rem
Wave 3	12.2 (2.0)	11.8 (2.8)	8.9 (3.3)	10.7 (2.9)	Family type, family type × gender	Nondiv > Rem; Boys (Nondiv > Rem)

Children's reports of fathers:						
Wave 1	10.8	9.6	8.1	9.8	. . .	
	(2.8)	(3.6)	(4.0)	(3.7)		
Wave 2	10.7	10.7	9.5	9.6	. . .	
	(2.3)	(3.0)	(4.3)	(3.3)		
Wave 3	9.9	10.4	10.2	10.6	. . .	
	(2.4)	(2.4)	(4.0)	(3.1)		
Mothers' reports of fathers:						
Wave 1	11.7	11.6	9.7	10.3	Family type	Nondiv > Rem
	(2.9)	(2.4)	(3.1)	(3.6)		
Wave 2	11.5	11.6	9.2	10.8	Family type	Nondiv > Rem
	(2.2)	(2.4)	(3.3)	(2.8)		
Wave 3	11.4	11.2	9.6	10.7	Family type	Nondiv > Rem
	(2.5)	(2.4)	(3.1)	(2.8)		
Fathers' dominance/power:						
Observers' ratings:						
Wave 1	4.0	4.0	3.8	3.8	Family type	Nondiv > Rem
	(.2)	(.2)	(.4)	(.4)		
Wave 2	3.7	3.7	3.6	3.5	. . .	
	(.6)	(.5)	(.5)	(.5)		
Wave 3	3.9	4.0	3.8	3.5	Family type	Nondiv > Rem
	(.4)	(.0)	(.7)	(.6)		
Fathers' parental influence:						
Observers' ratings:						
Wave 1	3.8	3.8	3.4	3.7	Family type	Nondiv > Rem
	(.5)	(.6)	(.6)	(.7)		
Wave 2	3.5	3.7	3.5	3.2	*Family type*	*Nondiv > Rem*
	(.8)	(.7)	(.8)	(.7)		
Wave 3	3.8	4.0	3.6	3.3	Family type	Nondiv > Rem
	(.8)	(.5)	(1.2)	(.9)		

NOTE.—Nondiv = Nondivorced; Rem = Remarried.

[a] Italicized contrasts denote planned comparisons.

[b] Univariate analyses.

TABLE 31

MEANS (Standard Deviations) FOR CHILDREN'S OBSERVED POSITIVITY AND NEGATIVITY TOWARD MOTHERS

	Nondivorced		Divorced		Remarried		Significant Main Effects and Interactions	Significant Contrasts and Planned Comparisons
	Boys	Girls	Boys	Girls	Boys	Girls		
Observers' ratings:[a]								
Positivity:								
Wave 1	2.6	2.7	2.3	2.6	2.6	2.6	...	*Boys (Rem > Div)*[b]
	(.5)	(.6)	(.4)	(.5)	(.4)	(.5)		
Wave 2	2.6	2.8	2.4	2.7	2.6	2.7	Gender	Girls > Boys
	(.4)	(.4)	(.5)	(.5)	(.5)	(.3)		
Wave 3	2.9	3.2	...	...	2.7	2.8	Family type	Nondiv > Rem
	(.5)	(.7)			(.7)	(.6)		
Negativity:								
Wave 1	1.7	1.8	2.2	2.0	1.8	2.0	Family type	Div > Nondiv
	(.5)	(.5)	(.7)	(.6)	(.6)	(.6)		
Wave 2	1.9	1.8	2.3	2.1	2.0	2.0	Family type	Div > Nondiv
	(.6)	(.6)	(.7)	(.6)	(.5)	(.6)		
Wave 3	1.8	1.9	...	...	2.2	2.1	...	
	(.7)	(.9)			(.8)	(.9)		

NOTE.—Nondiv = Nondivorced; Rem = Remarried.

[a] Univariate analyses.

[b] t test, $p \leq .05$. Italicized contrast denotes planned comparison.

TABLE 32

MEANS (Standard Deviations) FOR CHILDREN'S OBSERVED POSITIVITY AND NEGATIVITY TOWARD FATHERS

	NONDIVORCED		REMARRIED		SIGNIFICANT MAIN EFFECTS AND INTERACTIONS	SIGNIFICANT CONTRASTS AND PLANNED COMPARISONS
	Boys	Girls	Boys	Girls		
Observers' ratings:[a]						
Positivity:						
Wave 1	2.5	2.6	2.5	2.5	. . .	
	(.4)	(.6)	(.4)	(.5)		
Wave 2	2.6	2.6	2.3	2.5	Family type	Nondiv > Rem
	(.5)	(.4)	(.7)	(.4)		
Wave 3	2.9	3.2	2.6	2.6	Family type	Nondiv > Rem
	(.6)	(.7)	(.7)	(.5)		
Negativity:						
Wave 1	1.5	1.7	1.8	1.9	Family type	Rem > Nondiv
	(.5)	(.4)	(.6)	(.7)		
Wave 2	1.7	1.7	1.9	1.9	. . .	
	(.6)	(.5)	(.6)	(.6)		
Wave 3	1.6	1.7	2.0	2.0	Family type	Rem > Nondiv
	(.8)	(.7)	(.9)	(.7)		

[a] Univariate analyses.

divorced, nonremarried mothers; these, and the differing perceptions of different reporters, are discussed below.

Family Differences in Mother-Child Relationships

The discussion to follow focuses on the analyses of the composite indices of parenting that were assumed to be less subject to individual biases than the separate reports of family members. However, some comments will also be made regarding differences in individual family members' views of parent-child relationships in the three types of families. Assessments represented by a single measure—namely, spouses' reports of rapport and observers' ratings of positivity, negativity, monitoring, power, and attempted influence—could not be subjected to multivariate analysis. These instances are noted on the tables.

Divorced versus nondivorced families.—The mother-child relationship in divorced families can be described as highly ambivalent, involved, and affectively charged. Especially as perceived by the children, it combined greater instrumental affection with greater levels of negativity, conflict, and punishment than those reported by children in nondivorced families.

Greater levels of maternal positivity were evident in the analyses of the multimethod/multirespondent composite indices and children's self-reports. Examination of single scales revealed that differences in positivity between nondivorced and divorced mothers were attributable largely to the reports of children in divorced families of greater instrumental affection in the form of shared activities in all three waves rather than to differences in expressive affection, which were found in children's reports only in Wave 3, or to differences in rapport or observed behavior, which never occurred (Wave 3, Tables 23–26). Greater levels of negativity and conflict were also evident. Although in Wave 1 these differences in negativity were attributable to the higher levels of conflict between boys and their divorced mothers, no gender differences were found in later waves; the divorced mothers were more acrimonious with both sons and daughters as the children moved further into adolescence. In Wave 1 (as shown in Table 24), the composite indices indicated that divorced mothers of sons not only were more negative but were also poorer monitors and had less control over the boys' behavior than their nondivorced counterparts. In contrast, t tests (planned comparisons) suggested that divorced mothers of daughters had more control and monitored their pre- and early adolescents' behavior more closely than nondivorced mothers. At the level of different respondents' reports, it was the observers and children rather than the mothers themselves who perceived the single mother-child relationship as troubled. Observers rated children as more negative in their interactions with their mothers at all available waves (Waves 1 and 2) and mothers as more negative and lower in monitoring and power at Wave 1 and less influential in Waves 1 and 2 (all available). In contrast, the reports of divorced mothers differed little from those of nondivorced ones—in fact, they viewed themselves as more adept in monitoring at all waves. Even by Wave 3, when children of divorced mothers perceived them as using more negative sanctions and nagging communication and engaging in more conflicts over daily routines and adolescent issues, the mothers' own reports of their negativity differed little from those of nondivorced mothers.

Remarried versus nondivorced families.—At the level of composite indices, reported in Table 24, the Wave 1 mother-child relationships in newly remarried families differed from those in nondivorced families with respect to monitoring and negativity. Remarried mothers emerged as poorer monitors of sons' behaviors, and their relationships with daughters were characterized by higher negativity. In the single-reporter analyses, observers also reported that married mothers exhibited more negative behaviors toward their children in this early stage of the remarriage than did nondivorced mothers.

The negativity of remarried mothers was no longer evident at Wave 2, but they continued to be poorer monitors and, for the first time, to exert less control than nondivorced mothers. Similarly, stepfathers saw their wives as less controlling and poorer monitors of their children's character and behavior. By Wave 3, there were no significant differences between mother-child relationships in nondivorced and remarried families on the composite indices, but stepfathers continued to see their wives as exhibiting less monitoring and control, and observers reported less positivity in stepchildren's behavior toward their mothers. Thus, a little over 2 years after the remarriage, the mother-child relationship seemed to have restabilized to some degree and appeared similar to that in nondivorced families.

Remarried versus divorced families.—At Wave 1, the only differences to emerge between the remarried and the divorced families were greater negativity/conflict of divorced mothers of boys, as indicated by the multimethod/multirespondent composite indices, and divorced mothers' self-reports of greater monitoring and control. At later waves, however, in comparison to remarried mothers, divorced mothers were more negative toward both their sons and their daughters but vigilantly monitored only their daughters' behavior. By Wave 3, the divorced mothers were also more positive toward their children than mothers in remarried families. In all, divorced mothers appeared to have been more involved than remarried mothers in their children's lives, perhaps because of partially shared responsibility and help from the stepfathers in remarried families.

Family Differences in Father-Child Relationships

The results of the within-wave analyses conducted on the composite scores of fathers' parenting are presented in Tables 27 and 28 and on the scale scores of fathers' parenting in Tables 29 and 30.

As might be expected from the lack of role definition for stepparents, the stepfathers' relationships with their new stepchildren were quite anomalous compared to those of fathers of children in nondivorced families. Although no differences were apparent at Wave 1 at the composite level on the affective scales, stepfathers demonstrated poorer monitoring—knowing less about their new stepchildren's interests and behaviors—and less control of children's behavior than nondivorced fathers, particularly when the new stepchildren were male.

A different picture emerged at the scale level (see Table 30). While neither stepchildren nor observers noted any less positivity on the part of stepfathers, the stepfathers perceived themselves to be less expressive and less involved and to have less rapport with their stepchildren than did fathers in nondivorced households, possibly because stepchildren were more hostile, coercive, and conflictual in their interactions with their new stepfathers than children in nondivorced families were with their fathers, according to the observers (see Table 32).

Thus, it appears that, despite the negative behavior of their stepchildren in the early months of remarriage, the new stepfathers were acting in ways that appeared overtly positive or friendly to others while they themselves felt a lack of affection and rapport—a finding supported by observers' anecdotal comments that the stepfathers interacted with their new stepchildren like "polite strangers." Contrary to what was expected, stepfathers did not become similar to biological fathers and more involved over time—in Waves 2 and 3 they remained less controlling and monitored less than nondivorced fathers. Furthermore, other family members began to agree with stepfathers' self-perceptions of being less affectionate; this agreement is indicated by stepfathers' lower scores on the multimethod/multirespondent composite positivity index. Not surprisingly, 26 months after remarriage, stepchildren's behavior toward their stepfathers was still significantly less positive and more negative than children's behavior toward nondivorced, biological fathers.

Summary of Parent-Child Relationships

The expectation that divorced mothers and their sons would continue to experience a troubled relationship was most evident with respect to negativity and conflict. At Wave 1, divorced mothers were both more negative toward sons than either nondivorced or remarried mothers were and more negative toward sons than toward daughters. By Wave 3, however, these gender differences in conflict eventually disappeared, as divorced mothers developed more negative and conflictual relationships with sons and daughters than did either nondivorced or remarried mothers. This conflict was tempered by the high levels of involvement sometimes reported by divorced mothers and consistently reported by their children. By Wave 3, children in divorced families saw their mothers as negative and coercive but also as warm and involved.

We had predicted that problems in parent-child relationships would emerge in response to the remarriage but that the differences between remarried and nondivorced families would decrease over time. The expectation that mother-child relationships in newly forming stepfamilies would deteriorate over the first year but recover over time was partially supported. Newly remarried mothers did monitor the behavior of both sons and daughters less than either nondivorced or divorced mothers, and at Wave 1 they were more negative with their children than were nondivorced mothers. However, whatever early differences existed between remarried mothers and their children appeared to be resolved with time, and mother-child relationships in remarried families look similar to those in nondivorced families by Wave 3. The only exceptions to this were the lower observed positivity of children toward their remarried mothers and stepfathers' reports of mothers' lesser control of children's character.

In contrast, stepfathers felt more alienated from their children, and although they exhibited little overt negativity, they were less positive and involved in controlling and monitoring their children's behavior than were nondivorced fathers. These differences, as well as the somewhat greater negativity and lesser positivity shown by children toward the stepfather, still remained 26 months after remarriage.

STABILITY AND CHANGES OVER TIME IN PARENT-CHILD RELATIONSHIPS

The across-wave analyses were conducted in two stages. First, the between-wave correlations of the composite and scale scores of parenting were calculated to assess the stability of parenting behaviors within groups; these were run separately on mother-child and on father-child measures for boys and for girls within each family group. Similar correlations were run to assess the stability of children's observed positivity and negativity toward mothers and fathers. Since observational data for divorced families at Wave 3 were not available, no correlations involving Wave 3 could be calculated for these two indices. All these correlations and their significance levels are presented in Table 33. Tests of the significance of differences

TABLE 33

Across-Time Correlations in the Parenting Composites and Children's Observed Positivity and Negativity

	Mothers' Positivity/Warmth			Mothers' Negativity/Conflict			Mothers' Monitoring			Mothers' Control		
	Wave 1	Wave 2	Wave 3	Wave 1	Wave 2	Wave 3	Wave 1	Wave 2	Wave 3	Wave 1	Wage 2	Wage 3
Nondiv boys:												
Wave 1	...			...			...			...		
Wave 2	.62***	...		.74***	...		.57***	...		.60***	...	
Wave 3	.68***	.68***	...	.64***	.78***	...	.59***	.53***	...	.56***	.58***	...
Nondiv girls:												
Wave 1	...			...			...			...		
Wave 2	.72***	...		.57***	...		.71***	...		.62***	...	
Wave 3	.61***	.68***	...	.42**	.59***	...	.71***	.73***	...	.68***	.77***	...
Div boys:												
Wave 1	...			...			...			...		
Wave 2	.60***	...		.50**	...		.52**	...		.40**	...	
Wave 3	.33*	.36*	...	.16	.57**	...	.21	.29	...	.45**	.68***	...
Div girls:												
Wave 1	...			...			...			...		
Wave 2	.25	...		.49**	...		.64***	...		.37**	...	
Wave 3	.36*	.32*	...	.65***	.69***	...	.28	.37*	...	.32*	.46**	...
Rem boys:												
Wave 1	...			...			...			...		
Wave 2	.66***	...		.23	...		.65***	...		.56**	...	
Wave 3	.29	.68***	...	.06	.43*	...	.79***	.58***	...	.63**	.87***	...
Rem girls:												
Wave 1	...			...			...			...		
Wave 2	.49**	...		.69***	...		.62***	...		.48**	...	
Wave 3	.44**	.52**	...	.25	.38*	...	.54**	.72***	...	.34*	.38*	...

	Fathers' Positivity/Warmth			Fathers' Negativity/Conflict			Fathers' Monitoring			Fathers' Control		
Nondiv boys:												
Wave 1	. . .			. . .			. . .			. . .		
Wave 2	.67***	. . .		.68***	. . .		.71***	. . .		.69***	. . .	
Wave 3	.71***	.71***	. . .	.74***	.71***	. . .	.73***	.64***	. . .	.68***	.67***	. . .
Nondiv girls:												
Wave 1	. . .			. . .			. . .			. . .		
Wave 2	.71***	. . .		.47***	. . .		.67***	. . .		.67***	. . .	
Wave 3	.42***	.72***	. . .	.44**	.52***	. . .	.62***	.67***	. . .	.62***	.67***	. . .
Rem boys:												
Wave 1	. . .			. . .			. . .			. . .		
Wave 2	.69***	. . .		.52**	. . .		.58***	. . .		.58**	. . .	
Wave 3	.69***	.81***	. . .	.70***	.65***	. . .	.46*	.71***	. . .	.52**	.74***	. . .
Rem girls:												
Wave 1	. . .			. . .			. . .			. . .		
Wave 2	.73***	. . .		.57***	. . .		.50**	. . .		.74***	. . .	
Wave 3	.61***	.79***	. . .	.67***	.21	. . .	.59***	.75***	. . .	.74***	.68***	. . .
	Positivity to Mother			Negativity to Mother			Positivity to Father			Negativity to Father		
Nondiv boys:												
Wave 1	. . .			. . .			. . .			. . .		
Wave 2	.57***	. . .		.57***	. . .		.54***	. . .		.71***	. . .	
Wave 3	.46**	.44**	. . .	.06	.00	. . .	.57***	.33*	. . .	.47**	.12	. . .
Nondiv girls:												
Wave 1	. . .			. . .			. . .			. . .		
Wave 2	.33*	. . .		.11	. . .		.30*	. . .		.38*	. . .	
Wave 3	.36*	.27*	. . .	.42**	.75***	. . .	.55***	.33*	. . .	.33*	.61***	. . .
Div boys:												
Wave 1	. . .			. . .								
Wave 2	.31*	. . .		.58***	. . .							
Wave 3	. . .	. . .	. . .	. . .	. . .	. . .						

TABLE 33 (*Continued*)

	Positivity to Mother			Negativity to Mother			Positivity to Father			Negativity to Father		
	Wave 1	Wave 2	Wave 3	Wave 1	Wave 2	Wave 3	Wave 1	Wave 2	Wave 3	Wave 1	Wage 2	Wage 3
Div girls:												
Wave 1	...			...								
Wave 2	.45**	...		.49**	...							
Wave 3	...	...	...	...	...	...						
Rem boys:												
Wave 1	...			...			...			...		
Wave 2	.25	...		.27	...		.27	...		.49**	...	
Wave 3	.47*	.44*	...	.00	.55**	...	.26	.46*	...	.19	.51**	...
Rem girls:												
Wave 1	...			...			...			...		
Wave 2	.34*	...		.09	...		.30	...		.15	...	
Wave 3	.01	.16	...	−.17	.51**	...	.11	−.16	...	−.03	.27	...

Note.—Nondiv = Nondivorced; Div = Divorced; Rem = Remarried.

* $p \leq .05$.

** $p \leq .01$.

*** $p \leq .001$.

between correlations were performed but are not given in the tables since so few were significant. Second, a series of repeated-measures MANOVAs were conducted to examine how the composite indices of parenting and children's observed positivity and negativity changed over time for boys and girls in each family group; these results are summarized in Tables 34 and 35.

Stability in Parent-Child Relationships

It is remarkable that for both mothers and fathers in nondivorced families on all parenting dimensions and for both boys and girls, the correlations were large and consistently significant. Furthermore, although more changes might have been expected in new stepfamilies, marked stability characterized stepfathers' parenting across time; only the correlation between their negativity toward stepdaughters from Wave 2 to Wave 3 was not significant. Although nonsignificant correlations were more frequent in the ratings of divorced and remarried mothers, considerable stability was found over time.

It was in the children's observed positivity and negativity toward their parents in remarried families that the fewest significant correlations were obtained. Only eight out of 24 correlations were significant for these children, in contrast to 20 out of 24 for children with nondivorced parents and four out of the four for children with a divorced, nonremarried mother. Nevertheless, when Fisher's r to Z transformations were used to test the significance of differences between correlations, the number did not exceed what would be expected by chance.

The repeated-measures analyses used to examine short-term changes from Wave 1 to Wave 2 and long-term changes from Wave 1 to Wave 3 are presented in Tables 34 and 35. Only wave effects and interactions will be discussed here since gender and family effects were already discussed for the within-wave analyses.

Changes in Mother-Child Relationships over Time

Short-term changes.—It can be seen in Table 34 that significant wave effects were found across all maternal parenting dimensions, indicating an overall Wave 1 to Wave 2 decrease in mothers' positivity, $F(1,177) = 11.41$, $p \leq .001$, negativity, $F(1,177) = 10.18$, $p \leq .01$, monitoring, $F(1,177) = 18.71$, $p \leq .001$, and control, $F(1,177) = 6.72$, $p \leq .01$. However, several interactions qualify this general trend toward lesser involvement in the parenting of older children. Mothers in remarried and divorced families, but not in nondivorced ones, were declining in positivity, $F(2,177) = 3.43$,

TABLE 34

MEANS (Standard Deviations) FOR REPEATED-MEASURES ANALYSES OF SHORT-TERM CHANGES IN PARENT-CHILD RELATIONSHIPS FROM WAVE 1 TO WAVE 2

	Nondivorced		Divorced		Remarried		Significant Main Effects and Interactions	Significant Contrasts
	Boys	Girls	Boys	Girls	Boys	Girls		
Mothers':								
Positivity/warmth:								
Wave 1	−.07 (.54)	−.10 (.55)	−.04 (.53)	.20 (.52)	−.06 (.70)	.05 (.61)	Wave	1 > 2
Wave 2	−.08 (.67)	−.08 (.53)	−.21 (.54)	.06 (.37)	−.36 (.48)	−.05 (.54)	Wave × family type	Div, Rem (1 > 2)
Negativity/conflict:								
Wave 1	.01 (.66)	−.25 (.46)	.17 (.65)	−.06 (.45)	−.10 (.43)	.03 (.64)	Wave	1 > 2
Wave 2	−.11 (.71)	−.43 (.50)	−.05 (.48)	.03 (.67)	−.14 (.43)	−.27 (.60)	Family type, wave × family type × gender	Div > Nondiv; Girls (Rem, Nondiv 1 > 2)
Monitoring:								
Wave 1	.12 (.58)	.10 (.67)	−.21 (.46)	.21 (.61)	−.41 (.62)	−.17 (.51)	Wave	1 > 2
Wave 2	−.18 (.53)	−.06 (.57)	−.13 (.57)	.04 (.50)	−.66 (.86)	−.42 (.84)	Family type, gender	Nondiv, Div > Rem; Girls > Boys
Control:								
Wave 1	.12 (.52)	−.05 (.51)	−.16 (.57)	.09 (.51)	−.11 (.49)	−.04 (.42)	Wave	1 > 2
Wave 2	.02 (.59)	−.08 (.54)	−.03 (.47)	−.06 (.46)	−.40 (.73)	−.25 (.74)		
Children's observed:								
Positivity to mothers:								
Wave 1	2.65 (.47)	2.72 (.57)	2.34 (.41)	2.66 (.49)	2.64 (.38)	2.69 (.43)	...	
Wave 2	2.55 (.44)	2.85 (.44)	2.41 (.53)	2.70 (.46)	2.59 (.45)	2.74 (.34)		

Negativity to mothers:								
Wave 1	1.70 (.51)	1.81 (.47)	2.25 (.73)	1.95 (.65)	1.73 (.47)	2.03 (.52)	Wave	1 < 2
Wave 2	1.90 (.62)	1.83 (.64)	2.31 (.71)	2.10 (.60)	2.05 (.52)	2.02 (.58)		
Fathers':								
Positivity/warmth:								
Wave 1	.09 (.58)	.15 (.53)			−.28 (.67)	−.08 (.69)	Wave	1 > 2
Wave 2	.05 (.63)	.14 (.54)			−.74 (.62)	−.38 (.75)	Family type, family type × wave	Nondiv > Rem; Rem (1 > 2)
Negativity/conflict:								
Wave 1	.09 (.71)	−.19 (.38)			−.03 (.59)	−.08 (.55)	Gender	Boys > Girls
Wave 2	−.02 (.79)	−.36 (.40)			−.04 (.68)	−.08 (.55)		
Monitoring:								
Wave 1	.21 (.62)	.17 (.41)			−.40 (.65)	−.19 (.60)	Family type	Nondiv > Rem
Wave 2	.05 (.55)	.13 (.54)			−.42 (.80)	−.24 (.70)		
Control:								
Wave 1	.28 (.50)	.13 (.42)			−.44 (.75)	−.22 (.62)	Wave	1 > 2
Wave 2	.14 (.56)	.08 (.56)			−.49 (.87)	−.37 (.68)	Family type	Nondiv > Rem
Children's observed:								
Positivity to fathers:								
Wave 1	2.50 (.45)	2.62 (.58)			2.48 (.46)	2.61 (.54)	. . .	
Wave 2	2.56 (.49)	2.65 (.42)			2.30 (.66)	2.47 (.41)		
Negativity to fathers:								
Wave 1	1.50 (.47)	1.62 (.42)			1.67 (.43)	1.86 (.62)	Wave	1 < 2
Wave 2	1.76 (.64)	1.68 (.45)			1.85 (.56)	1.91 (.62)		

NOTE.—Nondiv = Nondivorced; Rem = Remarried.

TABLE 35

MEANS (Standard Deviations) FOR REPEATED-MEASURES ANALYSES OF LONG-TERM CHANGES IN PARENT-CHILD RELATIONSHIPS FROM WAVE 1 TO WAVE 3

	NONDIVORCED		DIVORCED		REMARRIED		SIGNIFICANT MAIN EFFECTS AND INTERACTIONS	SIGNIFICANT CONTRASTS
	Boys	Girls	Boys	Girls	Boys	Girls		
Mothers':								
Positivity/warmth:								
Wave 1	−.08 (.55)	−.04 (.53)	.07 (.50)	.19 (.52)	.10 (.50)	.05 (.61)	Wave	1 > 3
Wave 3	−.19 (.64)	−.21 (.57)	−.11 (.61)	.01 (.63)	−.26 (.60)	−.18 (.59)		
Negativity/conflict:								
Wave 1	−.01 (.66)	−.23 (.46)	.14 (.68)	−.06 (.48)	−.13 (.45)	.03 (.62)	Wave	1 > 3
Wave 3	−.34 (.67)	−.54 (.38)	.02 (.76)	.01 (.91)	−.30 (.48)	−.35 (.49)	Family type, wave × family type	Div > Nondiv, Rem; Rem, Nondiv (1 > 3)
Monitoring:								
Wave 1	.12 (.60)	.10 (.68)	−.13 (.45)	.22 (.62)	−.34 (.63)	−.08 (.53)	Wave	1 > 3
Wave 3	−.23 (.60)	−.08 (.58)	−.22 (.74)	.24 (.64)	−.34 (.64)	−.33 (.64)	Family type, gender	Nondiv, Div > Rem; Girls > Boys
Control:								
Wave 1	.11 (.54)	−.02 (.53)	−.12 (.53)	.12 (.48)	−.14 (.51)	.05 (.44)	Family type × wave	No significant contrasts
Wave 3	−.03 (.49)	−.06 (.62)	.04 (.60)	.30 (.62)	−.15 (.72)	−.25 (.53)		
Children's observed:								
Positivity to mothers:								
Wave 1	2.61 (.47)	2.70 (.54)	...	...	2.64 (.43)	2.71 (.46)	Wave	1 < 3
Wave 3	2.88 (.46)	3.14 (.67)	...	...	2.74 (.67)	2.80 (.61)		

Negativity to mothers:								
Wave 1	1.65	1.77	. . .	. . .	1.67	2.10	Family type	Rem > Nondiv
	(.48)	(.44)			(.49)	(.53)		
Wave 3	1.77	1.95	. . .	. . .	2.21	2.08		
	(.68)	(.89)			(.76)	(.93)		
Fathers':								
Positivity/warmth:								
Wave 1	.06	.21			−.20	.04	Wave, family type	1 > 3; Nondiv > Rem
	(.57)	(.52)			(.66)	(.69)		
Wave 3	−.04	.16			−.77	−.30	Family type × wave	Rem (1 > 3)
	(.59)	(.57)			(.64)	(.53)		
Negativity/conflict:								
Wave 1	.09	−.18			−.03	.05	Wave	1 > 3
	(.72)	(.37)			(.59)	(.69)		
Wave 3	−.16	−.43			−.14	−.20	Gender	Boys > Girls
	(.67)	(.38)			(.70)	(.53)		
Monitoring:								
Wave 1	.18	.17			−.40	−.04	Wave	1 > 3
	(.62)	(.42)			(.62)	(.68)		
Wave 3	.00	.03			−.46	−.25	Family type	Nondiv > Rem
	(.52)	(.64)			(.72)	(.54)		
Control:								
Wave 1	.27	.15			−.48	−.04	Family type	Nondiv > Rem
	(.51)	(.41)			(.74)	(.68)		
Wave 3	.17	.13			−.36	−.27	Family type × wave × gender	Rem (Boys 1 < 3); Rem (Girls 1 > 3)
	(.45)	(.45)			(.86)	(.72)		
Children's observed:								
Positivity to fathers:								
Wave 1	2.48	2.60			2.55	2.65	Wave	1 > 3
	(.46)	(.53)			(.48)	(.53)		
Wave 3	2.82	3.18			2.59	2.64	Wave × family type	Nondiv (1 < 3)
	(.55)	(.70)			(.75)	(.55)		
Negativity to fathers:								
Wave 1	1.52	1.64			1.64	1.89	. . .	
	(.47)	(.43)			(.56)	(.60)		
Wave 3	1.62	1.69			2.04	2.00		
	(.79)	(.65)			(.89)	(.71)		

NOTE.—Nondiv = Nondivorced; Rem = Remarried.

$p \leq .05$. The nondivorced and remarried but not the divorced mothers of daughters were less negative at Wave 2 than at Wave 1, $F(2,177) = 4.18$, $p \leq .05$. Thus, it appears that the divorced mothers were sustaining a constant degree of conflict, while other mothers were showing a decrement on this as well as all other dimensions. In contrast to the trend toward increasing disengagement found for mothers, all groups of children were increasing in observed negativity as they moved into adolescence, $F(1,155) = 5.36$, $p \leq .05$.

Long-term changes.—The pattern of the Wave 1 to Wave 2 decline on all maternal parenting measures was sustained over the 26-month period from Wave 1 to Wave 3 (see Table 35). Once again, conflict declined significantly only for nondivorced and remarried mothers with daughters but not for divorced mothers with daughters, $F(2,157) = 3.33$, $p \leq .05$. This pattern was also now found for boys. Furthermore, although there were no significant contrasts in the significant family type × wave interaction for maternal control, this significant interaction might be attributable to increases in the control of daughters by divorced mothers and decreases by remarried mothers ($p \leq .10$ in both cases). Over this 26-month period, as mothers were tending to become somewhat less involved and active in parenting, children were increasing in positivity toward them, $F(1,87) = 10.33$, $p \leq .01$.

Changes in Father-Child Relationships over Time

Short-term changes.—Few short-term changes were found in father-child relationships (see Table 34). Stepfathers, but not nondivorced fathers, showed a significant decline in positivity from Wave 1 to Wave 2 (for the wave × family type interaction, $F[1,116] = 22.09$, $p \leq .001$). As noted earlier, the within-wave analyses revealed that, relative to nondivorced fathers, stepfathers rated themselves low on positivity at both waves but that family members and observers did not concur until Wave 2. Thus, this significant decline in positivity seen in the current analysis appears to reflect changes in spouses', children's, and observers' ratings of the stepfathers' warmth and involvement rather than changes in the latter's self-perceptions. The general absence of significant Wave 1 and Wave 2 differences, particularly in nondivorced families, may indicate that, as children began to make the transition into adolescence, adjustments in father-child relationships occurred more slowly than in mother-child relationships. Children, however, were increasing in observed negativity toward their fathers just as they had toward their mothers during this period, $F(1,95) = 5.59$, $p \leq .05$.

Long-term changes.—As is the case with mother-child relationships, nondivorced fathers and stepfathers also became more disengaged from their children over time. However, adjustments in these relationships occurred more slowly. Both stepfathers and fathers declined in negativity, $F(1,107) = 22.58$, $p \leq .001$, and monitoring, $F(1,107) = 8.32$, $p \leq .01$, and stepfathers decreased more than nondivorced fathers in positivity (for the wave × family type interaction, $F[1,107] = 19.60$, $p \leq .001$).

A family type × gender × wave interaction was found for paternal control, $F(1,107) = 4.54$, $p \leq .05$. Stepfathers appeared to exert more control with boys, but less with girls, at the later wave. Despite these changes, however, stepfathers of both boys and girls continued to exert significantly less control than their nondivorced counterparts. In this 26-month period, there was also an increase in children's positivity toward their nondivorced fathers but not toward their stepfathers (for the family type × wave interaction, $F[1,87] = 10.73$, $p < .01$).

Summary

All parents appeared to retreat from active involvement with their children as the latter advanced into adolescence, although divorced mothers sustained some degree of conflict with their daughters. However, these changes over time may mean different things for children in different family types. In nondivorced households, the parents' disengagement may reflect a normal response to the increased competence of their children. In divorced families, mothers may be "giving up" on relatively troubled mother-son relationships and on emerging problems of antisocial behavior in daughters. The within-wave analyses indicated that, by Wave 3, remarried and nondivorced mothers resembled each other across parenting dimensions. However, this similarity appeared to be due to a greater disengagement by nondivorced mothers relative to remarried ones. Rather than concluding that remarried mothers were "recovering" and becoming more competent parents over time, it may be more accurate to conclude that nondivorced mothers with competent, responsible adolescent children could afford to withdraw to the lower levels of involvement characterizing remarried families. Remarried mothers, who were not as involved and authoritative at the outset and who had children with more behavior problems, may not be in a position to withdraw farther. The implications that such interpretations have for children's adjustment are examined in the last chapter. Fathers also seemed to be distancing themselves, but at a somewhat delayed pace compared to mothers and with more marked declines in positivity occurring for stepfathers than for fathers.

As they first entered adolescence, children showed increasingly negative behavior; eventually, however, children became increasingly positive toward all parents except stepfathers as their parents became less emotionally involved and granted them greater autonomy.

PARENTING TYPOLOGIES

These typologies were developed to gain an understanding of configurations of parenting variables that characterized mothers and fathers in each family type. Both mothers and fathers could be classified as either authoritative, disengaged, or conflictual/authoritarian. The means and standard deviations of the parenting composites for each cluster as well as the percentages of parents within each family type who fell into each typology are presented in Table 36.

Authoritative/harmonious parents were identified by higher levels of positivity and monitoring, moderate to high levels of control, and low negativity. However, at Wave 3, the negativity scores of mothers considered authoritative were at the level of the grand mean, possibly representing a slight increase in levels of negativity and conflict as the children moved into early adolescence. Disengaged parents were identified by moderate levels of negativity and lower levels of monitoring, control, and positivity. Conflictual parents were characterized by higher levels of conflict and monitoring but moderate to low levels of positivity. By the third wave, however, mothers with the highest levels of negativity had the lowest levels of monitoring, control, and positivity and thus probably represented a different parenting style, which we have called "conflictual/disengaged" rather than "authoritarian"; because of the very high levels of negativity relative to the other groups, the term "conflictual" was retained. Thus, at Wave 3, no classic authoritarian parenting style emerged, and for neither mothers nor fathers did a permissive cluster with moderate to high warmth and low control and monitoring emerge at any time.

Table 37 presents a cross-tabulation of parenting type and family type; since children's gender was not significantly associated with the parenting typology in any analysis, it was not included in comparisons. Family type was not associated with parenting types for mothers at Wave 1; at later waves, however, a significant association emerged. At Wave 2, mothers in remarried families were more likely to be disengaged, whereas nondivorced mothers were most likely to be authoritative and divorced mothers to be conflictual or authoritative. By the third wave, however, mothers in nondivorced families most often fell into the disengaged/nonconflictual group, whereas mothers in remarried families were found about equally in all three parenting styles. It may be that the parenting style represented by the disengaged/nonconflictual category at Wave 3 is associated with mothers' attempts to promote the independence and individuation of their adolescent children. In contrast, the authoritative mothers maintained a higher level of control and monitoring of their children.

The large number of divorced mothers falling in the authoritative group at Wave 3 is puzzling in view of our previous findings that these mothers were the highest of the maternal groups in negativity. Their placement in this category seems likely to have been due to their relatively high scores on warmth, control, and monitoring.

The results for fathers were quite consistent over time. Nondivorced fathers were most likely to be authoritative at all three waves. Stepfathers, in contrast, were more likely to be disengaged than nondivorced fathers, with the largest differences between family type occurring at Wave 1, when half the stepfathers were classified as disengaged. By the third wave, about two-fifths of stepfathers were classified as disengaged, compared to about one-fifth of nondivorced fathers.

Thus, although by Wave 3 there was an increase in the proportion of stepfathers classified as authoritative and a decrease in the proportion classified as disengaged, these parents remained higher in disengagement and lower in authoritativeness relative to nondivorced fathers even 26 months after their remarriage.

SUMMARY AND CONCLUSIONS

Previous research has shown that relationships between most parents and children become less involved as children move into early adolescence and become more autonomous (Steinberg, 1987a, 1988). Many parents seem to give children their head in this period—from the entry into adolescence to its mid-period—with a temporary increase in conflict followed by decreasing levels of conflict, monitoring, and control. However, family structure superimposes particular patterns on this general trend. Adolescence can be a difficult time for parents as well as for children. Homes with a lone, divorced mother or where the mother is adjusting to a new husband appear to be vulnerable to the emergence of disrupted, unstable parent-child relationships during this time (Bray, 1988; Hetherington, 1989).

Our findings indicated that relationships in divorced families were characterized by high involvement as well as high negativity and conflict. Although children and observers reported ineffectual control and negative relations between divorced mothers and their children, the mothers viewed this relationship more optimistically in that they saw themselves as monitoring and controlling their children's behavior more than nondivorced mothers did. This study was in accord with the results of other studies in finding more conflict and less control over sons by divorced than nondivorced mothers; however, it also indicated that the divorced mother–daughter relationship became more troubled in the later waves of the study as daughters moved into adolescence. These findings were consistent with other studies of family relationships in stabilized divorced families (Hetherington, 1972, 1988, 1989; Kalter, 1977; Wallerstein, 1982; Wallerstein & Kelly, 1980). It

TABLE 36

MEANS (Standard Deviations) OF MULTIMEASURE/MULTIRESPONDENT PARENTING COMPOSITES BY PARENTING CLUSTER

Cluster Label	Positivity/Warmth	Negativity/Conflict	Monitoring	Control
Mothers:				
Wave 1:				
Authoritative/harmonious	.29	−.31	.30	.08
	(.38)	(.32)	(.39)	(.40)
Conflictual/authoritarian	−.01	.73	.20	.37
	(.48)	(.47)	(.45)	(.39)
Disengaged	−.43	−.05	−.59	−.38
	(.42)	(.45)	(.55)	(.51)
Wave 2:				
Authoritative/harmonious	.40	−.41	.44	.05
	(.42)	(.35)	(.38)	(.51)
Conflictual/authoritarian	−.02	.58	.07	.29
	(.42)	(.52)	(.51)	(.40)
Disengaged	−.44	−.17	−.51	−.34
	(.42)	(.45)	(.54)	(.56)
Wave 3:				
Authoritative/harmonious	.46	−.02	.54	.47
	(.48)	(.71)	(.38)	(.44)
Conflictual/disengaged	−.19	.51	−.67	.44
	(.60)	(.68)	(.51)	(.58)
Disengaged	−.24	−.26	.00	−.07
	(.43)	(.37)	(.38)	(.42)

Fathers:				
Wave 1:				
Authoritative/harmonious	.22	−.32	.24	.19
	(.48)	(.32)	(.38)	(.34)
Conflictual/authoritarian	.30	.87	.52	.54
	(.50)	(.43)	(.48)	(.49)
Disengaged	−.49	−.04	−.64	−.58
	(.49)	(.44)	(.48)	(.57)
Wave 2:				
Authoritative/harmonious	.36	−.26	.31	.19
	(.44)	(.33)	(.41)	(.48)
Conflictual/authoritarian	−.33	.93	−.01	.37
	(.47)	(.53)	(.47)	(.43)
Disengaged	−.59	−.21	−.84	−.87
	(.48)	(.34)	(.70)	(.54)
Wave 3:				
Authoritative/harmonious	.33	−.22	.36	.27
	(.47)	(.34)	(.40)	(.47)
Conflictual/authoritarian	−.04	1.04	.10	.36
	(.64)	(.62)	(.40)	(.30)
Disengaged	−.53	−.14	−.70	−.56
	(.46)	(.36)	(.54)	(.60)

TABLE 37

CROSS-TABULATION OF PARENTING TYPE AND FAMILY TYPE

	Mothers				Fathers		
	Nondivorced	Divorced	Remarried	Total	Nondivorced	Remarried	Total
Wave 1:							
Authoritative	38	35	23	96	47	17	64
	(50.7)	(50.7)	(39.7)	(47.5)	(62.7)	(29.3)	(48.1)
Conflictual	16	15	13	44	15	10	25
	(21.3)	(21.7)	(22.4)	(21.8)	(20.0)	(17.2)	(18.8)
Disengaged	21	19	22	62	13	31	44
	(28.0)	(27.5)	(37.9)	(30.7)	(17.3)	(53.5)	(33.1)
Total	75	69	58	202	75	58	133
		χ^2 = 2.5 (N.S.)				$\chi^2 = 20.6, p \leq .001$	
Wave 2:							
Authoritative	30	23	11	64	54	16	70
	(41.1)	(36.5)	(23.4)	(35.0)	(74.0)	(34.0)	(58.3)
Conflictual	21	27	12	60	13	12	25
	(28.8)	(42.9)	(25.5)	(32.8)	(17.8)	(25.5)	(20.8)
Disengaged	22	13	24	59	6	19	25
	(30.1)	(20.6)	(51.1)	(32.2)	(8.2)	(40.4)	(20.8)
Total	73	63	47	183	73	47	120
		$\chi^2 = 13.6, p \leq .05$				$\chi^2 = 22.9, p \leq .001$	
Wave 3:							
Authoritative	23	25	12	60	43	17	60
	(33.8)	(48.1)	(27.9)	(36.8)	(63.2)	(39.5)	(54.1)
Conflictual	12	15	15	42	10	8	18
	(17.7)	(28.9)	(34.9)	(25.8)	(14.7)	(18.6)	(16.2)
Disengaged	33	12	16	61	15	18	33
	(48.5)	(23.1)	(37.2)	(37.4)	(22.1)	(41.9)	(29.7)
Total	68	52	43	163	68	43	111
		$\chi^2 = 11.3, p \leq .05$				$\chi^2 = 6.5, p \leq .05$	

NOTE.—Numbers in parentheses indicate the percentage of parents within the family type who demonstrated each parenting type. For example, at Wave 1, 50.7% of the 75 nondivorced mothers were authoritative, 21.3% were conflictual, and 28% were disengaged.

should be noted that this conflict, at least in the view of the children, was also accompanied by high levels of instrumental affection in all waves and expressive affection in Wave 3.

In remarried families, mother-child relationships appeared disrupted by the remarriage, but, as predicted, these were recovering 2 years later. Although in comparison to nondivorced fathers stepfathers continued to see their wives as not very adept at monitoring and controlling their children's behavior, the composite indices and other individual reports indicated few between-group differences on any of the four maternal parenting dimensions 26 months after remarriage. The greater observed negativity shown by children toward remarried than toward nondivorced mothers that was found in the first two waves had also disappeared, although children in the remarried families were less positive at that time. By 26 months after remarriage, however, mother-child relationships in remarried and nondivorced families were generally quite similar.

In contrast, there were large and enduring differences between nondivorced fathers and residential stepfathers. Even 26 months after remarriage, stepfathers were less positive, controlling, and vigilant about their children's behavior, and children remained less positive and relatively more negative toward their stepfathers.

A stepfather's role is ambiguous with children of any age, but building a new relationship with a teenaged stepchild may be especially fraught with pitfalls. Younger children are more likely to accept a stepparent as a parent figure, while older children can accept a stepparent as a companion and support for their biological parent. Teenaged stepchildren may resist being responsive and obedient toward someone they sometimes view as an intruder at the very time when their own development requires that they become more autonomous from the family, test limits, and establish their independence (Hetherington & Anderson, 1987; Hetherington, Arnett, & Hollier, 1987; Hetherington et al., 1989).

Stepfather-stepchild relationships were as awkward initially as might be expected for two people who are suddenly thrust into an intimate relationship not of their own making, and many such pairs in our sample continued to reject this relationship and refused to get involved. Two years seemed to do little to draw them closer, although the decrease over time in the proportion of stepfathers falling into a disengaged parenting typology may give reason for optimism about the further development of these relationships.

Remarriage involves many adaptive challenges and requires changes in family relationships. The preponderance of our evidence indicates that, if remarriage occurs in conjunction with children's transition to adolescence, close and congenial relationships between stepchildren and stepfathers may develop very slowly, if at all. The 26-month period of this study may not have been sufficiently long for stepfamilies to adapt to their new situation, especially as the children were also going through the normative changes associated with early adolescence.

This suggests some difficulties for remarriages involving early adolescent children; however, it should be pointed out that, although stepfathers and stepchildren had more problems on average than fathers and children in nondivorced families, there was also considerable diversity in the remarried group. Some of these families made the transition to becoming a stepfamily smoothly and functioned well with few apparent difficulties, and others may yet adapt given more time.

The scattered and modest differences found in the parenting of boys and girls leave us with rather a puzzle as to why the boys were doing consistently less well on the measures of adjustment reported in Chapter III. There were a few indications, at some time periods, that boys were involved in more cycles of maternal nagging and the imposing of negative sanctions and that they were somewhat less well monitored, but these differences were scattered and were minor compared to the more pervasive differences between family types on the parenting measures. The parenting differences in adolescence were insufficient to explain the marked gender differences in adjustment. Either the contributions of parenting to differences in boys' and girls' adjustment occur largely in preadolescence, or genetic and biological factors, social roles, and/or extrafamilial influences are more important in shaping gender differences in adolescents' behavior.

VI. SIBLING RELATIONSHIPS DURING REMARRIAGE

Edward R. Anderson and Alyson M. Rice

In this chapter, we examine differences in sibling relationships among boys and girls in nondivorced, divorced, and remarried families. The changes in these relationships as the children moved further into adolescence and as children in remarried families adapted to their new family situation were also explored. On the basis of previous research, the following hypotheses regarding sibling relationships were investigated.

First, it was expected that, in general, girls would show more positive, supportive, and empathic behavior but no less negative aggressive behavior toward their siblings than boys (Abramovitch et al., 1982; Dunn, 1983).

Second, the behavior of children toward their siblings was expected to be more negative and less positive in divorced and remarried families than in nondivorced families because of the stresses associated with family transitions. Specifically, target children in divorced and remarried families were expected to be more distant, aggressive, and rivalrous and less involved and empathic toward their siblings than target children in nondivorced families (Berkowitz, 1983; Hetherington, 1988; MacKinnon, 1989; Patterson, 1982).

Third, compared to remarried families, children in divorced families were expected to display less negative and more positive behavior because of the more recent marital transition and family reorganization that had been experienced in remarried families (Hetherington, 1988; Hetherington, Cox, & Cox, 1978, 1982; Radke-Yarrow, Richters, & Wilson, 1987).

Fourth, the pattern of less positive and more negative behavior was expected to be more pronounced in sibling dyads containing a boy (Hetherington, 1988; MacKinnon, 1989; Wallerstein et al., 1988).

Finally, it was expected that all sibling relationships would show signs of increased negativity and disengagement—that is, less involvement, more avoidance, aggression, and rivalry, but not necessarily less empathy—as children moved further into adolescence over the course of the study (Steinberg, 1988).

An overview of our findings reveals that these hypotheses were generally supported, but not on all measures or by all respondents.

OVERVIEW OF FINDINGS

Analyses of sibling relationships yielded five main findings.

1. Gender differences occurred primarily in interview reports of positive behavior; raters concurred that girls displayed more positive behavior toward their siblings than did boys. With respect to negative behavior, except for mothers' reports at Wave 1 that girls tended to avoid their siblings more, no differences were established.

2. Differences among family types occurred in both positive and negative behavior, with children in remarried families displaying more negative and less positive behavior toward their siblings compared to children in nondivorced families. Means for children in divorced families usually fell in between but were not significantly different from either of the other two groups.

3. Observational data indicated that children in divorced families displayed more negative and less positive behavior in interactions with their siblings than children in other family types, a finding that differs from results obtained through interview reports.

4. There are few effects of gender composition; however, according to some types of respondents, same-gender sibling dyads showed more involvement/companionship, and less support was offered to brothers in remarried families than to other siblings. Mothers reported the most negative and the least positive behavior for boys in remarried families, but this finding was not supported by other respondents' reports.

5. Over time, mean levels of both positive and negative behavior toward siblings declined significantly for children in all family groups. Because fathers reported significant increases in avoidance over time as well, these changes were interpreted as showing increasing disengagement from siblings as children entered adolescence.

METHOD

As noted in Chapter II, not all the children in this study had siblings. The numbers of male and female siblings, by family type and gender of target child, are presented in Table 38 (information on sibling ages is presented in Chap. II). For these analyses, all siblings were full biological siblings from the original marriage. The size of the sample unfortunately precluded a full analysis of spacing, birth order, and sibling composition;

TABLE 38

NUMBER OF MALE AND FEMALE TARGET SIBLINGS, BY FAMILY TYPE AND GENDER OF TARGET CHILD

	NONDIVORCED		DIVORCED		REMARRIED		
	Boys	Girls	Boys	Girls	Boys	Girls	TOTAL
Wave 1:							
Brothers	18	21	12	13	6	8	78
Sisters	16	12	12	16	12	12	80
Total	34	33	24	29	18	20	158
Wave 2:							
Brothers	17	21	12	12	6	7	75
Sisters	16	11	12	16	10	8	73
Total	33	32	24	28	16	15	148
Wave 3:							
Brothers	16	19	12	10	4	8	69
Sisters	15	10	7	13	8	6	59
Total	31	29	19	23	12	14	128

however, as will be seen, the contributions of gender composition of dyads and birth order to sibling interactions proved to be minor compared to those of family type.

In contrast to the many measures used to assess children's adjustment and parent-child relationships, the sibling relationship was assessed only by parents' and children's reports on an expanded version of Schaefer and Edgerton's (1981) Sibling Inventory of Behavior (SIB) and by observers' rating of behavior seen during the sibling interaction sessions. From the six subscales of the SIB, a positivity factor and a negativity factor were derived for each respondent. The total positivity scale included involvement/companionship, teaching/guidance, and empathy/support, and the total negativity scale was composed of aggression (active unkindness/anger), avoidance/embarrassment, and rivalry. Positivity and negativity factors were also derived from the observational ratings. In addition, multimethod/multirespondent composite measures of positivity and negativity based on parents' and children's SIB responses as well as observers' ratings were derived. (There are no composite measures of sibling interactions in divorced families at Wave 3, as observers' and children's reports were unavailable for this time. Thus, at the last wave of the study, the only reports of sibling interaction for these children came from their mothers.) The construction of these measures is described in greater detail in Chapter II and Appendix Table A3.

Reports from mothers, fathers, and children were related at all waves. Observational ratings were correlated with parents' reports only at Wave 3 but with children's reports at all waves, except for positivity at Wave 1. The correlations among respondents' reports of positivity and negativity are presented in Table 39.

WITHIN-WAVE DIFFERENCES IN SIBLING RELATIONSHIPS

Three sets of within-wave analyses were conducted, beginning with the general and then moving to the more specific measures. Composite measures were used as summary indices and to provide continuity with other chapters. First, multivariate analyses of variance (MANOVAs) were conducted on the composite indices of positive and negative behavior developed from combining across raters and methods. This analysis identified whether any differences in behavior toward siblings existed among the different families. Second, separate MANOVAs were conducted on the total SIB scores of positivity and negativity reported by mothers, fathers, and children and on the total positivity and total negativity scores derived from the observational ratings. This analysis identified the particular informant's contribution to the differences identified above. Third, MANOVAs were conducted on each of the six subscales of the SIB, separately for mothers, fathers, and children. This final analysis identified more specifically the negative or positive behaviors that contributed to the differences.

Results from the multivariate analyses of the multimethod/multirespondent composites as well as each respondent's report of the overall sibling relationship are presented in Table 40. Means, standard deviations, and significant main and interaction effects of family type and gender for the follow-up univariate analyses of positivity and negativity are shown in Tables 41 and 42. Results from the multivariate analyses of the six subscales of the SIB for each respondent are given in Table 43. Finally, results from the follow-up univariate analyses of the individual subscales are presented in Tables 44 and 45. In examining these tables, it should again be kept in mind that italicized results indicate that differences were tested when no significant multivariate effects were obtained but planned comparisons had been made. For the most part, these results confirm hypotheses and results found in other waves but perhaps should be viewed with more caution than nonitalicized findings.

Gender differences.—An overview of gender differences indicates that, when present, they tended to show girls as directing more positive behavior (empathy, teaching, involvement) toward their siblings than boys. Gender differences occurred less frequently with respect to negative behavior (aggression, rivalry, avoidance). Only mothers reported that boys were more aggressive than girls toward their siblings at Waves 2 and 3 and were more rivalrous at Wave 3. Mothers also reported that girls were more avoidant

TABLE 39

CORRELATIONS ACROSS RATERS ON SIBLING RELATIONSHIP DIMENSIONS

	WAVE 1				WAVE 2				WAVE 3			
	Mothers	Fathers	Children	Observers	Mothers	Fathers	Children	Observers	Mothers	Fathers	Children	Observers
Positivity:												
Mothers	...				...				...			
Fathers	.54**	...			.53**	...			.63**	...		
Children	.50**	.45**	...		.53**	.47**	...		.69**	.52**	...	
Observers	−.08	−.08	.03	...	.10	.19	.24**	...	.35**	.36**	.42**	...
Negativity:												
Mothers	...				...				...			
Fathers	.49**	...			.51**	...			.56**	...		
Children	.32**	.37**	...		.40**	.40**	...		.49**	.46**	...	
Observers	.16	.07	.20**	...	.18	.19	.23**	...	.41**	.24	.40**	...

** $p \leq .01$.

TABLE 40

F VALUES AND SIGNIFICANCE LEVELS FOR MULTIVARIATE ANALYSES OF SIBLING RELATIONSHIP DIMENSIONS

	WAVE 1			WAVE 2			WAVE 3		
EFFECT	Family	Children's Gender	Interaction	Family	Children's Gender	Interaction	Family	Children's Gender	Interaction
Multimethod/ multirespondent overall composite:									
Multivariate	4.06**	4.28*	1.40	2.14	4.98**	.73	2.49*	3.88*	.35
Multivariate *df*	(4,302)	(2,151)	(4,312)	(4,282)	(2,141)	(4,282)	(4,242)	(2,121)	(4,242)
Positivity	5.00**	2.91	2.39	2.03	7.87**	1.15	2.82	7.00**	.04
Negativity	5.94**	1.99	.93	3.59*	.06	.85	3.08*	.07	.63
Univariate *df*	(2,152)	(1,152)	(2,152)	(2,142)	(1,142)	(2,142)	(2,122)	(1,122)	(2,122)
Total score: Observational measures:									
Multivariate	3.01*	.98	1.00	2.56*	1.00	.59	2.44	.16	1.52
Multivariate *df*	(4,280)	(2,140)	(4,280)	(4,234)	(2,117)	(4,234)	(2,64)	(2,64)	(2,64)
Positivity	2.95	.09	1.70	4.44*	.70	.79	4.41*	.31	.59
Negativity	5.65**	1.03	1.32	3.59*	.28	.08	3.92	.10	.39
Univariate *df*	(2,141)	(1,141)	(2,141)	(2,118)	(1,118)	(2,118)	(1,65)	(1,65)	(1,65)

Total SIB:									
Mothers' reports:									
Multivariate	2.83*	3.47*	1.16	3.70**	8.26**	5.43***	1.57	5.95**	2.12
Multivariate *df*	(4,302)	(2,151)	(4,302)	(4,278)	(2,139)	(4,278)	(4,242)	(2,121)	(4,242)
Positivity	3.44*	3.78	1.06	5.98**	16.28***	7.15***	2.90	11.90***	1.61
Negativity	3.43*	1.30	1.92	3.05*	2.37	6.93***	1.04	1.59	3.70*
Univariate *df*	(2,152)	(1,152)	(2,152)	(2,140)	(1,140)	(2,140)	(2,122)	(1,122)	(2,122)
Fathers' reports:									
Multivariate	4.08*	.26	.62	1.78	2.30	.70	3.30*	.56	.12
Multivariate *df*	(2,100)	(2,100)	(2,100)	(2,90)	(2,90)	(2,90)	(2,80)	(2,80)	(2,80)
Positivity	4.83*	.02	.07	1.70	4.65*	1.03	3.13	1.14	.21
Negativity	6.79*	.50	1.20	3.28	1.08	.01	6.42*	.37	.14
Univariate *df*	(1,101)	(1,101)	(1,101)	(1,91)	(1,91)	(1,91)	(1,81)	(1,81)	(1,81)
Children's reports:									
Multivariate	2.85*	3.16*	2.53*	.70	4.57*	1.33	1.33	4.95**	.25
Multivariate *df*	(4,298)	(2,149)	(4,298)	(4,276)	(2,138)	(4,276)	(2,80)	(2,80)	(2,80)
Positivity	3.70*	2.39	3.94*	.49	4.42*	2.06	2.50	5.87*	.19
Negativity	4.51*	1.30	1.01	1.06	1.47	1.55	.63	1.97	.43
Univariate *df*	(2,150)	(1,150)	(2,150)	(1,139)	(1,139)	(2,139)	(1,81)	(1,81)	(1,81)

NOTE.—Multivariate test is Wilks's lambda. SIB = Sibling Inventory of Behavior.

* $p \leq .05$.

** $p \leq .01$.

*** $p \leq .001$.

TABLE 41

MEANS (Standard Deviations) FOR VARIOUS MEASURES OF SIBLING POSITIVITY

	Nondivorced		Divorced		Remarried		Significant Main Effects and Interactions[a]	Significant Contrasts and Planned Comparisons[a]
	Boys	Girls	Boys	Girls	Boys	Girls		
Positivity:								
Multimethod/ multirespondent composite:								
Wave 1	.22 (.53)	.10 (.66)	−.20 (.82)	−.18 (.72)	−.41 (.68)	−.12 (.54)	Family type	Nondiv > Rem
Wave 2	−.05 (.65)	.10 (.73)	−.35 (.77)	−.01 (.85)	−.65 (1.1)	.03 (.78)	Gender	Girls > Boys
Wave 3	−.13 (.75)	.28 (.88)	−.34 (.91)	.06 (.95)	−.68 (1.1)	−.16 (.90)	Gender	Girls > Boys
Observers' reports:								
Wave 1	2.58 (.44)	2.49 (.38)	2.26 (.39)	2.44 (.42)	2.47 (.39)	2.44 (.32)	. . .	
Wave 2	2.41 (.39)	2.62 (.55)	2.16 (.49)	2.27 (.51)	2.38 (.52)	2.29 (.56)	Family type	Nondiv > Div
Wave 3	2.67 (.60)	2.91 (.75)			2.43 (.67)	2.39 (.83)	*Family type*	*Nondiv > Rem*

Mothers' reports:								
Wave 1	3.35	3.38	3.27	3.40	2.95	3.27	Family type	Nondiv, Div > Rem
	(.44)	(.44)	(.59)	(.52)	(.58)	(.50)		
Wave 2	3.27	3.28	3.25	3.44	2.58	3.38	Family type, gender	Nondiv, Div > Rem; Girls > Boys;
	(.44)	(.45)	(.47)	(.47)	(.49)	(.58)	Family type, × gender	Rem (Girls > Boys); Boys (Nondiv, Div > Rem)
Wave 3	3.12	3.30	3.12	3.33	2.65	3.24	Gender	Girls > Boys
	(.49)	(.49)	(.47)	(.49)	(.55)	(.59)		
Fathers' reports:								
Wave 1	3.23	3.24			3.04	3.00	Family type	Nondiv > Rem
	(.49)	(.54)			(.45)	(.47)		
Wave 2	3.10	3.23			2.83	3.20	*Gender*	*Girls > Boys*
	(.52)	(.47)			(.65)	(.47)		
Wave 3	3.03	3.21			2.87	2.95	. . .	
	(.45)	(.51)			(.61)	(.50)		
Children's reports:								
Wave 1	3.27	3.06	2.79	3.26	2.65	3.04	Family type, family type × gender	Nondiv, Div > Rem; Boys (Nondiv > Rem)
	(.62)	(.58)	(.65)	(.54)	(.53)	(.60)		
Wave 2	3.11	3.09	2.93	3.10	2.72	3.26	Gender	Girls > Boys
	(.58)	(.53)	(.60)	(.64)	(.71)	(.64)		
Wave 3	2.91	3.14			2.67	3.01	Gender	Girls > Boys
	(.43)	(.51)			(.59)	(.47)		

NOTE.—Nondiv = Nondivorced; Div = Divorced; Rem = Remarried.

[a] Italicized contrasts denote planned comparisons.

TABLE 42

MEANS (Standard Deviations) FOR VARIOUS MEASURES OF SIBLING NEGATIVITY

	Nondivorced		Divorced		Remarried		Significant Main Effects and Interactions[a]	Significant Contrasts and Planned Comparisons[a]
	Boys	Girls	Boys	Girls	Boys	Girls		
Negativity:								
Multimethod/ multirespondent composite:								
Wave 1	−.35 (.52)	−.07 (.72)	.16 (.57)	.11 (.80)	.08 (.80)	.32 (.66)	Family type	Div, Rem > Nondiv
Wave 2	−.25 (.68)	−.06 (.75)	.12 (.51)	.23 (.75)	.26 (.91)	.05 (.77)	*Family type*	*Div > Nondiv*
Wave 3	−.27 (.72)	−.08 (.82)	−.25 (1.1)	−.32 (.95)	.38 (1.0)	.13 (.91)	Family type	Rem > Nondiv, Div
Observers' reports:								
Wave 1	1.93 (.42)	2.17 (.71)	2.50 (.62)	2.37 (.77)	1.98 (.57)	2.20 (.66)	Family type	Div > Nondiv, Rem
Wave 2	2.16 (.87)	2.28 (.79)	2.65 (.73)	2.65 (.74)	2.47 (.98)	2.60 (.86)	Family type	Div > Nondiv
Wave 3	2.20 (.87)	2.28 (.75)			2.83 (.72)	2.61 (1.2)	. . .	

Mothers' reports:								
Wave 1	2.41	2.67	2.65	2.74	2.82	2.72	Family type	Rem > Nondiv
	(.37)	(.48)	(.44)	(.54)	(.54)	(.40)		
Wave 2	2.43	2.61	2.56	2.56	3.01	2.49	Family type	Rem > Nondiv;
	(.39)	(.48)	(.31)	(.47)	(.48)	(.44)	Family type × gender	Rem (Boys > Girls); Boys (Rem > Nondiv, Div)
Wave 3	2.45	2.59	2.53	2.49	2.88	2.44	. . .	
	(.34)	(.45)	(.52)	(.45)	(.66)	(.38)		
Fathers' reports:								
Wave 1	2.52	2.48			2.67	2.85	Family type	Rem > Nondiv
	(.46)	(.44)			(.61)	(.52)		
Wave 2	2.56	2.44			2.75	2.65	. . .	
	(.50)	(.47)			(.59)	(.51)		
Wave 3	2.53	2.40			2.82	2.79	Family type	Rem > Nondiv
	(.56)	(.54)			(.59)	(.55)		
Children's reports:								
Wave 1	2.36	2.54	2.58	2.51	2.69	2.89	Family type	Rem > Nondiv, Div
	(.49)	(.60)	(.44)	(.50)	(.61)	(.72)		
Wave 2	2.33	2.59	2.49	2.72	2.56	2.41	. . .	
	(.47)	(.60)	(.49)	(.61)	(.62)	(.51)		
Wave 3	2.33	2.58			2.50	2.59	. . .	
	(.46)	(.57)			(.50)	(.43)		

NOTE.—Nondiv = Nondivorced; Div = Divorced; Rem = Remarried.

[a] Italicization denotes planned comparisons.

TABLE 43

F Values and Significance Levels for Multivariate Analyses of the Sibling Inventory of Behavior

	Wave 1			Wave 2			Wave 3		
	Family	Children's Gender	Interaction	Family	Children's Gender	Interaction	Family	Children's Gender	Interaction
Mothers' reports:									
Multivariate	1.34	3.76**	.94	2.28**	4.18***	2.34**	1.26	5.41***	1.02
Multivariate *df*	(12,294)	(6,147)	(12,294)	(12,270)	(6,135)	(12,270)	(12,234)	(6,117)	(12,234)
Involvement	1.67	1.04	1.35	2.93	8.79**	5.45**	.82	5.11*	1.05
Empathy	3.94*	2.35	.61	6.19**	15.11***	6.72**	3.29*	17.06***	3.36*
Teaching	1.52	3.52	.49	2.36	6.63*	2.11	1.80	4.00*	.26
Rivalry	4.73**	.59	2.30	5.60**	2.35	5.87**	3.07*	3.88*	3.84*
Aggression	2.38	.62	1.97	2.17	6.25*	1.90	.64	4.13*	1.90
Avoidance	.81	8.10**	.50	2.28	.19	6.05**	.16	1.27	1.90
Univariate *df*	(2,152)	(1,152)	(2,152)	(2,140)	(1,140)	(2,140)	(2,122)	(1,122)	(2,122)
Fathers' reports:									
Multivariate	1.90	1.80	.91	1.25	3.77**	1.02	2.54*	2.72*	.88
Multivariate *df*	(6,96)	(6,96)	(6,96)	(6,86)	(6,86)	(6,86)	(6,76)	(6,76)	(6,76)
Involvement	2.00	.10	.19	1.30	2.23	1.28	1.99	.21	.00

Empathy	5.06*	.18	.11	2.03	4.88*	2.32	2.97	2.79	.04
Teaching	2.25	.15	.28	.39	2.12	.01	1.09	.07	1.68
Rivalry	8.97**	.00	.33	5.76*	3.54	.06	11.53***	2.88	.00
Aggression	4.41*	.03	1.36	2.30	3.21	.06	3.99*	1.43	.03
Avoidance	1.99	6.00*	1.36	.50	1.45	.10	1.81	1.54	.74
Univariate *df*	(1,101)	(1,101)	(1,101)	(1,91)	(1,91)	(1,91)	(1,81)	(1,81)	(1,81)
Children's reports:									
Multivariate	1.36	2.07	1.56	.70	2.18*	1.19	2.30*	2.50*	.73
Multivariate *df*	(12,290)	(6,145)	(12,290)	(12,268)	(6,134)	(12,268)	(6,76)	(6,76)	(6,76)
Involvement	3.42*	.04	3.10*	.16	4.85*	4.44*	4.10*	1.63	.09
Empathy	5.12**	3.55	3.71*	.32	3.47	2.85	1.52	6.43*	1.41
Teaching	.48	2.38	1.62	.85	1.49	.06	.32	2.82	.15
Rivalry	1.82	.63	1.64	1.26	3.79	.99	1.32	.42	1.72
Aggression	3.25*	2.26	1.94	1.24	1.86	.66	3.44	2.85	.20
Avoidance	5.31**	.42	.05	.68	.01	2.01	1.18	1.37	.00
Univariate *df*	(2,150)	(1,150)	(2,150)	(2,139)	(1,139)	(2,139)	(1,81)	(1,81)	(1,81)

NOTE.—Multivariate test is Wilks's lambda.

* $p \leq .05$.

** $p \leq .01$.

*** $p \leq .001$.

TABLE 44

MEANS (Standard Deviations) FOR THE SUBSCALES OF THE SIBLING INVENTORY OF BEHAVIOR

	NONDIVORCED		DIVORCED		REMARRIED		SIGNIFICANT MAIN EFFECTS AND INTERACTIONS[a]	SIGNIFICANT CONTRASTS AND PLANNED COMPARISONS[a]
	Boys	Girls	Boys	Girls	Boys	Girls		
Involvement:								
Mothers' reports:								
Wave 1	3.39 (.42)	3.31 (.43)	3.28 (.56)	3.35 (.52)	3.06 (.59)	3.30 (.29)	...	
Wave 2	3.26 (.54)	3.21 (.42)	3.25 (.48)	3.39 (.53)	2.70 (.58)	3.38 (.46)	Gender, family type × gender	Girls > Boys; Boys (Nondiv, Div > Rem); Rem (Girls > Boys)
Wave 3	3.13 (.56)	3.22 (.49)	3.10 (.53)	3.24 (.53)	2.79 (.63)	3.25 (.53)	Gender	Girls > Boys
Fathers' reports:								
Wave 1	3.33 (.50)	3.26 (.54)			3.15 (.43)	3.16 (.36)	...	
Wave 2	3.20 (.54)	3.25 (.48)			2.95 (.67)	3.24 (.33)	...	
Empathy:								
Mothers' reports:								
Wave 1	3.83 (.59)	3.90 (.53)	3.74 (.76)	3.82 (.65)	3.33 (.76)	3.67 (.64)	*Family type*	*Nondiv, Div > Rem*
Wave 2	3.75 (.50)	3.78 (.53)	3.74 (.63)	3.95 (.61)	2.91 (.61)	3.87 (.72)	Family type, gender, family type × gender	Nondiv, Div > Rem; Girls > Boys; Rem (Girls > Boys); Boys (Nondiv, Div > Rem)
Wave 3	3.63 (.61)	3.81 (.60)	3.60 (.56)	3.94 (.65)	2.93 (.78)	3.86 (.53)	*Family type*, gender	*Nondiv, Div > Rem;* Girls > Boys
Fathers' reports:								
Wave 1	3.58 (.59)	3.68 (.68)			3.32 (.82)	3.33 (.62)	*Family type*	*Nondiv > Rem*
Wave 2	3.52 (.68)	3.63 (.59)			3.07 (.94)	3.64 (.66)	Gender	Girls > Boys
Wave 3	3.39 (.67)	3.64 (.63)			3.07 (.92)	3.39 (.76)	...	

Children's reports:								
Wave 1	3.78	3.58	3.44	3.81	2.97	3.47	*Family type*	*Nondiv, Div > Rem*
	(.69)	(.73)	(.81)	(.63)	(.74)	(.73)		
Wave 2	3.61	3.51	3.38	3.51	3.13	3.86	...	
	(.77)	(.71)	(.73)	(.75)	(.96)	(.78)		
Wave 3	3.37	3.57			3.00	3.57	Gender	Girls > Boys
	(.62)	(.61)			(.68)	(.70)		
Teaching:								
Mothers' reports:								
Wave 1	2.83	2.92	2.79	3.03	2.44	2.84	...	
	(.67)	(.68)	(.92)	(.83)	(.72)	(.89)		
Wave 2	2.80	2.86	2.76	2.96	2.13	2.88	Gender	Girls > Boys
	(.71)	(.77)	(.80)	(.80)	(.53)	(.91)		
Wave 3	2.59	2.87	2.66	2.80	2.23	2.63	Gender	Girls > Boys
	(.65)	(.73)	(.73)	(.75)	(.60)	(.92)		
Fathers' reports:								
Wave 1	2.78	2.80			2.64	2.50	...	
	(.69)	(.77)			(.56)	(.77)		
Wave 2	2.57	2.81			2.48	2.70	...	
	(.68)	(.76)			(.62)	(.79)		
Wave 3	2.56	2.81			2.60	2.44	...	
	(.57)	(.73)			(.60)	(.76)		
Children's reports:								
Wave 1	2.70	2.60	2.45	2.85	2.30	2.66	...	
	(.84)	(.77)	(.83)	(.80)	(.61)	(.90)		
Wave 2	2.59	2.75	2.47	2.70	2.39	2.50	...	
	(.66)	(.78)	(.80)	(.83)	(.61)	(.90)		
Wave 3	2.36	2.72			2.33	2.56	...	
	(.67)	(.86)			(.66)	(.61)		
Rivalry:								
Mothers' reports:								
Wave 1	2.55	2.80	2.86	3.10	3.12	2.87	*Family type*	*Div, Rem > Nondiv*
	(.52)	(.60)	(.68)	(.66)	(.76)	(.53)		
Wave 2	2.49	2.60	2.72	2.82	3.23	2.59	Family type, family type × gender	Div, Rem > Nondiv; Rem (Boys > Girls); Boys (Rem > Nondiv, Div)
	(.45)	(.58)	(.39)	(.58)	(.62)	(.62)		
Wave 3	2.51	2.65	2.68	2.51	3.17	2.60	*Family type,* gender	*Rem > Nondiv, Div;* Boys > Girls
	(.44)	(.56)	(.66)	(.58)	(.65)	(.39)		

TABLE 44 (*Continued*)

	Nondivorced		Divorced		Remarried		Significant Main Effects and Interactions[a]	Significant Contrasts and Planned Comparisons[a]
	Boys	Girls	Boys	Girls	Boys	Girls		
Fathers' reports:								
Wave 1	2.66	2.58			2.98	3.05	*Family type*	*Rem > Nondiv*
	(.58)	(.58)			(.76)	(.73)		
Wave 2	2.67	2.45			3.03	2.74	*Family type*	*Rem > Nondiv*
	(.61)	(.59)			(.74)	(.59)		
Wave 3	2.60	2.35			3.12	2.86	Family type	Rem > Nondiv
	(.69)	(.55)			(.70)	(.60)		
Children's reports:								
Wave 1	2.21	2.41	2.36	2.20	2.41	2.59	. . .	
	(.48)	(.63)	(.49)	(.52)	(.74)	(.62)		
Wave 2	2.09	2.40	2.23	2.47	2.18	2.16	. . .	
	(.41)	(.49)	(.47)	(.62)	(.60)	(.48)		
Wave 3	2.17	2.42			2.19	2.10	. . .	
	(.46)	(.56)			(.62)	(.58)		
Aggression:								
Mothers' reports:								
Wave 1	2.95	3.12	3.27	3.08	3.38	3.17	. . .	
	(.49)	(.60)	(.58)	(.66)	(.62)	(.45)		
Wave 2	3.00	2.97	3.16	2.95	3.50	2.99	Gender	Boys > Girls
	(.49)	(.66)	(.49)	(.55)	(.62)	(.55)		
Wave 3	2.94	2.97	3.08	2.88	3.38	2.85	Gender	Boys > Girls
	(.46)	(.65)	(.79)	(.63)	(.79)	(.60)		
Fathers' reports:								
Wave 1	3.12	2.96			3.23	3.35	*Family type*	*Rem > Nondiv*
	(.60)	(.50)			(.75)	(.57)		
Wave 2	3.07	2.81			3.24	3.04	. . .	
	(.60)	(.52)			(.65)	(.61)		
Wave 3	2.98	2.78			3.25	3.10	Family type	Rem > Nondiv
	(.61)	(.59)			(.71)	(.58)		

Children's reports:								
Wave 1	2.87 (.61)	3.10 (.66)	3.20 (.53)	3.07 (.64)	3.13 (.57)	3.51 (.81)	*Family type*	*Rem > Nondiv*
Wave 2	2.82 (.64)	3.03 (.79)	2.95 (.59)	3.28 (.63)	3.12 (.80)	3.08 (.67)	. . .	
Wave 3	2.70 (.53)	3.00 (.71)			3.02 (.58)	3.20 (.50)	. . .	
Avoidance:								
Mothers' reports:								
Wave 1	1.73 (.46)	2.10 (.62)	1.81 (.37)	2.03 (.69)	1.96 (.50)	2.13 (.53)	Gender	Girls > Boys
Wave 2	1.82 (.63)	2.25 (.50)	1.79 (.51)	1.91 (.61)	2.31 (.63)	1.88 (.47)	Family type × gender	Rem (Boys > Girls); Nondiv (Girls > Boys); Boys (Rem > Nondiv, Div); Girls (Nondiv > Div, Rem)
Wave 3	1.89 (.60)	2.16 (.49)	1.83 (.55)	2.12 (.51)	2.08 (.73)	1.88 (.47)	. . .	
Fathers' reports:								
Wave 1	1.77 (.49)	1.90 (.46)			1.80 (.48)	2.15 (.50)	. . .	
Wave 2	2.94 (.55)	2.05 (.51)			1.99 (.55)	2.17 (.48)	. . .	
Wave 3	2.02 (.56)	2.08 (.68)			2.09 (.67)	2.41 (.69)	. . .	
Children's reports:								
Wave 1	1.99 (.61)	2.12 (.74)	2.19 (.68)	2.25 (.75)	2.53 (.79)	2.58 (.99)	*Family type*	*Rem > Nondiv, Div*
Wave 2	2.06 (.63)	2.35 (.75)	2.28 (.74)	2.42 (.92)	2.37 (.79)	1.98 (.73)	. . .	
Wave 3	2.12 (.66)	2.31 (.70)			2.30 (.60)	2.47 (.54)	. . .	

NOTE.—Nondiv = Nondivorced; Div = Divorced; Rem = Remarried.

[a] Italicized contrasts denote planned comparisons.

TABLE 45

ACROSS-TIME CORRELATIONS FOR SIBLING RELATIONSHIP DIMENSIONS

	MULTIMETHOD/ MULTIRESPONDENT COMPOSITE			OBSERVERS' REPORTS			POSITIVITY: Mothers' Reports			POSITIVITY: Fathers' Reports			POSITIVITY: Children's Reports		
	Wave 1	Wave 2	Wave 3	Wave 1	Wave 2	Wave 3	Wave 1	Wave 2	Wave 3	Wave 1	Wave 2	Wave 3	Wave 1	Wave 2	Wave 3
Nondiv boys:															
Wave 1	...			...			...			...			...		
Wave 2	56***	...		20	...		69***	...		68***	...		78***	...	
Wave 3	61***	76***	...	21	11	...	76***	82***	...	76***	80***	...	56***	76***	...
Nondiv girls:															
Wave 1	...			...			...			...			...		
Wave 2	67***	...		33	...		81***	...		83***	...		63***	...	
Wave 3	67***	79***	...	36	36	...	76***	89***	...	89***	75***	...	47**	85***	...
Div boys:															
Wave 1	...			...			...			...			...		
Wave 2	82***	...		53**	...		75***	...			...		80***	...	
Wave 3	51*	56**	...	N.A.	N.A.	...	50*	78***	...			...	N.A.	N.A.	...
Div girls:															
Wave 1	...			...			...			...			...		
Wave 2	41***	...		31	...		87***	...			...		62***	...	
Wave 3	33	10	...	N.A.	N.A.	...	70***	62***	...			...	N.A.	N.A.	...
Rem boys:															
Wave 1	...			...			...			...			...		
Wave 2	81***	...		08	...		78***	...		67**	...		58*	...	
Wave 3	65*	91***	...	−20	47	...	66***	85***	...	79**	93**	...	47	89***	
Rem girls:															
Wave 1	...			...			...			...			...		
Wave 2	75***	...		−02	...		89***	...		73**	...		47	...	
Wave 3	61**	77**	...	−13	46	...	75***	82***	...	59*	89***	...	47	50	...

	Negativity														
Nondiv boys:															
Wave 1	...			...			...			...			...		
Wave 2	66***	...		46**	...		56***	...		83***	...		68***	...	
Wave 3	59***	66***	...	55**	38*	...	59***	57***	...	79***	79***	...	42**	53***	...
Nondiv girls:															
Wave 1	...			...			...			...			...		
Wave 2	69***	...		56**	...		73***	...		74***	...		56***	...	
Wave 3	73***	83***	...	38*	41*	...	82***	89***	...	78***	78***	...	50**	72***	...
Div boys:															
Wave 1	...			...			...			...			...		
Wave 2	58***	...		48*	...		59***	...			...		39*	...	
Wave 3	57***	66***	...	N.A.	N.A.	...	66***	62***	...			...	N.A.	N.A.	...
Div girls:															
Wave 1	...			...			...			...			...		
Wave 2	43*	...		40*	...		75***	...			...		43*	...	
Wave 3	22	01	...	N.A.	N.A.	...	53**	62***	...			...	N.A.	N.A.	...
Rem boys:															
Wave 1	...			...			...			...			...		
Wave 2	79***	...		−11	...		73***	...		71**	...		45	...	
Wave 3	50*	81***	...	−76[a]*	34	...	70**	78***	...	70**	94***	...	27	65*	...
Rem girls:															
Wave 1	...			...			...			...			...		
Wave 2	37	...		09	...		77***	...		38	...		05	...	
Wave 3	71**	51*	...	−59[a]*	19	...	69**	60*	...	73**	82***	...	50*	46	...

NOTE.—Nondiv = Nondivorced; Div = Divorced; Rem = Remarried. N.A. = not available.

[a] These large negative correlations may be partially attributable to the small number of children in remarried families with siblings at Wave 3. Notice that, even though their numerical value is large, they are significant only at the .05 level.

* $p \leq .05$.

** $p \leq .01$.

*** $p \leq .001$.

of their siblings at Wave 1. Significant gender differences occurred primarily in mothers' and children's reports rather than in fathers' reports or observers' ratings.

On the multimethod/multirespondent composite indices of negativity and positivity, significant multivariate gender differences emerged at all three waves. These differences lay primarily in positive rather than negative behavior, although at Wave 1 neither univariate test was significant (see Table 40). In general, the results indicated that girls were perceived as behaving more positively toward their siblings than were boys.

When reports from different informants were examined, only those obtained from mothers and children showed significant multivariate gender differences; again, the follow-up univariate tests showed that the differences occurred only with respect to positive behavior. In each of these significant cases, the direction of differences indicated that girls demonstrated more positive behavior toward their siblings than did boys (see Table 41). Reports from fathers and observers showed no multivariate gender differences.

Examination of the subscales of the SIB showed significant multivariate gender differences at all three waves for maternal reports and at Waves 2 and 3 for fathers' and children's reports (see Table 40). Thus, for fathers, only the subscales but not the total score showed gender differences. The particular measures that accounted for the multivariate effect, however, differed according to respondent and wave. In mothers' reports, the direction of difference indicated that girls directed more positive behavior (involvement, empathy, teaching) and less negative behavior (aggression) toward their siblings than did boys at Waves 2 and 3. However, at Wave 1, mothers reported girls to be more avoidant of their siblings.

In fathers' and children's reports, gender differences were more sparse. Fathers reported that girls were more empathic at Wave 2, and girls reported that they were more involved with their siblings at Wave 2 and more empathic at Wave 3.

Thus, as expected, girls demonstrated more positive behavior toward their siblings than did boys. However, in general, the magnitude of these gender differences was not large. Although reports from mothers and children indicated that girls offered more positive behavior, such as support, empathy, and involvement, toward their siblings, this effect was tempered by the fact that fathers' and observers' reports did not concur.

Family-type differences and interactions.—Although gender differences occurred primarily with respect to positive behavior, family differences were found in both positive and negative behaviors. In all instances, the direction of the significant effects revealed that children in nondivorced families were seen as having better sibling relationships. The multimethod/multirespondent composite measure showed significant differences between family types at Waves 1 and 3 (the comparison at Wave 2 was marginally significant at $p < .10$). At Wave 1, family-type differences occurred in both positivity and negativity, but only negativity was associated with family-type differences by Wave 3 on this measure. Results indicated that children in remarried families were viewed as behaving less positively at Wave 1 and more negatively at Waves 1 and 3 toward their siblings than were children in nondivorced families. Moreover, children in divorced families engaged in significantly more negative behavior at Waves 2 and 3, but not in less positive behavior with their siblings, than did children in nondivorced families (see Tables 41 and 42).

Examination of the total SIB scores of positivity and negativity from different respondents identified main effects of family type at Wave 1. In each of these reports, the same pattern of more negative and less positive sibling relationships in remarried than in nondivorced families was indicated. Sibling relationships in remarried families were also viewed as less positive than those in divorced families according to both mothers and children and as more negative according to children at the initial assessment.

The differences identified at Wave 1 on the total scores of the SIB were not always replicated at later waves. At Wave 2, family-type differences were found only in mothers' reports and, at Wave 3, only in fathers' reports. The pattern of mean differences was identical to that found at Wave 1, except that fathers no longer saw stepchildren as being less positive than biological children at the last wave.

When the subscales of the SIB were examined, significant multivariate effects of family type were found at Wave 2 for maternal reports and Wave 3 for paternal and children's reports (see Table 40). Results from the follow-up univariate analyses presented in Tables 43 and 44 indicated that mothers perceived children from remarried families as being less empathic with their siblings than children from nondivorced or divorced families. Mothers also perceived siblings from remarried and divorced families as more rivalrous than their counterparts from nondivorced families. Fathers and stepfathers saw differences in their children's levels of rivalry and aggression—stepchildren appeared more negative—and children reported differences in involvement, with children from remarried homes emerging as less involved. Other planned comparisons provided support for the general notion of more negative and less positive behavior in remarried families as compared to nondivorced families.

Significant differences also emerged in observational ratings of the children's behavior toward their siblings. However, in contrast to the interview ratings, observational ratings described children in divorced families as being significantly more negative than those in remarried families at Wave 1 and more negative than children in nondivorced families at both of the available waves (Waves 1 and 2). Children in divorced families were also seen as less positive than those in nondivorced families at Wave 2. Thus, a different pattern of results emerged from the observational data than from the reports of family members. It should be noted, however, that these discrepancies parallel those found in other areas of children's adjustment (see Chap. III). In no case were children from nondivorced families rated as less positive or more negative in sibling relationships than were those in divorced or remarried families.

Significant multivariate interactions between family type and children's gender emerged only in maternal reports of the sibling relationship at Wave 2. Comparisons of the means for total positivity and negativity and for the subscales of involvement, empathy, rivalry, and avoidance indicated that mothers perceived boys in remarried families to be the most negative in interactions with siblings; there was some indication that this pattern persisted through Wave 3. There was also some indication that girls from nondivorced families were more avoidant of their siblings than other groups of children, but only at Wave 2. Thus, our results indicated that, according to mothers, the family differences were primarily the result of more negative and less positive behavior on the part of boys, but not of girls, in remarried families.

Gender-of-sibling effects.—Analyses were also conducted using gender of target sibling as a between-subjects factor; the scarcity of effects identified in these analyses could be attributable to the reduction of sample sizes by the additional factor as well as to the large age range of the siblings. Even so, a significant family type × gender of sibling interaction was found in the reports of children on the total positivity score of the SIB at Wave 1, $F(2,144) = 6.90, p \leq .001$. Both boys and girls in remarried families reported showing less positive behavior toward their brothers than the other combinations of children and their siblings. Thus, children saw boys in stepfamilies as getting less support from their siblings in the early stage of remarriage, but this finding was not confirmed by other respondents' reports.

In addition, significant interactions between children's and siblings' gender were identified in maternal reports at all three waves (Wave 1, $F[6,141] = 3.14, p \leq .001$; Wave 2, $F[6,129] = 2.82, p \leq .05$; Wave 3, $F[6,111] = 3.01, p \leq .01$). Boys were more involved with brothers than with sisters, and girls were involved with brothers and sisters to a similar degree. Generally, however, involvement was higher in same-gender dyads than opposite-gender dyads, a result upheld in the reports of children at Wave 2, $F(1,133) = 6.71, p \leq .001$. A significant multivariate effect was identified in fathers' reports at Wave 3, $F(6,72) = 2.58, p \leq .05$, which confirmed the pattern of higher involvement in same-gender dyads.

In summary, gender pairing did not appear to have a large effect on the differences identified. The large age range of siblings probably precluded significant findings; unfortunately, because of reduced sample size, children's gender, siblings' gender, family type, and age could not be examined simultaneously.

STABILITY AND CHANGE OVER TIME IN SIBLING RELATIONSHIPS

Correlations of the multimethod/multirespondent composite indices of positivity and negativity across time are presented in Table 45 to determine the stability of behavior in the different family groups. The total scores of positivity and negativity derived from family members' ratings on the SIB and the total positivity and negativity scores from observational data are also included to compensate for the absence of observational data and children's reports for divorced families at Wave 3.

Composite ratings of positive and negative behavior demonstrated considerable within-group stability: within family types, positive and negative behavior at later waves was strongly predicted by behavior at earlier waves. This was true for all groups except divorced families with girls, where the number of significant correlations was less than in the other groups. However, correlations of the multimethod/multirespondent composites for this subgroup did not differ significantly from correlations in other family types.

Observational ratings showed less stability than reports of family members: this could be expected because the observational ratings were based on much briefer samplings than the ratings of family members. Correlations among observational reports differed significantly from correlations obtained among the multimethod/multirespondent composite in remarried families but not in the other family groups. Significant correlations were less frequent in reports of children than of parents, although in most cases these latter still showed considerable stability, ranging from .43 to .76. These correlations, however, do not give any indication of mean-level changes that might have occurred between groups.

Repeated-measures MANOVAs were conducted on the multimethod/multirespondent composite measures of positivity and negativity for boys and girls in each family type in order to examine mean-level short-term (Wave 1 to Wave 2, Table 46) and long-term (Wave 1 to Wave 3, Table 47) changes. Because of space limitations, repeated-measures MANOVAs for individual subscales are not presented; however, these are discussed in the text in order to clarify results of analyses of the composite measures.

Short-term changes in sibling relationships.—Short-term declines in positive behavior in sibling interactions were indicated by significant wave effects on the multimethod/multirespondent composite of positive behavior (Table 46), on mothers' total positivity score on the SIB, $F(1,140) = 5.24$, $p \leq .05$, and on the observational total positivity score, $F(1,111) = 6.73$, $p \leq .05$. No short-term changes were identified on either the multimethod/

TABLE 46

MEANS (Standard Deviations) FOR REPEATED-MEASURES ANALYSES OF SHORT-TERM CHANGES (Wave 1 to Wave 2) IN SIBLING RELATIONSHIP DIMENSIONS

	NONDIVORCED		DIVORCED		REMARRIED		SIGNIFICANT MAIN EFFECTS AND INTERACTIONS	SIGNIFICANT CONTRASTS
	Boys	Girls	Boys	Girls	Boys	Girls		
Multimethod/multi-respondent composite:								
Positivity:								
Wave 1	.21 (.54)	.15 (.60)	−.20 (.82)	.19 (.73)	−.53 (.62)	−.08 (.53)	Wave	1 > 2
Wave 2	−.05 (.65)	.10 (.73)	−.35 (.77)	−.01 (.85)	−.65 (1.1)	.03 (.78)	Family type, gender	Nondiv > Rem; Girls > Boys
Negativity:								
Wave 1	−.34 (.53)	−.12 (.68)	.16 (.57)	.07 (.79)	.26 (.55)	.15 (.56)	Family type	Div, Rem > Nondiv
Wave 2	−.25 (.68)	−.06 (.75)	.12 (.51)	.23 (.75)	.26 (.91)	.05 (.77)	...	

NOTE.—Nondiv = Nondivorced; Div = Divorced; Rem = Remarried.

multirespondent composite or the total scores of negative behavior; however, in the observational reports, there was an increase in negativity across time, $F(1,111) = 15.61, p \leq .001$. Fathers also reported short-term changes in positive behavior; these, however, were modified by a wave × gender interaction, $F(1,91) = 5.14, p \leq .05$. According to fathers, levels of positive behavior remained the same for girls (Wave 1 = 3.20; Wave 2 = 3.22) but declined for boys (Wave 1 = 3.15; Wave 2 = 3.01). This change was accounted for primarily by changes in the level of children's teaching and guidance. The declines in positive behavior seen in mothers' reports appeared to be accounted for by declines in the level of involvement and companionship rather than in empathy and support. Put simply, children were spending less time with their siblings as they entered adolescence and invested more time with their peers. Moreover, fathers reported a significant decrease in rivalry and aggression but a significant increase in avoidance, suggesting a general pattern of disengagement.

In the reports of children, a significant interaction of wave with family type was identified both in the SIB total positivity, $F(2,138) = 4.26$, $p \leq .01$, and the SIB total negativity, $F(2,138) = 3.66, p \leq .05$. According to children in nondivorced and divorced families, their positive behavior (empathy and involvement) declined, and their negative behavior (rivalry and avoidance) remained the same, whereas, in remarried families, positive behavior increased, and negative behavior decreased over this short term. Thus, in contrast to the patterns of disengagement identified by children in other families and by other informants, children in remarried families saw themselves increasing in their involvement with their siblings and offering them emotional support and empathy while decreasing in avoidance and rivalry.

Long-term changes in sibling relationships.—In the multimethod/multirespondent composite index of positivity, there were no changes from Wave 1 to Wave 3. With respect to the negativity composite, a significant family type × wave interaction (see Table 47) indicated that, whereas children in nondivorced and remarried families showed no change (nondivorced mean change = .06; remarried mean change = .01), children in divorced families were declining in negativity (Wave 1 = .051; Wave 3 = −.290). However, this finding is more likely to be an artifact of measurement than a true indication of improvement because there was considerable lack of consensus among informants as to changes in sibling relationships. Recall that neither observers' nor children's data were available for the third wave for divorced families; thus, the overall "composite" across methods for this family group consists only of maternal reports. Because observers rated children in divorced families as more negative than other children at Wave 1, absence of observational data at Wave 3 may give a false impression of improvement.

TABLE 47

Means (Standard Deviations) for Repeated-Measures Analyses of Long-Term Changes (Wave 1 to Wave 3) in Sibling Relationship Dimensions

	Nondivorced		Divorced		Remarried		Significant Main Effects and Interactions	Significant Contrasts
	Boys	Girls	Boys	Girls	Boys	Girls		
Multimethod/multi-respondent composite:								
Positivity:								
Wave 1	.19 (.54)	.17 (.62)	−.18 (.71)	.11 (.63)	−.51 (.55)	−.10 (.56)	Family type	Nondiv > Rem
Wave 3	−.13 (.75)	.28 (.88)	−.34 (.91)	.06 (.95)	−.68 (1.1)	−.16 (.90)	Gender	Girls > Boys
Negativity:								
Wave 1	−.37 (.50)	−.10 (.70)	.04 (.54)	.06 (.69)	.37 (.51)	.13 (.53)	Family type	Rem > Nondiv, Div
Wave 3	−.27 (.72)	−.08 (.82)	−.25 (1.1)	−.32 (.95)	.38 (1.0)	.13 (.91)	Family type × wave	Div (1 > 3)

Note.—Nondiv = Nondivorced; Div = Divorced; Rem = Remarried.

As in the short term, the long-term analysis showed significant main effects of wave, indicating a decline in total positive behavior as reported by mothers, $F(1,122) = 13.57, p \leq .001$, and fathers, $F(1,81) = 4.07, p \leq .05$. Moreover, significant main effects of wave indicated declines in total negative behavior according to both mothers, $F(1,122) = 6.57, p \leq .05$, and children, $F(1,81) = 5.17, p \leq .05$. In the reports of children, there was also a significant interaction between wave and family type, $F(1,81) = 5.38, p \leq .05$, which indicated that the decline in negative behavior was particularly pronounced in remarried families. Again, children perceived greater improvement in their sibling relationships than did other informants.

It should be noted, however, that observational reports showed a significant increase in level of negative behavior in both the short and the long term, $F(1,59) = 13.50, p \leq .001$, a pattern that appears to conflict with that found in the interview reports. What might explain this discrepancy? The decrease in both positive and negative behavior reported by informants other than observers might be interpreted as a pattern of increasing disengagement. Thus, as children entered adolescence, they may have been disengaging from their siblings, a pattern parallel to the pattern of disengagement, or "distancing" (Steinberg, 1987a, 1988), noted during this period in other family relationships. When, however, the children were required to interact with their siblings in the observational setting, this pattern of distancing and disengagement may have been difficult to maintain and may have been transformed into more conflictual or rejecting behavior.

SUMMARY AND CONCLUSIONS

The hypotheses we presented at the outset were partially supported by the findings. As reported in other studies, girls displayed more positive behavior—empathy, support, involvement, and teaching—toward their siblings than did boys. Gender differences were not as apparent with respect to such negative behavior as aggression and rivalry.

As was found in the measures of children's adjustment (reported in Chap. III), children in remarried families were described by family members as demonstrating less positive and more negative behavior toward their siblings—none of the significant differences favored these children as compared to children in nondivorced families. The largest differences occurred in empathy and support (about one point on a five-point scale used for maternal reports). Raters were consistent in the direction of reported differences; however, the particular subscales that reflected the significant differences varied across raters. Overall, the results indicated that, at least during adolescence, no stronger bonding between siblings who are undergoing family transitions occurred. Stepchildren, who were experiencing increased levels of stress in coping with the recent remarriages of their mothers, directed higher levels of negative behavior toward siblings than children in the longer-established nondivorced families. In contrast, children in stabilized divorced families, who were not currently undergoing a nonnormative transition, generally did not differ from either group with respect to sibling relationships. According to stepchildren, relationships with their siblings improved over time as they adjusted to their new family situations, although this report was not supported by those of other informants.

It might be proposed that increased bonding would be more evident in younger children, who do not have the opportunity to disengage from a stressful family situation and seek sources of support and buffering outside the family. However, the work of Hetherington (1989) and MacKinnon (1989) indicates that, even with younger children, conflictual or ambivalent sibling relationships are more common in families that have undergone marital transitions than in nondivorced families and that these negative forms of relating are more common in divorced and stepfamilies than are cohesive, mutually supportive relationships.

In accordance with other reports from Hetherington (1988), there was some suggestion that brothers in remarried families were offered less support from their siblings than other children; this result, however, was not consistent across reporters. There was a large age range of siblings who could be included in this study, and this made it difficult to examine the effects of gender composition and age systematically.

There were indications that children disengaged from their siblings during the transition to adolescence, showing both less negative and less positive behavior toward them. Consistent with patterns found in parent-child relationships (e.g., Steinberg, 1987a, 1988), sibling relationships in this study showed the same increased distancing in early adolescence. Entering adolescence, children may become embarrassed by their siblings and disengage from them more actively as they distance themselves from other family relationships and form significant bonds outside the family. In contrast to the decreases over time in negativity reported by family members, observers rated adolescents as increasing in negative behavior. During enforced interactions, disengagement seems difficult to sustain and may have been transformed into more direct confrontational and acrimonious behavior.

This pattern of distancing may be accelerated in families that have undergone marital transitions. It should be noted that, although the mean scores of children in divorced families most often fell somewhere between those in nondivorced and in remarried families on interview reports, observational ratings indicated that children in divorced families were more negative than those in nondivorced families even at the first wave. If this negative behavior reflected the children's attempts to distance themselves from their siblings, then perhaps those in divorced families were demonstrating the pattern of disengagement earlier than children in nondivorced families, who had not undergone this transition. It may be that, because of the non-normative family rearrangements, children in divorced and remarried families begin this period of distancing at an earlier age than children in non-divorced families. Patterns of distancing need to be examined in further research to determine how their course may differ for siblings of differing ages. It should be noted, however, that, despite indications of increasing distance in sibling relationships, children in all family groups still demonstrated overall relatively positive behavior to their siblings.

VII. THE EFFECT OF FAMILY RELATIONSHIPS ON ADOLESCENT DEVELOPMENT DURING FAMILY REORGANIZATION

Edward R. Anderson, Marjorie S. Lindner, and Layne D. Bennion

Thus far this report has described mean differences in children's adjustment and family relationships among nondivorced, divorced, and remarried families as well as how these changed with the onset of adolescence. In this chapter, we examine characteristics of family relationships that were associated with adaptive and with maladaptive child functioning in each type of family. From the outset, we had assumed that family relationships were a primary causal factor in children's development—that the quality of the marital, parent-child, and sibling relationships would have significantly shaped the long-term adjustment of the children. However, we now believe that this assumption merits further development; family relationships do affect children's adjustment, but that is only part of the picture.

A consistently strong association between acting-out noncompliant behavior in children and conflictual family relationships marked by high levels of negative affect has been uncovered by many researchers. Currently, children's exposure to or their involvement in marital conflict (e.g., Emery, 1982, 1988; Hetherington et al., 1982) and coercive exchanges between parents and children (e.g., Patterson, 1982) are believed to result in elevated levels of externalizing, acting-out behavior. In addition, coercive relationships between siblings may initiate and sustain aggressive behavior (Patterson, 1982).

Alternatively, it has been noted that a warm, supportive relationship with one family member can buffer a child against the adverse consequences of punitive, conflictual relationships with other family members (Rutter, 1981; Werner & Smith, 1982). Authoritative parenting, characterized by legitimate parental authority combined with high levels of expressive involvement and emotional support, has been shown to be very beneficial for children (for a review, see Steinberg, Mounts, Lamborn, & Dornbusch, 1991), and positive relationships with their siblings may provide an important resource for children involved in a stressful parent-child relationship or exposed to acrimony between their parents (Ihinger-Tallman, 1987).

Studies of family relationships and children's adjustment following divorce and remarriage have suggested that much of children's externalizing behavior can be attributed to the higher levels of parent-child and marital conflict that existed both prior to and following the divorce (Block et al., 1986; Cherlin, Chase-Lansdale, Furstenberg, Kiernan, Robins, Morrison, & Teitler, 1991; Emery, 1982, 1988). Moreover, negativity expressed in parent-child and marital relationships is likely to be reflected in sibling relationships (Hetherington, 1988; MacKinnon, 1989). Such increased levels of aggressive behavior are in accordance with traditional theories of aggression. For example, Berkowitz (1983) argues that adverse situations that arouse both "flight" and "fight" responses result in aggression toward individuals who are associated with the adverse situation when flight is restricted. These effects of conflict and stress appear to be particularly strong for boys (Emery, 1982; Zaslow & Hayes, 1984), who tend to be exposed to conflict more frequently than girls (Hetherington, 1988; Zaslow & Hayes, 1984).

Family relationships can be further exacerbated when high levels of marital conflict lead to disruption in parenting (Belsky, 1981, 1984). Thus, in addition to higher levels of conflict and coercive interchanges, children experiencing family transitions are often less likely than their peers from nonstressed homes to be receiving authoritative parenting (Baumrind, 1989; Hetherington, 1989). Divorced, nonremarried mothers, who are dealing with task overload and high levels of stress, are prone to breakdowns in monitoring and control or to acting in a manner that is reactive to children's problems rather than proactive and preventative. In addition, frequency of positive involvement and expressions of warmth between divorced mothers and their children may decline. To the extent that these changes occur, increases in antisocial behavior displayed by the children appear likely (Patterson & Bank, 1989).

In the case of remarriage, however, aversive marital and parent-child relationships may have different implications for the child. For example, some studies of younger children have shown that higher externalizing in children occurs in stepfamilies where there is little marital conflict (Brand et al., 1988; Bray, 1987, 1988), suggesting that some stepchildren resent a harmonious remarriage. Other studies have suggested that, with preadolescents, both authoritative and authoritarian stepfathers, who make immediate attempts to control and discipline the child, may be less successful in preventing externalizing behavior than stepfathers who begin more slowly by supporting the mother in her parenting and discipline while attempting to establish positive relationships with the children (Hetherington, 1989).

The importance of examining the interdependence of family relationships is apparent; a summary of the constructs used to do so in this study is presented in Figure 2, along with our basic hypotheses about the order of effects. These hypotheses depict the common "top-down" model in which a positive, supportive marital relationship marked by low levels of conflict serves as the cornerstone for supportive relationships elsewhere in the family, all of which subsequently have a positive effect on children's adjustment. Dashed lines indicate potential effects on the sibling relationship that we believe are important but not central to the analyses presented in this chapter. Our belief that the strength of these effects is likely to differ depending on the gender of the child involved, the type of family situation, and the length of time these relationships have been established is not indicated in the figure. Moreover, although the diagram implies a unidirectional pattern, we now believe that the true process is one of bidirectional influences.

Based on previous research, the following effects were hypothesized.

First, we expected that, in nondivorced families, the quality of the marital relationship would be positively related to that of the parent-child relationship. In stepfamilies, however, we expected no such association, at least in the initial months following remarriage, when family subsystems had not yet become integrated. In addition, we believed that the association between

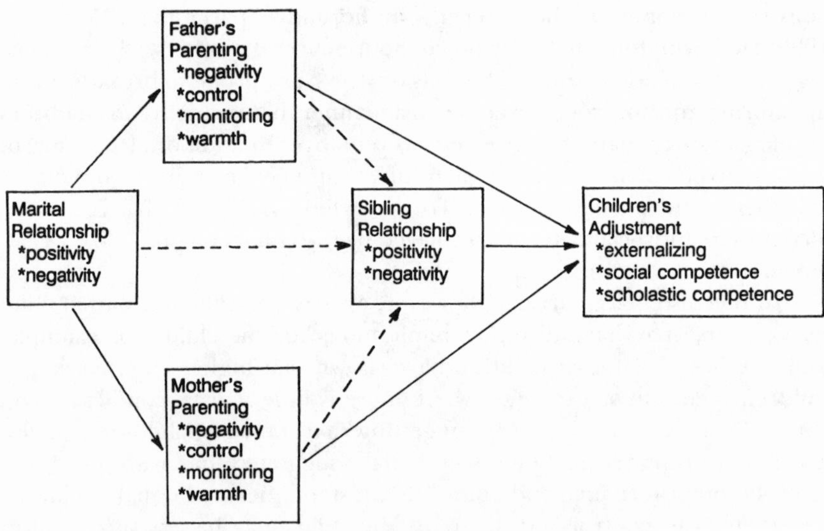

FIG. 2.—Summary of constructs and proposed hypotheses

the marital relationship and parenting would be stronger for fathers than for mothers.

Second, we expected authoritative parenting (i.e., higher levels of both warmth and control or monitoring) to be correlated generally with the most positive child adjustment (Baumrind, 1989). In remarried families, however, we predicted that higher levels of control by the stepfather, regardless of the accompanying level of warmth, would be associated with poorer adjustment (Hetherington et al., 1985).

Third, we hypothesized that, in all families, sibling relationships would reflect the quality of the parent-child relationship (Hetherington, 1988; Radke-Yarrow et al., 1987) and would be strongly associated with the child's adjustment. Because some previous research has indicated the presence of more acrimonious sibling relationships in divorced (Hetherington, 1988; MacKinnon, 1989) and in remarried families (Hetherington, 1988), we expected the association between sibling negativity and children's adjustment to be particularly strong in these two groups.

METHOD

Measures

In addressing our hypotheses, we relied on the multimethod/multirespondent composite measures of children's adjustment and family functioning noted in Figure 2 and described in Chapter II (cf. also Chap. III for child adjustment, Chap. V for parent-child relationship, and Chap. VI for sibling relationship dimensions). We also used the parenting typologies of authoritative, authoritarian/conflictual, and disengaged that emerged from the previously described cluster analyses (cf. Chap. V). Positivity and negativity composites for marital relationships were created for use in the current analyses and are described in a later section.

Overview of Analyses

The links between marital, parent-child, and sibling relationships and the adjustment of boys and girls in different family situations were investigated through multivariate regression. Ideally, we would have liked to test the model depicted in Figure 2 separately for each family type × gender group as well as to investigate relations over time among these dimensions; unfortunately, the limited sample size precluded this possibility. As a feasible alternative, the model was instead investigated through a series of stages in which individual paths were tested within a wave. In order to identify possible interactions of obtained associations with family type and children's gender, we conducted tests of homogeneity of regression slopes over groups, a procedure that tests whether the regression coefficients between an independent variable and a set of dependent variables differ depending on the family type or child gender group. This multivariate test was followed by univariate tests aimed at identifying whether a particular dependent variable contributed to the effect.

Three components of the overall model were tested separately. First, we examined the concurrent associations between marital relationships and parent-child relationships. Second, concurrent associations between parenting styles as well as individual parenting dimensions and children's adjustment were investigated. Third, we focused on concurrent relations between the dimensions of the sibling relationship and the children's adjustment. Finally, in the last section of this chapter, we investigated the reciprocal relations between children's adjustment and family relationships.

WITHIN-WAVE ASSOCIATIONS BETWEEN FAMILY RELATIONSHIPS AND CHILDREN'S ADJUSTMENT

The Marital Relationship and Parenting

Table 48 presents the concurrent (i.e., within-wave) regression coefficients between the dimensions of mothers' and fathers' parenting and the newly created composite dimensions of positivity and negativity in marital relationships. The composite dimension of marital positivity was indexed by the average Z score of husbands' and wives' ratings on the Spanier Dyadic Adjustment scale and the observational ratings of husbands' and wives' positivity in marital interactions (Cronbach's alpha = .72, .61, .51 for Waves 1, 2, and 3, respectively) and the composite dimension of marital negativity by the average Z score of ratings of husbands' and wives' conflict over child-rearing issues and the observational ratings of their negativity in marital interactions (Cronbach's alpha = .75, .61, .66).

In all waves, marital negativity was associated with parental negativity, and marital positivity with parental warmth, to a similar extent, and for both mothers and fathers. Relations with parental control and monitoring were less consistent: marital negativity was positively associated with parental control (Wave 1 only), whereas marital positivity was related to parental monitoring (Wave 2; also Wave 3 for fathers). The significant differences between family types in regression slopes are listed in Table 49. At Wave 1, marital positivity was associated with higher monitoring by mothers only for boys in nondivorced families. At Wave 2, marital negativity and marital positivity related differently to mothers' parenting-negativity depending on

TABLE 48

STANDARDIZED REGRESSION COEFFICIENTS RELATING COMPOSITE MARITAL RELATIONSHIP DIMENSIONS OF MOTHERS' AND FATHERS' PARENTING

	MARITAL NEGATIVITY			MARITAL POSITIVITY		
	Wave 1	Wave 2	Wave 3	Wave 1	Wave 2	Wave 3
Mothers' parenting:						
Negativity	.38***	.36[a]***	.54***	−.17*	−.26[a]**	−.17
Control	.23**	.10	.02	−.04	.12	.11
Monitoring	−.07	−.11	−.07	.09[a]	.28**	.06
Warmth	−.29***	−.27**	−.05	.39***	.50[a]***	.31***
Fathers' parenting:						
Negativity	.38***	.48***	.59***	−.28***	−.31***	−.23*
Control	.22*	.10	.05	−.02	.28**	.14
Monitoring	.02	−.07	−.13	.06	.38**	.26**
Warmth	−.25**	−.21*	−.11	.40***	.49***	.33***
Multivariate *df*	(4,125)	(4,112)	(4,103)	(4,125)	(4,112)	(4,103)
Univariate *df*	(1,128)	(1,115)	(1,106)	(1,128)	(1,115)	(1,106)

[a] Significant interaction between family types on regression slopes.
* $p \leq .05$.
** $p \leq .01$.
*** $p \leq .001$.

TABLE 49

SIGNIFICANT INTERACTIONS BETWEEN FAMILY TYPES ON REGRESSION SLOPES BETWEEN MARITAL AND PARENTING DIMENSIONS

	NONDIVORCED		REMARRIED	
	Boys	Girls	Boys	Girls
Marital positivity, Wave 1,[a] with mothers' monitoring[b] (beta)	.51**	−.19	.03	.01
Marital negativity, Wave 2,[c] with mothers' negativity[d] (beta)	.59**	−.25	.04	.54**
Marital positivity, Wave 2,[e] with:				
Mothers' negativity[f] (beta)	−.34*	−.00	.28	.67**
Mothers' warmth[g] (beta)	.69**	.65**	.19	.17

NOTE.—F values are for multivariate tests (Wilks's lambda) and follow-up univariate tests.
[a] $F(12,323) = 2.14, p = .014$.
[b] $F(3,125) = 3.34, p = .021$.
[c] $F(12,289) = 2.47, p = .004$.
[d] $F(3,112) = 5.69, p = .001$.
[e] $F(12,289) = 2.77, p = .001$.
[f] $F(3,112) = 4.22, p = .007$.
[g] $F(3,112) = 5.05, p = .003$.
* $p \leq .05$.
** $p \leq .01$.

family type; the associations were strongest for nondivorced families with boys and for remarried families with girls. In addition, marital positivity at Wave 2 was associated with mothers' warmth only in nondivorced families.

Although the results outlined above indicated the extent to which the marital relationship was associated with parents' treatment of their children, the extent to which this relationship was linked to children's treatment of parents was also of interest. We hypothesized that children in remarried families would direct more negative behavior toward their parents if the new marital relationship was close since we expected them to resent and actively to resist the closeness of the new couple. Consequently, we used marital positivity and negativity to predict scores on the observational composite scales of child-to-parent negativity; the results of these analyses are presented in Table 50. At all waves, negativity in marital relationships predicted higher negativity on the part of the children toward both parents, whereas positivity in that relationship showed essentially no significant associations. Contrary to our hypothesis concerning stepfamilies, the absence of interactions indicated consistency across family types in these associations.

TABLE 50

STANDARD REGRESSION COEFFICIENTS RELATING COMPOSITE MARITAL RELATIONSHIP DIMENSIONS TO COMPOSITE OBSERVATIONAL DIMENSIONS OF CHILD-TO-PARENT NEGATIVITY

	MARITAL NEGATIVITY			MARITAL POSITIVITY		
	Wave 1	Wave 2	Wave 3	Wave 1	Wave 2	Wave 3
Child to mother ...	.27***	.25*	.40***	.05	−.15	−.20
Child to father	.30***	.35***	.48***	.01	−.23*	−.19
Multivariate *df*	(2,123)	(2,96)	(2,89)			
Univariate *df*	(1,124)	(1,97)	(1,90)			

* $p \leq .05$.
*** $p \leq .001$.

Parent-Child Relationships and Children's Adjustment

Parenting style and children's adjustment.—The three parenting typologies (authoritative, authoritarian/conflictual, and disengaged; cf. Chap. V) were included with family type as a between-subjects factor in a series of multivariate analyses of variance (MANOVAs); the multimethod/multirespondent composite child adjustment indices (externalizing, social competence, and scholastic competence; cf. Chap. III) served as dependent variables. Because the correlational data indicated little evidence of different effects of parenting on boys and girls, children's gender was not included as a factor in these analyses. MANOVAs were conducted separately for mothers and fathers and at each wave of assessment.

Table 51 presents multivariate and follow-up univariate results from within-wave analyses investigating the relation between parenting style and children's adjustment; the means, standard deviations, and significant effects are shown in Table 52. Main effects of maternal parenting style and of family type were identified at all waves; no interactions between the two emerged in any of the comparisons. Post hoc contrasts indicated that an authoritative parenting style was associated with significantly higher levels of both social and scholastic competence and with lower levels of externalizing behavior than either the authoritarian/conflictual or disengaged styles.

Results for fathers paralleled those for mothers. Main effects of family type and parenting style were identified for both externalizing and social competence at all waves; however, only parenting style, not family type, was related to scholastic competence at Waves 1 and 2. Both fathers and stepfathers who demonstrated authoritative parenting had children with the lowest levels of externalizing and the highest levels of competence.

TABLE 51

F VALUES AND SIGNIFICANCE LEVELS FOR MULTIVARIATE ANALYSES OF FAMILY TYPE AND PARENTING STYLE ON COMPOSITE DIMENSIONS OF CHILDREN'S ADJUSTMENT

	WAVE 1			WAVE 2			WAVE 3		
	Family	Parenting	Interaction	Family	Parenting	Interaction	Family	Parenting	Interaction
Mothers' parenting:									
Multivariate	8.42***	11.12***	1.16	5.12***	7.31***	.55	3.23**	5.46***	1.45
Externalizing	15.86***	22.04***	2.02	9.32***	6.42**	.85	5.60**	10.44***	1.11
Social competence	19.55***	20.99***	1.03	13.16***	17.95***	.35	6.48**	9.96***	.50
Scholastic competence	6.21**	6.01**	1.23	3.47*	5.12**	.52	3.83*	4.19*	2.07
Fathers' parenting:									
Multivariate	4.76**	3.78***	1.11	4.47**	5.21***	.62	4.24**	5.54***	.65
Externalizing	6.81**	8.32***	.36	4.92*	11.75***	.85	10.75***	15.99***	.10
Social competence	13.11***	4.10*	.39	12.00***	9.01***	1.08	7.25**	9.27***	.85
Scholastic competence	1.94	5.41**	2.07	.12	5.64**	.09	2.52	2.15	.52

* $p \leq .05$.
** $p \leq .01$.
*** $p \leq .001$.

Parental behavior and children's adjustment.—To examine the particular dimensions of parenting potentially associated with children's adjustment, we conducted multivariate regression analyses; results of these analyses are shown in Table 53. Tests of homogeneity of regression slopes across family types yielded no significant differences, indicating that parenting was related to children's adjustment in similar ways across family-type/child-gender groups.

Both paternal negativity and maternal negativity were associated positively with externalizing and negatively with social competence at all waves. Parental negativity was also inversely related to scholastic competence at all waves for mothers and at two waves for fathers. It should be noted, however, that associations between negativity and externalizing were higher in absolute value than those between negativity and either social or scholastic competence. Warmth by either parent was associated positively with social competence and inversely with externalizing at all waves. Results for monitoring generally paralleled those found for warmth, with higher monitoring associated with lower externalizing and higher social and scholastic competence. Fewer significant associations prevailed between scholastic competence and parental behavior than in the case of either externalizing or social competence, and there were few consistent relations between parental control and children's adjustment.

In light of the absence of significant interactions of these relations with family type or children's gender, these analyses supported the benefits of authoritative parenting, regardless of family type. Even so, family type still predicted children's adjustment at all waves of the study. In both divorced and remarried families, children whose parents demonstrated an authoritative style scored higher on externalizing and lower on competence than their counterparts in nondivorced families with similarly authoritative parents. Also, any differences in the effects of authoritarian/conflictual and disengaged parenting were always in the direction of disengagement being less damaging to children's adjustment than authoritarianism; thus, for instance, children of mothers who displayed a disengaged style had higher levels of scholastic competence than children of authoritarian/conflictual mothers.

Sibling Relationships and Children's Adjustment

Table 54 presents the concurrent (within-wave) regression coefficients between children's adjustment and the composite sibling relationship dimensions (cf. Chap. VI). Both negativity and positivity in these relationships were consistently associated with externalizing and with social competence in the expected directions, but there were few relations with scholastic com-

TABLE 52

MEANS (Standard Deviations) AND SIGNIFICANT EFFECTS OF PARENTING STYLES ON CHILDREN'S ADJUSTMENT

	NONDIVORCED			DIVORCED			REMARRIED			SIGNIFICANT MAIN EFFECTS AND INTERACTIONS	SIGNIFICANT CONTRASTS
	Atative	Atarian	Diseng	Atative	Atarian	Diseng	Atative	Atarian	Diseng		
Mothers' parenting:											
Externalizing:											
Wave 1	−.42	−.02	−.06	−.17	.69	.39	.00	.49	.13	Family type,	Rem, Div > Nondiv;
	(.49)	(.49)	(.56)	(.52)	(.22)	(.65)	(.41)	(.49)	(.49)	parenting type	Atarian, Diseng > Atative
Wave 2	−.45	.10	−.19	−.07	.27	.34	.08	.28	.17	Family type,	Rem, Div > Nondiv;
	(.44)	(.62)	(.64)	(.49)	(.47)	(.48)	(.67)	(.52)	(.55)	parenting type	Atarian, Diseng > Atative
Wave 3	−.24	.15	−.29	−.14	.57	.09	−.08	.43	.30	Family type,	Rem, Div > Nondiv;
	(.60)	(.60)	(.46)	(.65)	(.81)	(.58)	(.30)	(.51)	(.43)	parenting type	Atarian > Diseng, Atative
Social competence:											
Wave 1	.34	.16	.05	.16	−.33	−.38	−.00	−.31	−.41	Family type,	Nondiv > Rem, Div;
	(.38)	(.40)	(.45)	(.40)	(.26)	(.32)	(.54)	(.52)	(.40)	parenting type	Atative > Diseng > Atarian
Wave 2	.42	.08	.02	.12	−.12	−.40	.09	−.24	−.42	Family type,	Nondiv > Rem, Div;
	(.34)	(.46)	(.47)	(.41)	(.39)	(.27)	(.59)	(.35)	(.47)	parenting type	Atative > Diseng > Atarian
Wave 3	.36	−.12	.13	.17	−.24	−.28	.00	−.33	−.34	Family type,	Nondiv > Rem, Div;
	(.52)	(.55)	(.44)	(.41)	(.72)	(.52)	(.45)	(.42)	(.46)	parenting type	Atative > Diseng, Atarian
Scholastic competence:											
Wave 1	.22	.28	.04	.08	−.26	−.56	.13	−.35	−.26	Family type,	Nondiv > Div, Rem;
	(.68)	(.47)	(.73)	(.77)	(.76)	(.86)	(.58)	(.51)	(.89)	parenting type	Atative > Diseng
Wave 2	.49	.00	−.11	−.08	−.16	−.41	.17	−.12	−.22	Family type,	Nondiv > Div;
	(.61)	(.58)	(.66)	(.87)	(.82)	(.66)	(.76)	(.51)	(.92)	parenting type	Atative > Diseng, Atarian
Wave 3	.50	−.08	.03	−.04	−.72	.08	−.15	−.16	−.09	Family type,	Nondiv > Div;
	(.53)	(.86)	(.70)	(.91)	(.75)	(.64)	(.73)	(.78)	(.61)	parenting type	Atative, Diseng > Atarian

Fathers' parenting:								
Externalizing:								
Wave 1	−.40	.00	.08	−.06	.26	.25	Family type,	Rem > Nondiv;
	(.49)	(.45)	(.58)	(.49)	(.31)	(.51)	parenting type	Atarian, Diseng > Atative
Wave 2	−.36	.40	−.25	−.06	.45	.21	Family type,	Rem > Nondiv;
	(.52)	(.56)	(.49)	(.54)	(.46)	(.59)	parenting type	Atarian > Diseng, Atative
Wave 3	−.37	.19	−.06	−.10	.57	.40	Family type,	Rem > Nondiv;
	(.48)	(.46)	(.68)	(.40)	(.33)	(.39)	parenting type	Atarian, Diseng > Atative
Social competence:								
Wave 1	.31	.09	.04	−.06	−.11	−.35	Family type,	Nondiv > Rem;
	(.38)	(.44)	(.48)	(.63)	(.36)	(.46)	parenting type	Atative > Diseng
Wave 2	.29	−.15	.14	.05	−.37	−.44	Family type,	Nondiv > Rem;
	(.43)	(.35)	(.53)	(.52)	(.30)	(.51)	parenting type	Atative > Diseng, Atarian
Wave 3	.35	−.21	−.13	−.08	−.36	−.34	Family type,	Nondiv > Rem;
	(.44)	(.41)	(.52)	(.46)	(.41)	(.46)	parenting type	Atative > Diseng, Atarian
Scholastic competence:								
Wave 1	.38	−.03	−.30	.02	−.40	−.12	Parenting type	Atative > Atarian, Diseng
	(.48)	(.75)	(.79)	(.76)	(.59)	(.73)		
Wave 2	.31	−.25	−.21	.19	−.22	−.28	Parenting type	Atative > Atarian, Diseng
	(.62)	(.50)	(.92)	(.62)	(.63)	(.97)		
Wave 3	.30	−.07	−.05	−.04	−.42	−.09	. . .	
	(.64)	(.53)	(.92)	(.76)	(.62)	(.64)		

NOTE.—Nondiv = Nondivorced; Div = Divorced; Rem = Remarried; Atative = Authoritative; Atarian = Authoritarian/Conflictual; Diseng = Disengaged.

TABLE 53

STANDARDIZED REGRESSION COEFFICIENTS RELATING COMPOSITE PARENTING DIMENSIONS TO COMPOSITE DIMENSIONS OF CHILD ADJUSTMENT

	NEGATIVITY			CONTROL			MONITORING			WARMTH		
	Wave 1	Wave 2	Wave 3	Wave 1	Wave 2	Wave 3	Wave 1	Wave 2	Wave 3	Wave 1	Wave 2	Wave 3
Mothers' parenting:												
Externalizing	.52***	.53***	.54***	−.02	−.10	−.13	−.21**	−.19*	−.23**	−.26***	−.28***	−.17*
Social competence	−.31***	−.26***	−.26***	.08	.09	.14	.27***	.23**	.29***	.50***	.45***	.42***
Scholastic competence	−.25***	−.23**	−.25**	.17*	.09	.12	.21**	.25***	.27***	.22**	.16*	.29***
Multivariate *df*	(3,193)	(3,174)	(3,154)									
Univariate *df*	(1,195)	(1,176)	(1,156)									
Fathers' parenting:												
Externalizing	.46***	.52***	.47***	.08	−.17	−.03	−.13	−.20*	−.20*	−.26**	−.39***	−.25**
Social competence	−.23**	−.24**	−.23*	.05	.22*	−.01	.18*	.34***	.27**	.41***	.49***	.39***
Scholastic competence	−.30***	−.24**	−.17	.03	.20*	−.07	.10	.36***	.22*	.11	.29**	.18
Multivariate *df*	(3,126)	(3,113)	(3,104)									
Univariate *df*	(1,128)	(1,115)	(1,106)									

* $p \le .05$.
** $p \le .01$.
*** $p \le .001$.

TABLE 54

STANDARDIZED REGRESSION COEFFICIENTS RELATING COMPOSITE SIBLING RELATIONSHIP DIMENSIONS TO COMPOSITE DIMENSIONS OF CHILD ADJUSTMENT

	SIBLING NEGATIVITY		
	Wave 1	Wave 2	Wave 3
Externalizing	.55***	.51[a]***	.57***
Social competence	−.41***	−.40[a]***	−.33***
Scholastic competence	−.14	−.05	−.02
Multivariate *df*	(3,149)	(3,138)	(3,118)
Univariate *df*	(1,151)	(1,140)	(1,120)
	SIBLING POSITIVITY		
	Wave 1	Wave 2	Wave 3
Externalizing	−.16*	−.19*	−.26**
Social competence	.34***	.45***	.47***
Scholastic competence	.21**	.16	.12

	EXTERNALIZING	SOCIAL COMPETENCE
Nondivorced boys	.70**	−.57*
Nondivorced girls	.66**	−.49**
Divorced boys	.16	−.01
Divorced girls	.39*	−.10
Remarried boys	.60*	−.54*
Remarried girls	.60*	−.61*

Multivariate, $F(15,368) = 1.80, p = .032$
Externalizing, $F(5,135) = 3.11, p = .011$
Social competence, $F(5,135) = 2.31, p = .047$

[a] Significant interaction between family types on regression slopes.
* $p \leq .05$.
** $p \leq .01$.
*** $p \leq .001$.

petence. Significant differences in regression slopes between family types were found at Wave 2 for negativity, indicating that, at this period, the associations between sibling negativity and children's externalizing and social competence were weaker for divorced families.

LONGITUDINAL ASSOCIATIONS BETWEEN FAMILY RELATIONSHIPS AND CHILDREN'S ADJUSTMENT

Our analyses of concurrent associations showed the different family types to be characterized more by their similarities than by their differences. In this section, we investigate transactions between family members and children over time, using cross-lagged regression analyses in which previous levels of behavior are partialed out. Because sample size was reduced by the inclusion of data from later waves, analyses were conducted separately for different family types, but with boys and girls combined. The resultant longitudinal *N*'s for these analyses of short-term (Wave 1 to Wave 2) and long-term (Wave 1 to Wave 3) change were, respectively, 73 and 68 nondivorced, 63 and 52 divorced, and 47 and 43 remarried families. In addition, the cross-lag regressions were limited to those between the negativity dimensions and externalizing and to those between the positivity dimensions and social competence because these had emerged as being the most important relations in the earlier analyses. Transactions between the negativity or positivity of mothers, fathers, and siblings and children's externalizing and social competence, respectively, were examined separately. In addition, cross-lagged regressions were conducted separately for short-term (Wave 1 to Wave 2) and long-term (Wave 1 to Wave 3) effects.

In all models, most of the variation in parenting or sibling relationships and children's adjustment was accounted for by previous levels of functioning. However, concurrent correlations between family members' negativity or positivity and children's externalizing or social competence remained significant. These were smaller at later waves because of the large autocorrelation with previous levels of functioning, implying that some of the variance in the concurrent correlations resulted from the previous history of family functioning. Although we discuss all the models, only those in which significant cross-lagged effects were found are depicted in the figures; the coefficients shown on the cross-lagged paths indicate whether the given variable had a significant effect after accounting for the level of previous functioning.

In both nondivorced and divorced families, stability, rather than change, in family relationships and in children's adjustment was the general rule. In divorced families, no significant longitudinal transactions of any kind were identified, but large autocorrelations were found in all cases. The single significant transactional finding in nondivorced families indicated that prior maternal negativity affected later child externalizing, but only in the short term (Fig. 3). Thus, the longitudinal effects of family members on one another appeared greatly reduced in comparison to the concurrent effects, particularly when one considers how significant the latter were in the associations between father and child as well as in sibling relationships and in both the externalizing and the social competence of children.

In remarried families, by contrast, longitudinal transactions prevailed between children's externalizing and family members' negativity as well as between children's social competence and family members' positivity. Specifically, stepchildren's externalizing appeared to be affecting changes in the negativity expressed by their stepfathers, at least in the short term (Fig. 4). Similarly, these children's social competence appeared to be affecting

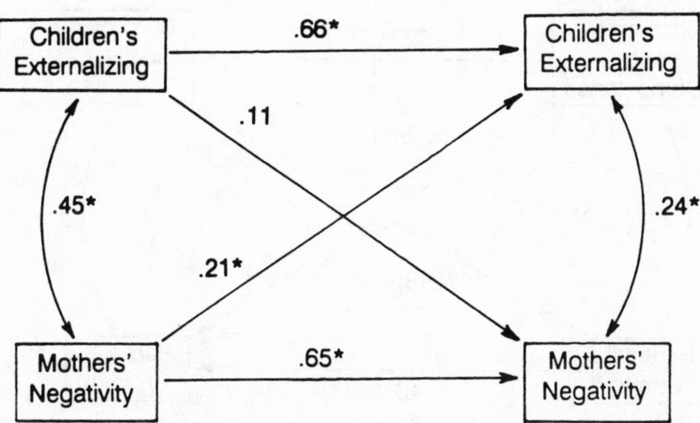

FIG. 3.—Cross-lagged regression model (Wave 1 × Wave 2) with maternal negativity and children's externalizing for nondivorced families (* $p \leq .05$).

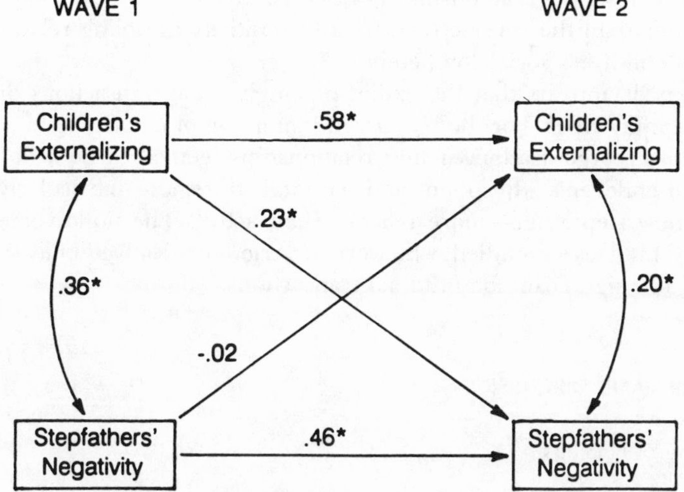

FIG. 4.—Cross-lagged regression model with paternal negativity and children's externalizing for remarried families (* $p \leq .05$).

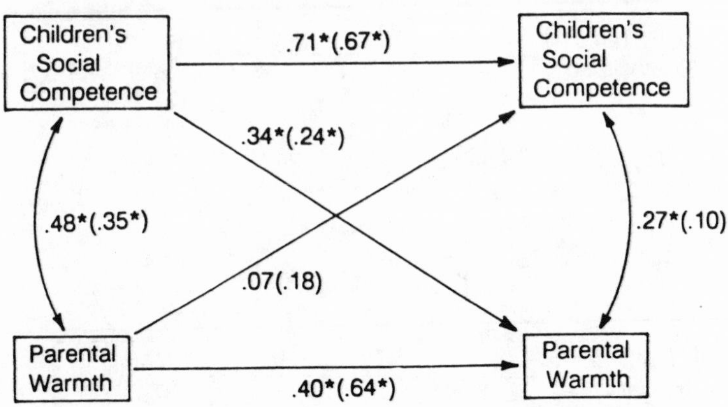

FIG. 5.—Cross-lagged regression model with parental warmth and children's social competence for remarried families. Coefficients for mothers are listed first, followed by coefficients for stepfathers in parentheses (* $p \leq .05$).

changes in the warmth and positivity expressed by both their stepfathers and their mothers (Fig. 5).

Significant transactions between siblings and children were also identified for remarried families both in the short term and in the long term. Negativity in sibling relationships affected children's subsequent externalizing, rather than the reverse (Fig. 6), and positivity in sibling relationships affected children's social competence (Fig. 7).

Thus, it appears that the extent of longitudinal transactions differed among family types. For the remarried families in our study, still undergoing family reorganization, sibling relationships seemed to be a dominant factor in children's adjustment and parental strategies—particularly those of the new stepfather—more reactive than active. The nondivorced and divorced families we studied, who were in periods of relative family stability, showed few significant longitudinal transactions.

SUMMARY AND DISCUSSION

Overview of Findings

With respect to family processes and children's adjustment, several of our findings were notable, and we summarize these first.

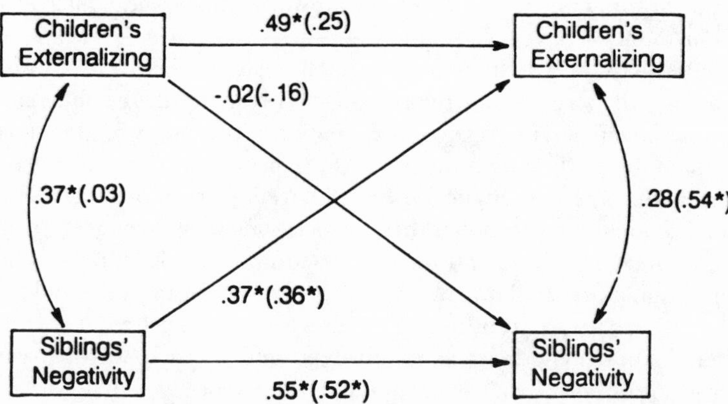

FIG. 6.—Cross-lagged regression model with sibling negativity and children's externalizing for remarried families. Coefficients for Wave 2 are listed first, followed by coefficients for Wave 3 in parentheses (* $p \leq .05$).

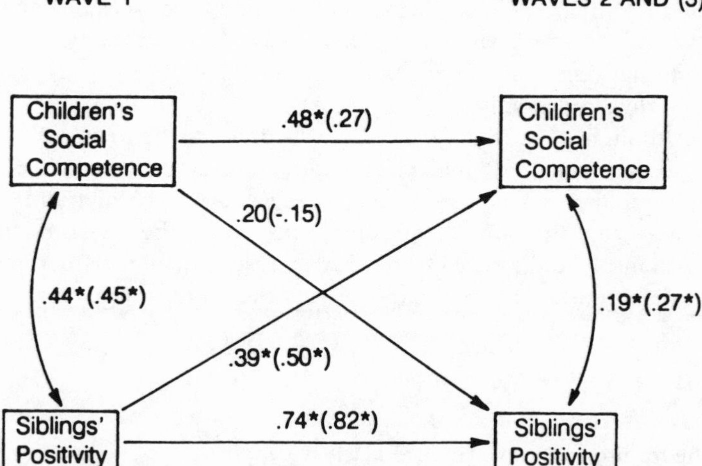

FIG. 7.—Cross-lagged regression model with sibling positivity and children's social competence for remarried families. Coefficients for Wave 2 are listed first, followed by coefficients for Wave 3 in parentheses (* $p \leq .05$).

1. In the analyses of concurrent relations between the quality of family relationships and children's adjustment, few interactions with either family type or children's gender were identified. That is, children's adjustment and marital, parent-child, and sibling relationships functioned similarly across different family types.

2. Positivity and negativity in marital relationships were consistently associated with parent-child relationships. Negativity in the marriage was related to negativity in parent-child relationships and to higher levels of parental control, whereas positivity was associated with warmth in parent-child relationships and higher levels of parental monitoring. Although a few interactions suggested that these associations were strongest for nondivorced families with boys and for remarried families with girls, the pattern was predominantly similar across family types and for mothers and fathers.

3. Authoritative parenting emerged as a strong concurrent correlate of children's adjustment in each family type and at each wave, predicting higher levels of both social and scholastic competence as well as lower levels of externalizing behavior in all children regardless of family type. With regard to specific dimensions of parent-child relationships, warmth and monitoring and (in the opposite direction) parental negativity were consistently related to children's externalizing, social competence, and scholastic competence. Absence of interactions with family type indicated that these parenting dimensions were related to children's adjustment in similar ways across family types and children's gender and for both mothers and fathers.

4. The quality of sibling relationships also correlated significantly with children's adjustment in all family types. Negativity in this relationship was associated with higher externalizing behavior and lower social competence, and positivity was associated with more socially competent behavior and lower externalizing. Some interactions indicated that these associations were weaker in divorced families.

5. Although analyses of concurrent associations between family relationship dimensions and children's adjustment indicated that family types were more similar than different, some of the analyses of longitudinal transactions suggested that long-term associations among these factors differed as a function of family type. In particular, results obtained for remarried families diverged from those characterizing the other two groups.

Discussion

The findings we have reported clearly support the view that, regardless of family circumstances, the quality of the marital relationship is linked to the quality of both the mother's and the father's relationships with their children. The pervasively beneficial effects of authoritative parenting were also reemphasized by our results. Regardless of family type, gender of child, or gender of parent, warmth, support, involvement, and monitoring were consistently related to high levels of social competence, and absence of coercion, conflict, and negativity were associated with lower levels of externalizing behavior and higher levels of social and scholastic competence in children.

The quality of sibling relationships was also consistently associated with children's adjustment across all family types. However, cross-lagged panel regression analysis suggested that sibling relationships directly affected later child outcomes only for children in remarried families. This finding warrants further research on sibling relationships during family transitions, in which the potential confounds of the siblings' gender, age differences, and different experiences could be investigated.

Family factors and family process are evidently important contributors to the long-term adjustment of children; however, our findings indicate a need for caution in making assumptions about the direction of effects: the types of transactions occurring across family subsystems may differ depending on family type. Undergoing family transitions may alter not only the level of stress experienced by individual family members but also the manner in which each affects the adjustment of the others. Thus, a disruptive, aggressive, noncompliant early adolescent may have a larger effect on parenting in remarried families than in nondivorced families, particularly for the stepfather. Results from the cross-lagged regression results suggested that stepchildren's externalizing and socially competent behavior were driving changes in the parenting of their new stepfathers and that children's socially competent behavior also affected changes in warmth expressed by mothers in remarried families. Thus, during the period of reorganization accompanying remarriage, parental strategies may become more reactive than active, a view supported by the absence of any such effects in the nondivorced and divorced families, who were in periods of relative stability.

Further evidence for differences among family types with regard to child-driven effects can be found in analyses that have been reported by Deal, Anderson, Ratliff, Hetherington, and Clingempeel (1990). These researchers applied the Social Relations Model[5] (Kenny & LaVoie, 1984) to

[5] This method is merely a special case of the more general multimethod/multitrait model where variance is partitioned into components attributable to method and trait. In this case, each individual is observed in a round-robin format with every other individual, which allows the different "traits" (actor, partner) to be observed in mutually exclusive "methods" (dyads, in this case). It should be noted, however, that, in a round-robin design with only three individuals (mother, father, child), the relationship in the Social Relations Model cannot be uniquely separated from the error term (Kenny & LaVoie, 1984) and hence is a limitation of this design.

the observational data obtained in this study in an attempt to disentangle confounds of actor and partner effects. For example, although remarried mothers displayed more negative behavior toward their children than biological mothers (see Chap. V), it could be that this negative behavior was elicited by the children rather than reflecting remarried mothers' predisposition toward them. In the Social Relations Model, which provides a method for partitioning such different effects, a child's behavior toward the mother is construed as comprising (*a*) the child's actor effect, (*b*) the mother's partner effect, (*c*) the mother-child relationship effect, and (*d*) random error or disturbance. Most central to this discussion are actor effects (the behavior that a person exhibits regardless of the partner) and partner effects (the behavior that a person tends to elicit from others). In this study, children's actor effects were derived from the child-mother and child-father scores, but mothers' partner effects were derived from the child-mother and father-mother scores. Thus, each component was uniquely identified by a combination of scores.

Significant child actor and child partner effects were identified in this Social Relations analysis of our observational data, and both these effects were significantly greater in remarried than in nondivorced families. Not only were children in remarried families acting significantly more negatively toward their parents than were children in nondivorced families, but they also *elicited* more negative behavior from them. Thus, the higher levels of negative behavior displayed by mothers and stepfathers resulted in part from children eliciting or provoking such behavior. A recent review by Lytton (1990) suggests that, as children grow older, they play an increasingly powerful role in shaping parental behavior and that this is particularly true with respect to externalizing, conduct-disorder problems.

Analyses of change scores in this data set (Hetherington et al., 1991) provided a third source of support for postulating child-driven effects specific to remarried families. In these analyses, change scores in children's externalizing and observed negativity (Wave 1 to Wave 3) were used to predict the four composite dimensions of parenting—warmth/involvement, negativity, control, and monitoring—at Wave 3. Effects of concurrent problem behavior were accounted for by entering Wave 3 externalizing or negativity into the equation prior to the change scores. These results suggested that nondivorced mothers and fathers responded to increases in adolescents' externalizing with higher levels of warmth and involvement and to increases in adolescent-to-father negativity with greater control attempts. Alternatively, remarried parents seemed to be responding to adolescents' increased externalizing with fewer attempts at control. These results support the claim that changes in the children's behavior are associated with different types of parental responses, depending on the family situation.

Further research is warranted to investigate the different ways in which adolescents' behavior shapes parenting. It may be that current top-down models of family process, in which positive marital relationships serve as the cornerstone for adaptive family functioning and especially for positive parenting, need to be altered to account for differences in family processes in remarried and divorced families. We had expected that the differences in the quality of family relationships across nondivorced, divorced, and remarried families would account for most of the differences in children's adjustment that were reported in Chapter III. They did not, however, and it therefore appears that children's adjustment is not entirely a function of differences in the quality of family relationships, although the negative effects associated with nonsupportive or conflictual sibling relationships appeared to have a more lasting effect on the adjustment of children in remarried families. In our speculation, one of the effects of family transition is children's increased vulnerability to socialization forces outside the family. This may be especially true for the age range studied here. Although there was generally a great deal of stability in children's adjustment over time, children in remarried families demonstrated less stable behavior than children in nondivorced families. It may be that the experience of one or more family transitions during early adolescence accelerates the normative adolescent process of individuation, and, as a result, factors other than family relationships become more critical for children in such families. In addition, factors associated with the parents' divorce, such as continued contact or conflict with the noncustodial parent, may also play an important role for children in these families.

VIII. SUMMARY AND DISCUSSION

E. Mavis Hetherington

CHARACTERISTICS OF DIVORCED AND REMARRIED FAMILIES

Our findings suggest that the course of adaptation to remarriage in stepfather families with an early adolescent child is a difficult one: little improvement in either the adjustment of children or stepfather-stepchild relationships was seen in the 26 months covered by our study. Moreover, the disruptions in family functioning were found to be pervasive and to extend beyond parent-child relationships to nonsupportive or even antagonistic sibling relationships. This stands in marked contrast to studies of divorce (e.g., Hetherington et al., 1982) and remarriage in families with younger children, where considerable positive change in family relationships and in children's behavior occurred within the first two years following a marital transition (Bray, 1987; Hetherington, 1988, 1989).

The Marital Relationship

In the face of disruptions in other family subsystems, it is remarkable that remarried women and their husbands were able to sustain a satisfying relationship. Developing a strong marital bond while negotiating changes in other family roles and relationships, especially parent-child relationships, has been identified as a major task for remarried couples (Bray, 1990; Hetherington, 1988; McGoldrick & Carter, 1980). Our remarried husbands and wives seemed to be dealing with this challenge well. Initially, in the honeymoon period following the remarriage, these couples expressed more satisfaction with their relationships than couples in never-divorced families did. Over time, however, the remarried couples' responses became similar to those of nondivorced couples, and, by Wave 3, few differences between groups were obtained. Given the difficulties that the remarried couples were confronting in parent-child relationships, acrimonious sibling relationships, and the behavior problems of their adolescent children, a high level of commitment to sustaining the marriage in these early years was suggested. Nevertheless, remarried couples did indicate higher levels of dysphoria than nondivorced spouses, which suggests that these stressors were not without effect.

Parent-Child and Sibling Relationships

The most difficult interpersonal challenges in stepfamily relations lay in the development of a constructive relationship between parents and children. Mothers in remarried families seemed able eventually to renegotiate their relationships with their children. Although remarried mothers and their children initially manifested higher levels of conflict and the mothers manifested lower levels of monitoring and control than nondivorced mothers, mother-child relationships in remarried families appeared similar to those in nondivorced families by Wave 3.

The complexity and ambiguity of society's definition of the stepfathers' role as well as the multiple challenges that stepfathers encounter have frequently been noted (Bray, 1990; Hetherington, 1989), suggesting that the course of adjustment is more difficult for these parents. Our stepfathers were trying to maintain a gratifying marital relationship while confronting wives they perceived as exhibiting little control over their children, quarrelsome siblings, and suspicious, resentful, antisocial stepchildren. It is perhaps not surprising that a disengaged parenting style characterized by low levels of involvement and rapport, little control over the stepchildren's behavior, lack of awareness of their activities, and little exertion of discipline was more common among stepfathers than among biological fathers.

At the outset, stepfathers appeared like polite strangers—they attempted to become involved, disclosed things about themselves, asked questions of the children, and remained relatively warm. Because the response of their stepchildren to such overtures was often more negative than that of children in nondivorced families, and because stepchildren exhibited higher levels of problem behaviors, it appears that many stepfathers eventually gave up attempting to engage and form a close relationship with their stepchildren.

The negative behavior of the stepchildren proved more effective in shaping the stepfathers' behavior than stepfathers were in altering negative behavior in their new stepchildren. When antisocial behavior in children became more frequent, stepfathers were unable to respond in a manner likely to reduce this behavior and became even less controlling. However, in spite of the influence exerted by stepchildren's behavior on stepfathers' parenting, authoritative parenting by the stepfather (in contrast to a disengaged or conflictual/authoritarian style) was associated—as it was for all parents—with greater competence and less externalizing in children even in the initial stage of the remarriage. This stands in contrast to findings with younger children where stepfathers found it advantageous first to establish a warm relationship with their new stepchildren while supporting the mother's discipline and only gradually to exert control and more authoritative parenting (Hetherington, 1989).

Anderson and White (1986) suggested that the quality of the children's relationships with their biological mothers should be especially important in remarried families. They reported that functional stepfamilies differed from functional nondivorced families in showing a close relationship between the biological mother and the child and a more distant one between the stepfather and child. In our study, we obtained no evidence that either mothers' or fathers' warmth and closeness with their children was associated differently with the latter's adjustment or with family functioning in nondivorced and in remarried families.

Even though our one-parent households were stabilized, reports from sons and observers supported previous findings of greater negativity and less control on the part of divorced, as compared to nondivorced, mothers of sons. Furthermore, although divorced mothers were actively involved with their children, conflict over adolescent issues such as alcohol and drug use, curfew, and dating or sexual activities and increased maternal efforts at control and monitoring emerged as the children moved into adolescence. By Wave 3, the comparatively greater degree of monitoring and control exerted by divorced mothers occurred only with girls; however, the extent of maternal negativity/conflict was similar with both sons and daughters in Waves 2 and 3. This supports reports that puberty often brings difficulties to a previously congenial relationship between mothers and daughters in divorced households (Hetherington, 1989; Kalter, 1977; Wallerstein et al., 1988). Although a similar pattern of increased conflict between mothers and daughters was present in nondivorced families, this declined by Wave 3.

These findings for early adolescent children contrast with studies of younger children in which divorced mothers have been found to exhibit lower levels of monitoring and control, in comparison to nondivorced mothers, and to have close congenial relationships with daughters but not sons (Hetherington et al., 1982). It has been suggested that the monitoring and control attempts of divorced mothers seen in the current study could be a response elicited by their adolescent daughters' antisocial behavior. However, the cross-lagged panel analyses showed no significant longitudinal transactions between parenting and externalizing in divorced families. Difficulty in adapting to the new stepfamily situation was also reflected in greater negativity and less positivity in sibling relations in stepfamilies compared to nondivorced families, and the quality of sibling relations played an important role in shaping subsequent adjustment in stepchildren.

THE RELATION BETWEEN PARENTING AND EARLY ADOLESCENT ADJUSTMENT

One of the notable findings in this study was the absence of either gender or family-type differences in the associations between parenting and children's adjustment. Authoritative parenting by both mothers and fathers was associated with better outcomes for both boys and girls and in all family types. Negativity and positivity in parenting showed the most pervasive relations with children's adjustment, by being associated with their externalizing behavior, social competence, and academic achievement; fathers' warmth was less consistently related to academic competence than was mothers' warmth.

There were few relations found between parental control and children's adjustment. If children have not established internal controls by early adolescence, it may be too late for externally imposed controls to be effective. Parental rule setting seems to be more important with younger children (Baumrind, 1991; Hetherington, 1988). It has been suggested that parental monitoring—knowing where children are, whom they are with, and what they are doing—becomes increasingly important in adolescence (Baumrind, 1991; Patterson & Bank, 1989). In our study, significant relations between maternal monitoring and children's externalizing and social and academic competence were obtained at all three waves. The effects for fathers' monitoring were somewhat delayed, emerging only in Waves 2 and 3. Thus, warm, supportive, noncoercive parents who monitored their adolescents' behavior but granted them considerable autonomy seemed to have the most well-adjusted children.

The scarcity of family type × gender interactions in analyses of our early adolescent children's adjustment was unexpected in view of the prevalence of such effects in studies of younger children (Emery, 1982; Hetherington, 1988; Zaslow, 1988, 1989). In this study, girls were usually perceived to be more well adjusted than boys, and children in divorced or remarried families were seen as less well adjusted than those in nondivorced families. These perceptions differed somewhat with the identity of the informant. Thus, while parents reported high levels of problem behavior for children in both divorced and remarried families, teachers tended to view only children from the divorced single-parent homes as exhibiting higher levels of problem behavior, and even these differences were not consistently reported across waves. However, the children from divorced families reported higher levels of delinquent activity than children from nondivorced homes. In nearly all comparisons that proved statistically significant, children from the nontraditional families appeared to be less competent and to have higher levels of deviant behavior than children from nondivorced families. These differences were most frequently found in the case of children in remarried families. Furthermore, few of these problems declined over time. That is, little adaptation was seen in the behavior of children over the 26-month course of this study.

MARITAL TRANSITIONS AND CHILDREN'S ADJUSTMENT

Even when their parents were authoritative, children in remarried and divorced families showed less optional adjustment than those in nondivorced families. This suggests that factors beyond the quality of parenting played an important role in effecting differences in the adjustment of these adolescents. The quality of the sibling relationship was one such factor established by our findings. We focused only on family relationships within the household; however, other studies have shown that relationships outside the family—with peers, grandparents, and noncustodial parents—can influence the adjustment of children in divorced and remarried families as well (Baumrind, 1991; Camara & Resnick, 1988; Hetherington, 1989).

Furthermore, it has been proposed that the normative changes and stresses encountered by children as they enter adolescence may be exacerbated by their parents' marital transitions (Hetherington & Anderson, 1987). As the early adolescent child's demands for autonomy increase, parents become increasingly disengaged, less controlling, and emotionally involved and spend less time with the child (Baumrind, 1991). Moreover, heightened conflict often tends to accompany this early surge of independence on the part of the child. For remarried and divorced mothers, this pattern of disengagement from their children may be accelerated and accompanied by more pronounced conflict and negative affect, and autonomy may occur earlier in children who go through their parents' divorce and spend time in a one-parent household (Weiss, 1979). The introduction of a stepfather may further complicate problems in the development of autonomy or lead to a precipitous or inappropriate disengagement from the family (Hetherington, 1989).

A second area in which the experience of parental divorce and remarriage may contribute to disruptions in adolescents' development is that of intimate relationships and sexuality. Many investigators have commented on the precocious sexual activity and concerns shown by children in divorced, mother-headed families (Hetherington, 1989; Newcomer & Udry, 1987;

Wallerstein & Kelly, 1982). This may be attributable in part to the poor control and monitoring of preadolescent children demonstrated by some divorced mothers. It may also follow as a consequence of the divorced spouses' use of their children as informants about each other's dating and sexual behavior and of children's exposure to multiple intimate relationships of their divorced parents (Wallerstein & Kelly, 1982). The introduction of a stepfather in early adolescence, a time when children are themselves becoming physically mature, may also heighten their sensitivity to issues of intimate relations. Many nondivorced fathers are disconcerted by their daughters' burgeoning sexuality (Hill et al., 1985a), and this problem may be more severe in the case of stepfathers and stepdaughters. The higher rates of sexual abuse in stepfamilies suggests that sometimes this problem is dealt with unsuccessfully (Parker & Parker, 1986).

As noted earlier, most of our measures showed that children from divorced and remarried families demonstrated problems of adjustment, especially in the form of externalizing disorders, that continued over the 26-month course of the study. Other studies have found that, even in long-established divorced and remarried families, behavior problems may emerge when the child reaches early adolescence (Baumrind, 1989; Bray, 1990; Hetherington, 1989). Thus, adolescence may be not only a time in which it is difficult for children to adjust to their parents' new marital transitions but also one that triggers latent problems in their social relationships and adjustment.

Although our findings indicate that it may be particularly difficult for children to deal with their parents' marital transitions during adolescence, our lack of evidence for positive adaptation may have been a function of the design of the study, in that 26 months may have provided insufficient time in which to adjust. The work of Hetherington (1989) and of Bray (1990) shows that younger children were able to adjust to their parents' remarriage in 2–2½ years, suggesting different sensitivities that are related to age. When remarriage occurs in early adolescence, adjustment appears to occur more slowly, and it may not take place at all.

The way children respond to their current family situation depends on preceding family relationships and experience. Children who enter a stepfamily face yet another in a series of family transitions. Many such children, particularly boys, may still be showing adjustment problems associated with the previous transition of divorce and of life in a single-mother home. In fact, it has been speculated that the difficulties that characterize children in remarried homes are largely attributable to their earlier experience of divorce (Furstenberg, 1988), and a recent study found that some behavior problems attributed to the divorce were already shown by children in the conflictual predivorce family (Cherlin, Chase-Lansdale, Furstenberg, Kiernan, & Robins, 1991). Our results indicated that children in remarried homes tended to exhibit more behavior problems than those in divorced homes; thus, as has been reported by Capaldi and Patterson (1991), there may be a linear increase in problem behavior associated with multiple family transitions.

With further advance into adolescence, many youngsters may find supports outside the home—in the neighborhood, school, work place, or peer groups—that are not available to younger children and that are able to buffer the experience of multiple family reorganizations or adverse family relationships. Previous work by Hetherington (1989) and by Patterson and his colleagues (Patterson, DeBaryshe, & Ramsey, 1989) supports the notion that social and academic competencies can provide a positive counter to the negative effects of disruptive family relationships. Hence, the disengagement reported to occur in about one-third of adolescent children who are confronting their parents' marital transitions may be a constructive way of coping with a stressful family situation when other sources of social and emotional gratification are available (Hetherington, 1989). However, other research has indicated that involvement on the part of a caring adult is critical for children in high-risk situations (Hetherington, 1989; Werner & Smith, 1982). In the case of children who disengage from their divorced or remarried families, this role may be played by the noncustodial parent, a grandparent, a teacher, or a neighbor (Hetherington, 1989); becoming attached to the family of a friend can also have salutary effects. Disengagement accompanied by high involvement in peer activities with no concomitant adult monitoring is more likely to be associated with the development of deviant behavior (Hetherington, 1989).

This *Monograph* has focused on relationships within the family and on their contributions to the adjustment of children who must cope with their parents' marital transitions. A broader ecological perspective that involves both familial and extrafamilial factors will be examined in future work and should yield further understanding of the diversity of children's responses to their parents' divorce or remarriage.

APPENDIX A

TABLE A1

SUMMARY OF INSTRUMENTS USED IN THIS REPORT

Instrument	No. of Items	Respondents/ Waves	Scales/Factors	Scale/ Range
I. Demographic measures: Eight measures constructed from items taken from Zill & Furstenberg (1981)		Mo123; Fa123		
II. Child adjustment measures:				
A. Child Behavior Checklist (Achenbach & Edelbrock, 1983):				
i. Part I	91	Mo123; Fa123; T123[a]	Standardized scales	*T* scores
			Internalizing	
			Externalizing	
			Total problem behaviors	
2. Part II	13	Mo123; Fa123	Standardized scales:	*T* scores
			Social competence	
			School scale	
B. Child Competence Inventory (adapted from Baumrind, 1979a, Q Sort)	56	Mo123; Fa123; C123	Derived through data reduction:	
			Social responsibility	1–4
			Cognitive agency	1–4
			Sociability	1–4
			Energetic/attractive/popular	1–4
C. Perceived Competence Scale for Children (Harter, 1982)	28	T123[a]	Standardized scales:	
			Scholastic competence	1–4
			Social competence	1–4
			Physical competence	1–4
			General self-worth	1–4
D. Behavior Events Inventory (adapted from Patterson, 1982, 24-Hour Behavior Checklist)	31	Mo123; Fa123; C123	Derived through data reduction:	
			Prosocial behavior (Mo, Fa, C)	0–1[b]
			Coercive behavior (Mo, Fa, C)	0–1[b]
			Depression (Mo, Fa, C)	0–1[b]
			Delinquent behavior (C)	0–1[b]

Measure	Items	Respondents	Scales	Range
III. Adult adjustment measure, Beck Depression Inventory (Beck, 1967)	21	Mo123; Fa123	Depression (total summed score)	0–21
IV. Marital relationship measures:				
A. Dyadic Adjustment scale (Spanier, 1976)	32	Mo123; Fa123	Standardized scales:	
			Satisfaction	0–20
			Expressiveness	0–12
			Consensus	0–60
			Cohesiveness	0–23
			Overall marital satisfaction	0–115
B. Child-rearing Issues: Self and Spouse (constructed for this study)	22	Mo123; Fa123	Derived through data reduction:	
			Conflict over daily routines	9–63
			Conflict over adolescent issues	8–56
C. Child-rearing Roles (Baumrind, 1979b)	7	Mo123; Fa123	Only first item used:	
			Relative husband/wife responsibility for child-rearing tasks	1–5
D. Housekeeping Roles (Baumrind, 1979b)	7	Mo123; Fa123	Only first item used:	
			Relative husband/wife responsibility for housekeeping tasks	1–5
V. Parent-child relationship measures:				
A. Expression of Affection (Patterson, 1982)	19	Mo123; Fa123; C123[c]	Derived through data reduction:	
			Expressive affection	7–49
			Instrumental affection	7–56
B. Assessment of Child Monitoring (Baumrind, 1978, 1979b)	Mo6; Fa6; C7	Mo123; Fa123; C123[c]	Derived through data reduction:	
			Monitoring: Character development	4–20
			Monitoring: Deviant behavior	3–15
			Control: Character development	4–20
			Control: Deviant behavior	3–15

TABLE A1 (*Continued*)

Instrument	No. of Items	Respondents/ Waves	Scales/Factors	Scale/ Range
C. Child-rearing Issues: Parent and Child (constructed for this study)	37	Mo123;	Derived through data reduction:	
		Fa123;	Conflict over daily routines	9–63
		C123[c]	Conflict over adolescent issues	8–56
			Discipline: Use of communication	6–42
			Discipline: Negative sanctions	10–70
D. Parenting Practices (constructed for this study)	10	Mo123;	Derived through data reduction:	
		Fa123	Rapport	6–30
IV. Sibling relationship measure: Sibling Inventory of Behavior (expanded version of Schaefer & Edgerton's, 1981, Sibling Inventory of Behavior)	49	Mo123;	Derived through data reduction:	
		Fa123;	Involvement	1–5
		C123	Empathy	1–5
			Rivalry	1–5
			Avoidance	1–5
			Aggression	1–5
			Teaching	1–5

NOTE.—Mo = Mother/Wife; Fa = Father/Husband; C = Child; T = Teacher; 1 = Wave 1; 2 = Wave 2; 3 = Wave 3. For example, Mo123 = Mother/Wife responded at all three waves. Full tables including alphas for each factor are available from the authors.

[a] Teacher data were not available for children in single-mother families at Wave 3.

[b] Percentages of items endorsed, averaged across all visits within a wave.

[c] Child completed this measure twice: once about his or her mother and once about his or her (step)father.

TABLE A2

Composition of Within- and Across-Wave Composite Variables

Dimension	Alphas for Composites: Wave 1	Wave 2	Wave 3	Child Adjustment Composites: Assessment Instruments	Scales	Informants
Externalizing	.80	.82	.72	Child Behavior Checklist	Externalizing	Mother, father, teachers
				Behavior Events Checklist	Coercive behavior	Mother, father, target child
					Delinquent behavior	Target child
				Observational coding	Antisocial behavior: Target child to mother; Target child to father; Target child to sibling	Observer
Social competence	.71	.66	.65	Child Behavior Checklist	Social competence	Mother, father
				Child Competence Inventory	Social responsibility	Mother, father, target child
				Perceived Competence Scale for Children	Social competence	Teachers
				Behavior Events Inventory	Prosocial behavior	Mother, father, target child
				Observational coding	Prosocial behavior: Target child to mother; Target child to father; Target child to sibling	Observer
Scholastic competence	.81	.71	.78	Child Behavior Checklist	School scale	Mother, father
				Child Competence Inventory	Cognitive agency	Mother, father, target child
				Perceived Competence Scale for Children	Scholastic competence	Teachers
				Marital Relationship Composites		
Positivity: Spouses' positivity to each other	.72	.61	.51	Spanier Dyadic Adjustment scale	Marital satisfaction	Wife, husband
				Observational coding	Positivity: Wife to husband; Husband to wife	Observer
Negativity: Spouses' negativity to each other	.75	.61	.66	Conflict: Child-rearing Issues	Marital conflict	Wife, husband
				Observational coding	Negativity: Wife to husband; Husband to wife	Observer

TABLE A2 (*Continued*)

Dimension	Alphas for Composites			Parent-Child Relationship Composites[a]		
	Wave 1	Wave 2	Wave 3	Assessment Instruments	Scales	Informants
Positivity/warmth:						
Mothers	.70	.67	.71	Expression of Affection	Expressive affection	Mother, target child (about mother)
				Parenting Practices	Rapport	Mother, target child (about mother)
				Observational coding	Positivity: Mother to target child	Observer
Fathers	.75	.80	.72	Expression of Affection	Expressive affection	Father, target child (about father)
				Parenting Practices	Rapport	Father, target child (about father)
				Observational coding	Positivity	Observer
Control:						
Mothers	.59	.71	.61	Assessment of Child Monitoring	Control of:	
					Character development	Mother, target child (about mother), father (about mother)
					Deviant behavior	Mother, target child (about mother), father (about mother)
				Observational coding	Dominance/Power: Mother to child	Observer
					Parental influence: Mother to child	Observer
Fathers	.78	.78	.76	Assessment of Child Monitoring	Control of:	
					Character development	Father, target child (about father), mother (about father)
					Deviant behavior	Father, target child (about father), mother (about father)
				Observational coding	Dominance/power: Father to child	Observer
					Parental influence: Father to child	Observer

Monitoring:						
Mothers	.73	.74	.69	Assessment of Child Monitoring	Monitoring of:	
					Character development	Mother, target child (about mother), father (about mother)
					Deviant behavior	Mother, target child (about mother), father (about mother)
				Observational coding	Monitoring: Mother to target child	Observer
Fathers	.73	.74	.69	Assessment of Child Monitoring	Monitoring of:	
					Character development	Father, target child (about father), mother (about father)
					Deviant behavior	Father, target child (about father), mother (about father)
				Observational coding	Monitoring: Father to target child	Observer
Negativity/conflict:						
Mothers	.78	.85	.74	Child-rearing Issues	Discipline:	
					Communication	Mother, target child (about mother)
					Negative sanctions	Mother, target child (about mother)
					Conflict:	
					Daily routines	Mother, target child (about mother)
					Adolescent issues	Mother, target child (about mother)
				Observational coding	Negativity: Mother to target child	Observer
Fathers	.80	.82	.81	Child-rearing Issues	Discipline:	
					Communication	Father, target child (about father)
					Negative sanctions	Father, target child (about father)
					Conflict:	
					Daily routines	Father, target child (about father)
					Adolescent issues	Father, target child (about father)
				Observational coding	Negativity: Father to target child	Observer

TABLE A2 (*Continued*)

Dimension	Alphas for Composites			Sibling Relationship Composites		
	Wave 1	Wave 2	Wave 3	Assessment of Instruments	Scales	Informants
Positivity	.78	.80	.83	Sibling Inventory of Behavior	Involvement	Mother, father, target child
					Empathy	Mother, father, target child
					Teaching	Mother, father, target child
				Observational coding	Positivity:	Observer
					Target child to sibling	
					Sibling to target child	
Negativity	.87	.84	.86	Sibling Inventory of Behavior	Rivalry	Mother, father, target child
					Avoidance	Mother, father, target child
					Aggression	Mother, father, target child
				Observational coding	Negativity:	Observer
					Target child to sibling	
					Sibling to target child	

[a] Separate composites were created for mother-child and (step)father-child relationships.

TABLE A3

SCALES INCLUDED IN EACH MULTIPLE ANALYSIS OF VARIANCE (MANOVA)

	CHILD ADJUSTMENT DIMENSIONS		
DIMENSION	Informant	Assessment Instruments	Scales
Externalizing	Parents[a]	Child Behavior Checklist	Externalizing
		Behavior Events Inventory	Coercive behavior
	Target child	Behavior Events Inventory	Coercive behavior
			Delinquent behavior
	Teachers	Child Behavior Checklist	Externalizing[b]
	Observer	Observational coding system	Antisocial behavior:
			Target child to mother
			Target child to father
			Target child to sibling
Internalizing	Parents[a]	Child Behavior Checklist	Internalizing
		Behavior Events Inventory	Depression
	Target child	Behavior Events Inventory	Depression[b]
	Teachers	Child Behavior Checklist	Internalizing
Social Competence	Parents[a]	Child Behavior Checklist	Social competence
		Behavior Events Inventory	Prosocial behavior
		Child Competence Inventory	Social responsibility
			Sociability
			Energetic/attractive/popular
	Target child	Behavior Events Inventory	Prosocial behavior
		Child Competence Inventory	Social responsibility
			Sociability
			Energetic/attractive/popular
	Teachers	Perceived Competence Scale for Children	Social competence
			Global self-worth
	Observer	Observational coding system	Prosocial:
			Target child to mother
			Target child to father
			Target child to sibling

TABLE A3 (*Continued*)

Dimension	Informant	Assessment Instruments	Scales
		Sibling Relationship Dimensions	
Scholastic competence . .	Parents[a]	Child Behavior Checklist	School scale
		Child Competence Inventory	Cognitive agency
	Target child	Child Competence Inventory	Cognitive agency[b]
	Teachers	Perceived Competence Scale for Children	Cognitive agency[b]
		Marital Relationship Dimensions	
Positivity	Spouses[a]	Dyadic Adjustment scale	Marital satisfaction[b]
	Observer	Observational coding system	Positivity:
			Mother to father
			Father to mother
Negativity	Spouses[a]	Child-rearing Issues	Conflict over daily routines
			Conflict over adolescent issues
		Family Conflict	Overall marital conflict[b]
	Observer	Observational coding system	Negativity:
			Mother to father
			Father to mother
Roles	Spouses[a]	Child-rearing Roles	Responsibility for child rearing
		Housekeeping Roles	Responsibility for housekeeping
		Parent-Child Relationship Dimensions	
Warmth	Parents[a]	Expression of Affection	Expressive affection
			Instrumental affection
		Parenting Practices and Parent-child relationship	Rapport (self- and spouse reports[c])
	Target child	Expression of affection[a]	Expressive affection
	Observer	Observational coding system	Positivity:
			Parent[a] to target child
			Target child to parent[a]

Control	Parents[a]	Assessment of Child Monitoring	Control of: Character development (self- and spouse reports[c]) Deviant behavior (self- and spouse reports[c])
	Target child	Assessment of Child Monitoring	Control of: Character development[c] Deviant behavior[c]
	Observer	Observational coding system	Dominance/power: Parent[a] to target child Parental influence: Parent[a] to target child
Monitoring	Parents[a]	Assessment of Child Monitoring	Monitoring of: Character development (self- and spouse reports[c]) Deviant behavior (self- and spouse reports[c])
	Target child	Assessment of Child Monitoring	Monitoring of: Character development[a] Deviant behavior[a]
	Observer	Observational coding system	Monitoring:[b] Parent[a] to target child
Negativity/conflict	Parents[a]	Child-rearing Issues	Conflict over daily routines Conflict over adolescent issues Nagging communication about discipline Use of negative sanctions
	Target child	Child-rearing Issues	Conflict over daily routines[a] Conflict over adolescent issues[a] Nagging communication about discipline[a] Use of negative sanctions[a]
	Observer	Observational coding system	Negativity: Parent[a] to target child Target child to parent[a]

TABLE A3 (*Continued*)

Dimension	Sibling Relationship Dimensions		
	Informant	Assessment Instruments	Scales
Positivity	Parent[a]	Sibling Inventory of Behavior	Involvement Empathy Teaching
	Target child	Sibling Inventory of Behavior	Involvement Empathy Teaching
	Observer	Observational coding system	Prosocial: Target child to sibling Sibling to target child Positivity: Target child to sibling Sibling to target child
Negativity	Parents[a]	Sibling Inventory of Behavior	Rivalry Avoidance Aggression
	Target child	Sibling Inventory of Behavior	Rivalry Avoidance Aggression
	Observer	Observational coding system	Antisocial: Target child to sibling Sibling to target child Negativity: Target child to sibling Sibling to target child

[a] Separate MANOVAs were conducted on the mother's reports of the child and the (step)father's reports of the child; the child's reports of the mother and the child's reports of the (step)father; or the wife's report of the husband and the husband's report of the wife.

[b] Analyses of variance (ANOVAs) were performed rather than MANOVAs.

[c] Self- and spouse reports were highly correlated and thus were both included in the MANOVA.

APPENDIX B

EXAMPLE OF AN OBSERVATIONAL SCALE

HOSTILITY/REJECTION

Rate: All.

This scale measures the degree to which the parent or child displays hostile, angry, rejecting behavior. Take the following into account: *nonverbal communication,* such as irritable, sarcastic, or curt tones of voice or shouting; *rejection,* such as actively ignoring the other or denying the other's needs; and the *content* of the statements themselves, such as denigrating or critical remarks (e.g., "You don't know anything," or, "You could never manage that"). Bear in mind that just because two people disagree does not necessarily mean that they are being hostile.

1. *Not at all characteristic.*—Across the interactions, the target displays virtually no examples of hostile, angry, or rejecting behavior.

2. *Mainly uncharacteristic.*—There is some evidence of low-intensity hostility, but it is quickly abated. Examples of low-intensity hostility are mild criticism with minimal negative affect, an occasional abrupt remark, a scowl or frown, a cynical smile, and, in children particularly, a taunt or tease.

3. *Between the two extremes.*—There are a few examples of moderately intense hostility, such as curt or irritable responses, mild rejection, or some moderately intense criticism or anger. (The intensity of the negative affect helps distinguish between a rating of 2 and one of 3.)

4. *Mainly characteristic.*—The target shows more frequent and intense hostility, such as several curt or disruptive remarks, more intense and prolonged critical comments, or some shouting. The target may also show more intense rejection or rebuffing of the other person's requests for assistance or affection. The target may also show more denigration or mocking.

5. *Highly characteristic.*—The target can be characterized as highly hostile, angry, and/or rejecting. There may be a high degree of shouting, angry tones of voice, heavy use of sarcasm to denigrate the other, and sharp and frequent criticism or mocking. The target may be highly rejecting.

REFERENCES

Abramovitch, R., Pepler, D., & Corter, C. (1982). Patterns of sibling interaction among preschool-age children. In M. E. Lamb & B. Sutton-Smith (Eds.), *Sibling relationships: Their nature and significance across the lifespan* (pp. 61–86). Hillsdale, NJ: Erlbaum.

Achenbach, T. M. (1978). The Child Behavior Profile: 1. Boys aged 6–11. *Journal of Consulting and Clinical Psychology,* **46,** 478–488.

Achenbach, T. M., & Edelbrock, C. S. (1979). The Child Behavior Profile: 2. Boys aged 12–16 and girls aged 6–11 and 12–16. *Journal of Consulting and Clinical Psychology,* **47,** 223–233.

Achenbach, T. M., & Edelbrock, C. S. (1983). *Manual for the Child Behavior Checklist and Revised Child Behavior Profile.* New York: Queen City Printers.

Ahrons, C. R. (1980). Joint custody arrangements in the post-divorce family. *Journal of Divorce,* **3,** 189–205.

Albrecht, S., Bahr, H., & Goodman, K. (1983). *Divorce and remarriage: Problems, adaptations, and adjustments.* Westpoint, CT: Greenwood.

Allison, P. D., & Furstenberg, F. F. (1989). How marital dissolution affects children: Variations by age and sex. *Developmental Psychology,* **25,** 540–549.

Anderson, E. R., Hetherington, E. M., & Clingempeel, W. G. (1989). Transformations in family relations at puberty: Effects of family context. *Journal of Early Adolescence,* **9**(3), 310–334.

Anderson, J. Z., & White, G. D. (1986). Dysfunctional intact families and stepfamilies. *Family Process,* **25,** 407–422.

Ball, D. W., Newman, J. M., & Scheuren, W. J. (1984). Teachers' generalized expectations of children of divorce. *Psychological Reports,* **54,** 345–353.

Bank, L., Forgatch, M. S., Patterson, G. R., & Fetrow, R. A. (1991). *Parenting practices: Mediators of negative contextual factors in divorce.* Manuscript submitted for publication.

Bank, S., & Kahn, M. (1982a). Intense sibling loyalties. In M. E. Lamb & B. Sutton-Smith (Eds.), *Sibling relationships: Their nature and significance across the lifespan* (pp. 251–266). Hillsdale, NJ: Erlbaum.

Bank, S., & Kahn, M. (1982b). *The sibling bond.* New York: Basic.

Baumrind, D. (1967). Child care practices anteceding three patterns of preschool behavior. *Genetic Psychological Monographs,* **75,** 43–88.

Baumrind, D. (1973). The development of instrumental competence through socialization. In A. D. Pick (Ed.), *Minnesota symposium on child psychology* (Vol. **7,** pp. 3–46). Minneapolis: University of Minnesota Press.

Baumrind, D. (1978). Parental disciplinary patterns and social competence in children. *Youth and Society,* **9,** 239–276.

Baumrind, D. (1979a). *Adolescent Q-Sort.* Berkeley: University of California, Institute of Human Development, Family Socialization and Developmental Competence Project.

Baumrind, D. (1979b). *Rating scales for parents of adolescent children.* Berkeley: University of California, Institute of Human Development, Family Socialization and Developmental Competence Project.

Baumrind, D. (1989, April). *Sex-differentiated socialization effects in childhood and adolescence in divorced and intact families.* Paper presented at the meeting of the Society for Research in Child Development, Kansas City, MO.

Baumrind, D. (1991). Effective parenting during the early adolescent transition. In P. A. Cowan & E. M. Hetherington (Eds.), *Family transitions* (pp. 111–163). Hillsdale, NJ: Erlbaum.

Beck, A. T. (1967). *Depression, causes and treatment.* Philadelphia: University of Pennsylvania Press.

Belsky, J. (1981). Early human experience: A family perspective. *Developmental Psychology,* **17,** 3–23.

Belsky, J. (1984). The determinants of parenting: A process model. *Child Development,* **55,** 83–96.

Berkowitz, L. (1983). Aversively stimulated aggression: Some parallels and differences in research with animals and humans. *American Psychologist,* **38,** 1135–1144.

Bernard, J. (1972). *The future of marriage.* New York: Bantam.

Biglan, A., Hops, H., Sherman, L., Arthur, J., & Osteen, V. (1985). Problem-solving interactions of depressed women and their husbands. *Behavior Therapy,* **16,** 431–451.

Block, J. H., Block, J., & Gjerde, P. F. (1986). The personality of children prior to divorce: A prospective study. *Child Development,* **57,** 827–840.

Block, J. H., Block, J., & Gjerde, P. F. (1988). Parental functioning and the home environment of families of divorce: Prospective and current analyses. *Journal of the American Academy of Child and Adolescent Psychiatry,* **27,** 207–213.

Bohannon, P. (1975). *Stepfathers and the mental health of their children* (Final report). La Jolla, CA: Western Behavioral Science Institute.

Bowerman, C., & Irish, D. (1962). Some relationships of stepchildren to their parents. *Marriage and Family Living,* **24,** 113–121.

Brand, E., & Clingempeel, G. (1987). Interdependency of marital and stepparent-stepchild relationships and children's psychological adjustment: Research findings and clinical implications. *Family Relations,* **36,** 140–145.

Brand, E., Clingempeel, W. G., & Bowen-Woodward, K. (1988). Family relationships and children's psychological adjustment in stepmother and stepfather families: Findings and conclusions from the Philadelphia Stepfamily Research Project. In E. M. Hetherington & J. D. Arasteh (Eds.), *Impact of divorce, single parenting and stepparenting on children* (pp. 299–324). Hillsdale, NJ: Erlbaum.

Bray, J. H. (1987, August). *Becoming a stepfamily.* Symposium presented at the meeting of the American Psychological Association, New York.

Bray, J. H. (1988). Children's development during early remarriage. In E. M. Hetherington & J. D. Arasteh (Eds.), *Impact of divorce, single parenting and stepparenting on children* (pp. 279–298). Hillsdale, NJ: Erlbaum.

Bray, J. H. (1990). *Developmental issues in stepfamilies: Research project final report.* Unpublished manuscript.

Bray, J. H., Berger, S., Mann, T., Silverblatt, A., & Gershenhorn, S. (1987, April). *Parenting practices and family process during early remarriage.* Paper presented at the meeting of the Society for Research in Child Development, Baltimore.

Bray, J. H., Berger, S., Silverblatt, A., & Hollier, E. A. (1987). Family process and organization during early remarriage: A preliminary analysis. In J. P. Vincent (Ed.), *Advances in family intervention, assessment and theory* (Vol. **4,** pp. 253–280). Greenwich, CT: JAI.

Bray, J., Gershenhorn, S., & Bennett, A. (1987, August). The role of the stepfather. In *Becoming a stepfamily.* Symposium conducted at the meeting of the American Psychological Association, New York.

Bryant, B. K. (1982). Sibling relationships in middle childhood. In M. E. Lamb & B. Sutton-Smith (Eds.), *Sibling relationships: Their nature and significance across the lifespan* (pp. 87–121). Hillsdale, NJ: Erlbaum.

Buchanan, C. M., Maccoby, E. E., & Dornbusch, S. M. (in press). Adolescents and their families after divorce: Three residential arrangements compared. *Journal of Research on Adolescence.*

Burchinal, L. G. (1964). Characteristics of adolescents from unbroken and reconstituted families. *Journal of Marriage and the Family,* **24,** 44–51.

Cairns, R. B., & Cairns, B. D. (1984). Predicting aggressive patterns in boys and girls: A developmental study. *Aggressive Behavior,* **11**(3), 227–242.

Camara, K. A., & Resnick, G. (1987). Marital and parental subsystems in mother-custody, father-custody, and two-parent households: Effects on children's social development. In J. P. Vincent (Ed.), *Advances in family intervention, assessment and theory* (Vol. **4,** pp. 165–196). Greenwich, CT: JAI.

Camara, K. A., & Resnick, G. (1988). Interparental conflict and cooperation: Factors moderating children's post-divorce adjustment. In E. M. Hetherington & J. D. Arasteh (Eds.), *Impact of divorce, single parenting and stepparenting on children* (pp. 169–195). Hillsdale, NJ: Erlbaum.

Capaldi, D. M., & Patterson, G. R. (1991). Relation of parental transitions to boys' adjustment problems: 1. A linear hypothesis; 2. Mothers at risk for transitions and unskilled parenting. *Developmental Psychology,* **27,** 489–504.

Centers, R., Raven, B., & Rodrigues, A. (1971). Conjugal power and structure: A re-examination. *American Sociological Review,* **36,** 264–278.

Chase-Lansdale, L., & Hetherington, E. M. (1990). The impact of divorce on life-span development: Short and long term effects. In P. B. Baltes, D. L. Featherman, & R. M. Lerner (Eds.), *Life-span development and behavior* (Vol. **10,** pp. 105–150). Hillsdale, NJ: Erlbaum.

Cherlin, A. J. (1981). *Marriage, divorce, remarriage: Changing patterns in the postwar United States.* Cambridge, MA: Harvard University Press.

Cherlin, A. J., Chase-Lansdale, P. L., Furstenberg, F. F., Kiernan, K., & Robins, P. K. (1991, April). *The effects of divorce on children's emotional adjustment: Two prospective studies.* Paper presented at the meeting of the Society for Research in Child Development, Seattle.

Cherlin, A. J., Chase-Lansdale, P. L., Furstenberg, F. F., Kiernan, K., Robins, P. K., Morrison, D. R., & Teitler, J. O. (1991, April). *How much of the effects of divorce on children occurs before the separation? Longitudinal evidence from Great Britain and the United States.* Paper presented at the meeting of the Society for Research in Child Development, Seattle.

Cohen, J. (1968). Weighted kappa: Nominal scale agreement with provision for scale disagreement or partial credit. *Psychological Bulletin,* **70,** 213–220.

Cowan, C. P., Cowan, P. A., Heming, G., & Miller, N. B. (1991). Becoming a family: Marriage, parenting, and child development. In P. A. Cowan & E. M. Hetherington (Eds.), *Family transitions* (pp. 79–109). Hillsdale, NJ: Erlbaum.

Cowan, P. A., Cowan, C. P., & Heming, G. (1989, April). *From parent adaption to child adaption in kindergarten.* Paper presented at the meeting of the Society for Research in Child Development, Kansas City, MO.

Cowan, P. A., Cowan, C. P., Schultz, M. S., & Heming, G. (in press). Prebirth to preschool family factors in children's adaptation to kindergarten. In R. D. Parke & S. G. Kellam (Eds.), *Exploring family relationships with other social contexts.* Hillsdale, NJ: Erlbaum.

Cox, M. J., Owen, M. T., Lewis, J. M., & Henderson, V. K. (1989). Marriage, adult adjustment, and early parenting. *Child Development,* **60,** 1015–1024.

Crosbie-Burnett, M. (1984). The centrality of the step relationship: A challenge to family theory and practice. *Family Relations,* **33**(3), 459–463.

Daniels, D. (1987). Sibling personality differences and differential experiences of siblings in the same family. *Journal of Personality and Social Psychology,* **51,** 339–346.

Daniels, D., Dunn, J., Furstenberg, F. F., & Plomin, R. (1985). Environmental differences within the family and adjustment differences within pairs of adolescent siblings. *Child Development,* **56,** 764–774.

Deal, J. E., Anderson, E. R., Ratliff, D., Hetherington, E. M., & Clingempeel, W. G. (1990, November). *A social relations model analysis of family behavior in remarried families.* Paper presented at the meeting of the National Council on Family Relations, Seattle.

Dixon, W. J., & Brown, M. B. (Eds.). (1979). *Biomedical computer programs: P-series.* Berkeley and Los Angeles: University of California Press.

Duberman, L. (1973). Step-kin relationships. *Journal of Marriage and the Family,* **35,** 283–292.

Duberman, L. (1975). *The reconstituted family: A study of remarried couples and their children.* Chicago: Nelson-Hall.

Dunn, J. (1983). Sibling relationships in early childhood. *Child Development,* **54,** 787–811.

Dunn, J., & Kendrick, C. (1982). *Siblings: Love, envy and understanding.* Cambridge, MA: Harvard University Press.

Edelbrock, C. S., & Achenbach, T. M. (1984). The teacher version of the Child Behavior Profile: 1. Boys aged 6–11. *Journal of Consulting and Clinical Psychology,* **52,** 207–217.

Emery, R. E. (1982). Interparental conflict and the children of discord and divorce. *Psychological Bulletin,* **92,** 310–330.

Emery, R. E. (1988). *Marriage, divorce, and children's adjustment.* Newbury Park, CA: Sage.

Forgatch, M. S., Patterson, G. R., & Skinner, M. L. (1988). A mediational model for the effect of divorce on antisocial behavior in boys. In E. M. Hetherington & J. D. Arasteh (Eds.), *Impact of divorce, single parenting and stepparenting on children* (pp. 135–154). Hillsdale, NJ: Erlbaum.

Furman, W., & Buhrmester, D. (1985). Children's perceptions of the qualities of sibling relationships. *Child Development,* **56,** 448–461.

Furstenberg, F. F. (1979). Recycling the family: Perspectives for researching a neglected family form. *Marriage and Family Review,* **2,** 12–22.

Furstenberg, F. F. (1982). Conjugal succession: Reentering marriage after divorce. In P. B. Baltes & O. G. Brim (Eds.), *Lifespan development and behavior* (Vol. **4,** pp. 107–146). New York: Academic.

Furstenberg, F. F. (1988). Child care after divorce and remarriage. In E. M. Hetherington & J. D. Arasteh (Eds.), *Impact of divorce, single parenting and stepparenting on children* (pp. 245–261). Hillsdale, NJ: Erlbaum.

Giles-Sims, J. (1984). The stepparent role: Expectations, behavior, and sanctions. *Journal of Family Issues,* **5**(1), 116–130.

Giles-Sims, J. (1987). Social exchange in remarried families. In K. Pasley & M. Ihinger-Talman (Eds.), *Remarriage and stepparenting today: Current research and theory* (pp. 141–163). New York: Guilford.

Glenn, N. (1981). The well-being of persons remarried after divorce. *Journal of Family Issues,* **2,** 61–75.

Glick, P. C. (1988). The role of divorce in the changing family structure: Trends and variations. In S. A. Wolchick & P. Karoly (Eds.), *Children of divorce: Empirical perspectives on adjustment* (pp. 3–34). New York: Gardner.

Glick, P. C. (1989a). The family life cycle and social change. *Family Relations,* **38,** 123–129.

Glick, P. C. (1989b). Remarried families, stepfamilies, and stepchildren: A brief demographic profile. *Family Relations,* **38,** 24–47.

Glick, P. C., & Lin, S. (1986). Recent changes in divorce and remarriage. *Journal of Marriage and the Family,* **48,** 737–747.

Gottman, J. M., & Levenson, R. W. (1988). The social psychophysiology of marriage. In P. Noller & M. A. Fitzpatrick (Eds.), *Perspectives on marital interaction* (pp. 182–200). Philadelphia: Multilingual Matters.

Grotevant, H. D., Scarr, S., & Weinberg, R. A. (1977). Intellectual development in family constellations with adopted and natural children. *Child Development,* **48,** 1699–1703.

Guidubaldi, J. (1988). Differences in children's divorce adjustment across grade level and gender: A report from the N.A.S.P.–Kent State Nationwide Project. In S. A. Wolchick & P. Karoly (Eds.), *Children of divorce: Empirical perspectives on adjustment* (pp. 185–231). New York: Gardner.

Harter, S. (1982). The Perceived Competence Scale for Children. *Child Development,* **53,** 87–97.

Hernandez, D. J. (1988). Demographic trends and the living arrangements of children. In E. M. Hetherington & J. D. Arasteh (Eds.), *Impact of divorce, single parenting and stepparenting on children* (pp. 3–22). Hillsdale, NJ: Erlbaum.

Hetherington, E. M. (1972). Effects of fathers' absence on personality development in adolescent daughters. *Developmental Psychology,* **7**(3), 313–326.

Hetherington, E. M. (1981). Divorce: A child's perspective. *American Psychologist,* **34,** 851–858.

Hetherington, E. M. (1988). Parents, children and siblings six years after divorce. In R. Hinde & J. Stevenson-Hinde (Eds.), *Relationships within families* (pp. 311–331). Cambridge: Cambridge University Press.

Hetherington, E. M. (1989). Coping with family transitions: Winners, losers, and survivors. *Child Development,* **60,** 1–14.

Hetherington, E. M. (1990, March). *Families, lies and videotapes.* Presidential address delivered at the meeting of the Society for Research in Adolescence, Atlanta.

Hetherington, E. M., & Anderson, E. R. (1987). The effects of divorce and remarriage on early adolescents and their families. In M. D. Levine & E. R. McAnarney (Eds.), *Early adolescent transitions* (pp. 49–67). Lexington, MA: Heath.

Hetherington, E. M., Arnett, J., & Hollier, E. A. (1987). Adjustment of parents and children to remarriage. In S. A. Wolchick & P. Karoly (Eds.), *Children of divorce: Empirical perspectives on adjustment* (pp. 67–107). New York: Gardner.

Hetherington, E. M., & Camara, K. A. (1984). Families in transition: The process of dissolution and reconstitution. In R. D. Parke (Ed.), *Review of child development research* (pp. 398–439). Chicago: University of Chicago Press.

Hetherington, E. M., Cox, M. J., & Cox, R. (1978). The development of children in mother-headed families. In H. Hoffman & D. Reiss (Eds.), *The American family: Dying or developing?* (pp. 117–145). New York: Plenum.

Hetherington, E. M., Cox, M. J., & Cox, R. (1982). Effects of divorce on parents and children. In M. E. Lamb (Ed.), *Nontraditional families* (pp. 233–288). Hillsdale, NJ: Erlbaum.

Hetherington, E. M., Cox, M. J., & Cox, R. (1985). Long-term effects of divorce and remarriage on the adjustment of children. *Journal of the American Academy of Psychiatry,* **24**(5), 518–530.

Hetherington, E. M., Lindner, M. S., Miller, N. B., & Clingempeel, W. G. (1991, April).

Work, marriage, parenting, and children's adjustment in nondivorced and remarried families. Paper presented at the meeting of the Society for Research in Child Development, Seattle.

Hetherington, E. M., Stanley Hagan, M., & Anderson, E. R. (1989). Marital transitions: A child's perspective. *American Psychologist,* **44,** 303–312.

Hill, J., Holmbeck, G., Marlow, L., Green, T., & Lynch, M. (1985). Menarcheal status and parent-child relations in families of seventh grade girls. *Journal of Youth and Adolescence,* **14,** 301–316.

Hill, J., Holmbeck, G., Marlow, L., Green, T., & Lynch, M. (1985b). Pubertal status and parent-child relations in families of seventh grade boys. *Journal of Early Adolescence,* **5,** 31–44.

Hobart, C. (1987). Parent-child relations in remarried families. *Journal of Family Issues,* **8,** 259–277.

Hobart, C. (1988). The family system in remarriage: An exploratory study. *Journal of Marriage and the Family,* **50,** 649–661.

Huston, A. (1983). Sex-typing. In E. M. Hetherington (Ed.), P. H. Mussen (Series Ed.), *Handbook of child psychology: Vol.* **4.** *Socialization, personality, and social development.* New York: Wiley.

Ihinger-Tallman, M. (1987). Sibling and stepsibling bonding in stepfamilies. In K. Pasley & M. Ihinger-Tallman (Eds.), *Remarriage and stepparenting today: Current research and theory* (pp. 164–182). New York: Guilford.

Jones, S. M. (1978). Divorce and remarriage: A new beginning, a new set of problems. *Journal of Divorce,* **2,** 217–227.

Kalter, N. (1977). Children of divorce in an outpatient psychiatric population. *American Journal of Orthopsychiatry,* **47,** 40–51.

Kenny, D. A., & LaVoie, L. (1984). The social relations model. In L. Berkowitz (Ed.), *Advances in experimental social psychology* (Vol. **18,** pp. 141–182). New York: Academic.

Krantzler, M. (1975). *Creative divorce.* New York: New American Library.

Kurdek, L. A. (1981). An integrative perspective on children's divorce adjustment. *American Psychologist,* **36,** 856–866.

Kurdek, L. A., Blisk, D., & Siesky, A. E. (1981). Correlates of children's long-term adjustment to their parents' divorce. *Developmental Psychology,* **17,** 565–579.

Levenson, R., & Gottman, J. M. (1985). Physiological and affective predictors of changes in relationship satisfaction. *Journal of Personality and Social Psychology,* **49,** 85–94.

Lewis, J. M., & Wallerstein, J. S. (1987). Family profile variables and long-term outcome in divorce research: Issues at a ten-year follow-up. In J. P. Vincent (Ed.), *Advances in family intervention, assessment and theory* (Vol. **4,** pp. 121–142). Greenwich, CT: JAI.

London, K. A. (1991). *Cohabitation, marriage, marital dissolution, and remarriage: United States, 1988* (Advanced data from vital and health statistics). Hyattsville, MD: National Center for Health Statistics.

Lutz, P. (1983). The stepfamily: An adolescent perspective. *Family Relations,* **32,** 367–375.

Lytton, H. (1990). Child and parent effects in boys' conduct disorder: A reinterpretation. *Developmental Psychology,* **26,** 683–697.

Maccoby, E., & Martin, J. (1983). Socialization in the context of the family: Parent-child interaction. In P. H. Mussen (Ed.), *Carmichael's manual of child psychology* (pp. 1–101). New York: Wiley.

MacKinnon, C. E. (1989). An observational investigation of sibling interactions in married and divorced families. *Developmental Psychology,* **25,** 36–44.

Martin, B. (1987). Developmental perspectives on family theory and psychopathology. In T. Jacob (Ed.), *Family interaction and psychopathology: Theories, methods, and findings* (pp. 163–202). New York: Plenum.

McGoldrick, M., & Carter, E. A. (1980). Forming a remarried family. In E. A. Carter & M. McGoldrick (Eds.), *The family life cycle: A framework for family therapy* (pp. 265–294). New York: Gardner.

Newcomer, S., & Udry, J. (1987). Parental marital status effects on adolescent sexual behavior. *Journal of Marriage and the Family,* **49,** 235–240.

Nie, N. H., Hull, C. H., Jenkins, J. G., Steinbrenner, K., & Bent, D. H. (1975). *SPSS: Statistical package for the social sciences* (2d ed.). New York: McGraw-Hill.

Olson, D. H., Portner, J., & Bell, R. (1982). FACES II: Family adaptability and cohesion evaluation scales. In D. H. Olson (Ed.), *Family inventories* (pp. 5–24). Saint Paul: University of Minnesota, Family Social Science.

Papernow, P. L. (1984). The stepfamily cycle: An experimental model of stepfamily development. *Family Relations,* **33,** 355–363.

Parker, H., & Parker, S. (1986). Father-daughter sexual abuse: An emerging perspective. *American Journal of Orthopsychiatry,* **56,** 531–549.

Patterson, G. R. (1982). *Coercive family process: Vol. 3. A social learning approach.* Eugene, OR: Castalia.

Patterson, G. R. (1989). *Multiple comparisons of intact, stepfather, and single-mother families in family management practices and parenting and child behaviors.* Unpublished manuscript, Oregon Social Learning Institute, Eugene.

Patterson, G. R., & Bank, L. (1986). Bootstrapping your way in the nomological thicket. *Behavioral Assessment,* **8,** 49–73.

Patterson, G. R., & Bank, L. (1987). When is a nomological network a construct? In D. R. Peterson & D. B. Fishman (Eds.), *Assessment for decision* (pp. 249–279). New Brunswick, NJ: Rutgers University Press.

Patterson, G. R., & Bank, L. (1989). Some amplifying mechanisms for pathologic process in families. In M. R. Gunnar & E. Thelen (Eds.), *Minnesota symposium on child psychology: Vol. 22. Systems and development* (pp. 167–209). Hillsdale, NJ: Erlbaum.

Patterson, G. R., DeBaryshe, B., & Ramsey, R. (1989). A developmental perspective on antisocial behavior. *American Psychologist,* **44,** 329–335.

Peek, C. W., Bell, N. J., Waldren, T., & Sorrell, G. T. (1988). Patterns of functioning in families of remarried and first-married couples. *Journal of Marriage and the Family,* **50,** 699–708.

Perry, J. B., & Pfuhl, E. H. (1963). Adjustment of children in "solo" and "remarriage" homes. *Marriage and Family Living,* **25,** 221–223.

Pink, J., & Wampler, K. (1985). Problem areas in stepfamilies: Cohesion, adaptability and the stepparent-adolescent relationship. *Family Relations,* **34,** 327–335.

Plomin, R. (1986). *Development, genetics and psychology.* Hillsdale, NJ: Erlbaum.

Plomin, R., & Daniels, D. (1987). Why are children in the same family so different from each other? *Behavioral and Brain Sciences,* **10,** 1–16.

Radke-Yarrow, M., Richters, J., & Wilson, E. (1987). Child development in a network of relationships. In R. Hinde & J. Stevenson-Hinde (Eds.), *Relationships within families* (pp. 48–67). Cambridge: Cambridge University Press.

Ransom, J. W., Schlesinger, S., & Derdeyn, A. P. (1979). A stepfamily in formation. *American Journal of Orthopsychiatry,* **49,** 36–43.

Raush, H. L., Barry, W. A., Hertel, R. K., & Swain, M. A. (1974). *Communication, conflict, and marriage.* San Francisco: Jossey-Bass.

Rodgers, J. L., & Rowe, D. C. (1985). Does contiguity breed similarity? A within-family analysis of nonshared sources of IQ differences between siblings. *Developmental Psychology,* **21**(5), 743–746.

Rosenberg, M. (1965). *Society and the adolescent self-image.* Princeton, NJ: Princeton University Press.

Rubin, L. B. (1979). *Worlds of Pain.* New York: Basic.

Rutter, M. (1981). Parent-child separation: Psychological effects on the children. *Journal of Child Psychology and Psychiatry,* **12,** 233–260.

Santrock, J. W., & Sitterle, K. A. (1987). Parent-child relationships in stepmother families. In K. Pasley & M. Ihinger-Tallman (Eds.), *Remarriage and stepparenting today: Current theory and research* (pp. 273–299). New York: Guilford.

Santrock, J. W., Warshak, R., Lindbergh, C., & Meadows, L. (1982). Children's and parents' observed social behavior in stepfather families. *Child Development,* **53,** 472–480.

SAS Institute. (1985). *SAS user's guide: Basics* (Version 5). Cary, NC: SAS Institute.

Scarr, S., & Grajek, S. (1982). Similarities and differences among siblings. In M. E. Lamb & B. Sutton-Smith (Eds.), *Sibling relationships: Their nature and significance across the lifespan* (pp. 357–382). Hillsdale, NJ: Erlbaum.

Schaefer, E., & Edgerton, M. (1981). *The Sibling Inventory of Behavior.* Chapel Hill: University of North Carolina.

Schooler, C. (1972). Birth order effects: Not here, not now. *Psychological Bulletin,* **78,** 161–175.

Spanier, G., & Furstenberg, F. F. (1987). Remarriage and reconstituted families. In M. B. Sussman & S. K. Steinmetz (Eds.), *Handbook of marriage and the family* (pp. 419–434). New York: Plenum.

Spanier, K. (1976). Dyadic Adjustment scale. *Journal of Marriage and the Family,* **38,** 27–37.

Steinberg, L. (1981). Transformations in family relations at puberty. *Developmental Psychology,* **17,** 833–840.

Steinberg, L. (1987a). The impact of puberty on family relations: Effects of pubertal status and pubertal timing. *Developmental Psychology,* **23,** 451–460.

Steinberg, L. (1987b). Recent research on the family at adolescence: The extent and nature of sex differences. *Journal of Youth and Adolescence,* **16,** 191–197.

Steinberg, L. (1988). Pubertal maturation and family relations: Evidence for the distancing hypothesis. In G. R. Adams, R. Montemayor, & T. P. Gullotta (Eds.), *Advances in adolescent development.* Beverly Hills, CA: Sage.

Steinberg, L., Mounts, N. S., Lamborn, S. D., & Dornbusch, S. M. (1991). Authoritative parenting and adolescent adjustment across varied ecological niches. *Journal of Research on Adolescence,* **1,** 19–36.

Stolberg, A. L., & Anker, J. M. (1983). Cognitive and behavioral changes in children resulting from parental divorce and consequent environmental changes. *Journal of Divorce,* **7**(2), 23–41.

Stoneman, Z., Brody, G. H., & MacKinnon, C. E. (1986). Same-sex and cross-sex siblings: Activity choices, roles, behavior, and gender stereotypes. *Sex Roles,* **15,** 495–511.

Strother, J., & Jacobs, E. (1984). Adolescent stress as it relates to stepfamily living. *School Counselor,* **32,** 97–103.

Touliatos, J., & Lindholm, B. W. (1980). Teachers' perceptions of behavior problems in children from intact, single-parent and stepparent families. *Psychology in the Schools,* **17,** 264–269.

Udry, J. (1987). Hormonal and social determinants of adolescent social initiation. In J. Bancroft (Ed.), *Adolescence and puberty.* New York: Oxford University Press.

Udry, J., Talbert, L., & Morris, N. (1986). Biosocial foundations for adolescent female sexuality. *Demography,* **23,** 217–230.

Walker, K. N., & Messinger, L. (1979). Remarriage after divorce: Dissolution and reconstruction of family boundaries. *Family Process,* **18**(2), 185–191.

Wallerstein, J. S. (1982). *Children of divorce: Preliminary report of a ten year follow-up.* Paper presented at the 10th international congress of the International Association for Child and Adolescent Psychiatry and Allied Professions, Dublin.

Wallerstein, J. S., Corbin, S. B., & Lewis, J. M. (1988). Children of divorce: A ten-year study. In E. M. Hetherington & J. D. Arasteh (Eds.), *Impact of divorce, single parenting and stepparenting on children* (pp. 198–214). Hillsdale, NJ: Erlbaum.

Wallerstein, J. S., & Kelly, J. B. (1980). *Surviving the breakup: How children and parents cope with divorce.* New York: Basic.

Wallerstein, J. S., & Kelly, J. B. (1982). The father-child relationship: Changes after divorce. In S. Cath, A. Gurwitt, & J. Ross (Eds.), *Father and child: Developmental and clinical perspectives* (pp. 451–466). Boston: Little Brown.

Weingarten, H. (1980). Remarriage and well-being: National survey evidence of social and psychological effects. *Journal of Family Issues,* **1,** 533–559.

Weiss, R. S. (1979). Growing up a little faster: The experience of growing up in a single-parent household. *Journal of Social Issues,* **35,** 97–111.

Werner, E. E., & Smith, R. S. (1982). *Vulnerable but invincible: A longitudinal study of resilient children and youth.* New York: McGraw-Hill.

Whiteside, M. F. (1982). Remarriage: A family developmental process. *Journal of Marriage and Family Therapy,* **4,** 59–68.

Williamson, D.S., & Bray, J. H. (1988). Family development and change across the generations: An intergenerational perspective. In C. J. Falicon (Ed.), *Family transitions: Continuity and change over the life cycle* (pp. 357–384). New York: Guilford.

Wilson, K. L., Zurcher, L. A., McAdams, D. C., & Curtis, R. L. (1975). Stepfathers and stepchildren: An explanatory analysis from two national surveys. *Journal of Marriage and the Family,* **37**(3), 526–536.

Zaslow, M. J. (1988). Sex differences in children's response to parental divorce: 1. Research methodology and postdivorce family forms. *American Journal of Orthopsychiatry,* **58,** 355–378.

Zaslow, M. J. (1989). Sex differences in children's response to parental divorce: 2. Samples, variables, ages and sources. *American Journal of Orthopsychiatry,* **59,** 118–141.

Zaslow, M. J., & Hayes, C. (1984). Sex differences in children's response to psychosocial stress: Toward a cross-context analysis. In M. E. Lamb, A. Brown, & B. Rogoff (Eds.), *Advances in developmental psychology* (Vol. **4,** pp. 285–337). Hillsdale, NJ: Erlbaum.

Zill, N. (1988). Behavior, achievement, and health problems among children in stepfamilies: Findings from a national survey of child health. In E. M. Hetherington & J. D. Arasteh (Eds.), *Impact of divorce, single parenting and stepparenting on children* (pp. 325–368). Hillsdale, NJ: Erlbaum.

Zill, N., & Furstenberg, F. F. (1981). *National Survey of Children: Wave 2.* Unpublished measure.

Zill, N., & Peterson, J. L. (1983, April). *Marital disruption, parent-child relationships, and behavior problems in children.* Paper presented at the meeting of the Society for Research in Child Development, Detroit.

Zimiles, H., & Lee, V. E. (1991). Adolescent family structure and educational progress. *Developmental Psychology,* **27,** 314–320.

COMMENTARY

FAMILY STRUCTURE AND CHILDREN'S ADJUSTMENT: IS QUALITY OF PARENTING THE MAJOR MEDIATOR?

Eleanor E. Maccoby

This *Monograph* tells us how three groups of young adolescents function in the context of three contrasting family environments. It explores how and whether family structure, family process, and within-family subsystems are linked to young people's adjustment as they traverse a 2-year period in early adolescence. Like the previous work by Hetherington and her colleagues, this *Monograph* constitutes a landmark contribution to the research literature on divorce and more specifically on the ways in which transitions into and out of single-parent status affect the well-being of children and youths. Specialists will find much to reread and mull over, but the less specialized reader will find a single sweep through the data and conclusions highly rewarding. The introduction provides an exceptionally comprehensive review of the literature on the effects of divorce and remarriage on young adolescents.

The study compares families in which a divorced mother has recently remarried with two other groups: "intact"[1] families and families headed by single mothers who have not remarried. It does not include families in which the children of divorced parents live with their fathers or in joint physical custody. However, these two groups are comparatively small among

I would like to thank Christy M. Buchanan for helpful suggestions on an earlier draft of this Commentary.

[1] I recognize that the authors have avoided using the label "intact" for the never-divorced families—perhaps on the grounds that some of these families may have fracture lines even though the parents have remained together. Nevertheless, defining this group in terms of what they are *not* is sometimes awkward, and I am using "intact" as an alternative to "nondivorced."

the population of divorced families. Since the large majority of divorcing families choose to have the children live with their mothers, the results of this study are broadly applicable. The fact that the study does not examine the relationship of children to noncustodial fathers or ask about the effects of this relationship on the functioning of the custodial family is potentially a more serious omission, considering how many mother-resident children do maintain relationships with their noncustodial fathers over a considerable number of years following divorce (Maccoby & Mnookin, in press; Buchanan, Maccoby, & Dornbusch, 1991). The intrusion or support from former spouses who maintain relationships with the children is an element in family functioning that has not yet been dealt with adequately in family systems theory. Still, one study cannot deal with all the issues relevant to divorce, and the present work considers more facets of within-family relationships than other research has done.

A central finding is that the children in intact families were doing better at each assessment period than those living with divorced mothers who had either remained single or remarried. This finding is consistent with a considerable body of literature pointing to the disruptive effects of divorce (and/or the familial conditions that precede divorce) on children's functioning. In general, the boys were functioning less well than the girls, but this sex difference was found in the intact families as well as in the nontraditional ones. Thus, unlike previous studies, this work indicates that, although sex differences are clearly present, they are generally independent of the effects of family structure. More specifically, this study does not find that boys react more negatively to divorce or girls to remarriage. The study does not support the hypothesis that boys are particularly affected by the loss of a male role model, even after living for 5 years with a single mother; nor are they found to be particularly benefited at remarriage by the availability of a new father figure.

It is difficult for readers of the divorce literature to maintain perspective on the size of effects. Clearly, there is a great deal of overlap among the groups of children who are living in different family structures. When we emphasize the differences between groups, it is easy to lose sight of the fact that some children in intact families are doing poorly and that many children whose parents are divorced and/or remarried are doing well despite their family disruption. Are the differences in group means large enough to be meaningful in any nonstatistical sense? Hetherington and her colleagues have taken this problem seriously, and in Figure 1 they show the proportion of children in each group who are reported by their parents to be manifesting behavior problems (on the Achenbach Child Behavior Checklist) at a rate above the clinical cutoff point for serious problems. We see that, in the intact families, the incidence of problems above this point is similar to that found in large, normative samples (10% or below). In the nontraditional families, the answer to our question depends greatly on whose perspective we accept. Stepfathers reported very high rates of problem behaviors in their stepdaughters and stepsons—nearly 50% above the clinical cutoff point. However, many of them had had little previous experience of daily living with young teenagers and may have overreported problem behaviors. If we rely on the mothers' reports for a comparison across all three family structures, we see that, in comparison to the intact families, a much higher proportion of the children in divorced families (between 25% and 30%) were showing behavior problems at rates above the clinical cutoff point. Rates among children in the remarried families were at least as high. According to the reports of remarried mothers, the rates of problems of their daughters were somewhat lower, and their sons higher, than in the single-mother group. It is important to note that the majority of the children in the nontraditional families (if we discount the stepfathers' reports) were functioning within the normal range—normal, that is, by comparison with the norms on the Achenbach behavior problems scale. Still, the effects documented in this report are large enough to be consequential. Furthermore, it is sobering that little improvement was seen during the 2-year life of the study.

Considering the adjustment data from all sources, it is surprising to see that children with remarried mothers were not more poorly adjusted, overall, than children whose divorced mothers had remained single. Previous studies had suggested that the effects of successive disruptions are cumulative. The children in the remarried families were being assessed in the midst of a second major disruption in their lives. Yet the composite adjustment scores that combined information from all available sources reveal only one instance (one measure at one assessment period) in which children living with divorced single mothers were doing better than those in remarried families (see Table 4).

We first ask, then, what accounts for the lower levels of adjustment found in the two groups of nontraditional families. In the divorce literature, it is a common hypothesis that the effects of divorce are mediated by a deterioration in the quality of parenting, at least during the immediate postdivorce period. Can the children's problems in the two nontraditional groups be traced to lower levels of parental competence? Chapters V and VII provide the information most directly relevant to this question, and the answers are in some ways surprising. In Chapter V, we see that, according to the observers' reports at Waves 1 and 2, the mothers in the intact families were monitoring the children more closely and showing less negativity toward them than the mothers in the other two groups, and both these aspects of parenting style are well established as being associated with competence and a relative absence of behavior problems of children. Thus far, then, the better adjustment of the children from intact families can be seen as an outcome of more effective parenting.

At the end of Chapter V, however, we find some data that are puzzling. Three parenting patterns are identified—authoritative, authoritarian-conflicted, and disengaged—and we see that at Time 3 the divorced mothers were more frequently authoritative and less often disengaged than the mothers in the other two groups. This is certainly not a picture that connotes ineffective parenting by single mothers. The parents in the remarried families were more conflictual and less disengaged than those in intact families, so the problems of children in these families might stem from parental negativity, although the fact that the parents were not disengaging would ordinarily be thought of as a positive factor.

In Chapter VII, the three parenting patterns are entered as joint predictors, along with the three family types, of children's outcome measures. If the effects of family type are mediated by parenting styles, we would expect to see that, once parenting styles are entered into a predictive analysis, family type would no longer matter—or, at least, its effect would be greatly weakened. We see, on the contrary, that both family type and parenting style prove to be strong independent predictors of children's adjustment, and there are no interactions. Within each family type, the quality of parenting clearly matters: in each, authoritative parenting is associated with better functioning in the children, and authoritarian-conflictual parenting is associated with poorer functioning. More important for our understanding of divorce and remarriage and their effects, the differences in adjustment between children in intact families and those in the two other groups are *not* explained by differences in parental competence. When one compares those families in the three different family structures who share a given parenting style, it remains true that the children of nondivorced parents are doing substantially better than children living with mothers who have been divorced and/or remarried.

It would appear that something else about living with a divorced mother (whether she is still single or remarried) is a risk factor for children of this age. What could the "something else" be? A possibility that springs immediately to mind is self-selection by families into nontraditional family status. As the authors note, prospective longitudinal studies (Block, Block, & Gjerde, 1986; Cherlin et al., 1991) have shown that children whose parents will later divorce are already showing signs of behavioral disturbance before the divorce occurs. The usual interpretation of these studies has been that the children were already doing badly before the divorce because their parents were already in conflict and functioning poorly in their parental roles. Undoubtedly, there is a good deal of truth to this, but it hardly helps us explain why children of well-functioning (authoritative) parents should be showing signs of dysfunction 5 years after the divorce, compared to children with equally competent parents in intact families.

It remains a plausible possibility that there is something about being in a nontraditional family, over and above diminished parenting, that contributes to the adjustment difficulties of children of this age. A first possibility is that experiencing parental conflict may have direct effects on children. These children were old enough at the time of their parents' divorce to remember a good deal about the conflict that occurred then. Furthermore, many divorcing couples continue in a conflicted relationship over a considerable span of time following divorce (Johnston, Kline, & Tschann, 1989; Maccoby & Mnookin, in press), and there is ample evidence that exposure to continued parental conflict is harmful to children.

If we think about aspects of family structure in nontraditional families that might be operative, we need to think about the single-parent and remarried families separately since their structures differ. Considering first the children living with divorced mothers who have not remarried, we see that these children have not attained, even 5 years later, a level of functioning comparable to those whose parents did not divorce. If they deteriorated initially, they have not recovered. Presumably, the parental functioning of still-single divorced mothers had had ample opportunity to stabilize during the 5 years since the divorce. Indeed, the data in this study indicate that the divorced single mothers were not showing the diminished parenting that has been observed in previous studies during the crisis period immediately after a divorce. The divorced mothers saw themselves as warm, vigilant in monitoring, and no higher in negativity than mothers in the other groups. From the mothers' perspective, then, the picture was one of competent parenting, and this was consistent with a good deal of what the observers saw.

From the *children's* perspective, however, the picture is a mixed one. The children of divorced mothers report high levels of both instrumental and expressive affection from their mothers—higher, indeed, than is reported by children in intact families. However, the children of divorced single mothers were more likely than other children to say that their mothers were given to nagging and the use of negative sanctions and that there was considerable conflict over daily routines and adolescent issues. Observers reported that the children in divorced families directed fairly high levels of negative behavior toward their mothers and that the still-single divorced mothers had less power and control in interacting with their adolescent children than did either never-divorced or remarried mothers. A reasonable interpretation is that children of still-single divorced mothers are less willing than other children to accept their mothers' authority, even though the parent-child relationship is a warm and close one and the mothers themselves are not behaving in ways that would be expected to incite children to negativity. Indeed, by Wave 3, the divorced mothers were higher than any other group in their rates of "authoritative" parenting. In short, 5 years after divorce, the quality of the mother's parenting appeared to have recovered (assuming that it did deteriorate during the postdivorce transitional period), while the quality of the children's functioning as interaction partners for their mothers had not.

It is understandable that children should be more defiant toward parental authority in divorced families than in never-divorced ones: in intact families, there are two parents to back up each other's authority, and the parental alliance has never been openly disrupted. In most cases, the parents will each have conveyed to the children the message that the other parent is worthy of respect. By comparison with such families, divorced single mothers are in a weaker position. Not only is a second adult voice missing, but in many cases the custodial parent has been the target of the other parent's anger and contempt, and children of this age are likely to know it. There is evidence that children (perhaps particularly boys) who have witnessed abusive behavior by their fathers toward their mothers are likely to show mother-directed coercive behavior (Jaffe, Wolfe, & Wilson, 1990). In any case, it is plausible that such experiences would weaken the authority of a single mother.

Quite evidently, the divorced mothers were maintaining close, affectionate relationships with their children while at the same time attempting to maintain effective management and control. The children acknowledged the close emotional tie, but when this was combined with the mothers' efforts to monitor and control closely, it may have seemed to the children that they were not being given enough room for the relatively high level of autonomy that they felt they had a right to demand. No doubt, in some of these families, a certain amount of role reversal had occurred, with the mothers relying on their children as confidants and thereby ceding to the children an inappropriate degree of control in the relationship with their mothers. It is difficult to say whether the mothers' control efforts were too strong or too intrusive—perhaps these mothers were only responding appropriately to the children's behavior. In any case, the children were evidently attempting to fight free of maternal control. It may seem strange to say that the failure of parents to guide adolescents effectively may stem largely from the adolescents' resistance to being socialized rather than from parental incompetence, but in this case it seems a distinct possibility.

There is another reason why good, authoritative parenting exercised by divorced mothers may not be as effective as in intact families: namely, the harsh economic realities of the single-mother situation. In most cases, support payments received from fathers do not begin to replace the income he provided to the family before the divorce, and the mother has had to become the major breadwinner. This usually means more hours away from the house, and there is less often a parent immediately available for the important "socialization moments" as they arise in the course of the children's daily lives. These mothers could be monitoring effectively during the times when they are available to their children while nevertheless not being available at many of the times when they are needed.

The case of the remarried families is quite different, and there are different assets and liabilities. The stepfather brings much-needed new income to the family. The mothers are generally happy in their new marriages, and their enhanced moods and sense of self-worth are no doubt experienced positively by the children so that they, in their turn, show less negativity toward her than do the children of single mothers. However, stepfathers, as is amply shown in this study, are in an ambiguous authority position with young adolescents; they are not readily accepted and can hardly provide the same kind of authority backup for mothers that is possible in never-divorced families. We see vividly in the remarried families that the ability of a parent to function effectively in the parental role with children who have reached adolescence depends on the readiness of the adolescent to take up the reciprocal role—the role of a younger person who accepts authority and trusts the older person to be supportive of the adolescent's interests. Evidently, trust of this kind toward stepfathers was lacking among many of the adolescents in the remarried families, and the situation did not improve over a 2-year period. I think that the authors are right in interpreting the disengagement by parents (both mothers and stepfathers) in these households as a form of giving up on efforts at control, out of frustration at being ineffective. By contrast, disengagement by parents in intact families—which occurred equally often, at least among the mothers—is more likely to reflect parental trust in the adolescents' competence at self-regulation, as the authors say.

It is a considerable challenge to family systems theory to understand the functioning of families in which children have an established child-to-parent relationship with their mothers but accept a stepfather as at best an uncle-like family friend who lives in the household. Is it that the adolescents are still hoping for a reconciliation between the mother and the children's natural father, even 5 years after the divorce and the mother's remarriage? This seems hardly plausible. Perhaps it is the children who are still maintaining relationships with their noncustodial fathers who, out of loyalty to him, are unwilling to accept a new "father." Or perhaps the children in some remarried families have previously seen a mother's partner (or partners) come and go so that, despite the commitment of a marriage ceremony, it takes more than 2 years for them to believe that the stepfather is a permanent part of their lives. Or perhaps the problem is centered in the mother herself, in that, despite a strong marital bond with her new partner, she is not fully willing to relinquish part of the parenting function to her new spouse and does not support the formation of a father-child relationship between him and the children. We need to know more about these processes. The work of Hetherington and her colleagues has laid an excellent foundation for the next phase of research, by delineating with great clarity and compassion the role strains experienced by both mothers and stepfathers in remarried families, vis-à-vis young adolescent children.

In the final data chapter (Chapter VII), the transactions among several family subsystems begin to be laid out, along with their relation to the children's adjustment. We see that the quality of the marital relationship affects the quality of parent-child relationships, which in turn affect the children's well-being. This *Monograph* gives us considerable insight into the sibling relationship, a unique contribution to our understanding of divorce and its effects. We see first of all that the quality of sibling relationships is related to children's adjustment. In most cases this connection no doubt reflects a circular process in which a child's adjustment affects reactions to siblings, as well as vice versa. However, in remarried families only, a direct causal link between earlier sibling conflict and children's later behavior difficulties are indicated. The data allow us to trace a process of disengagement between siblings over time—a process that is more acrimonious in remarried families than in intact ones. It is clear that siblings are not able to rely on one another very extensively for positive support at times of stressful family reorganization. We know that, as time passes, young adolescents are orienting their lives more and more toward extrafamilial same-age friendships, and the age differences between siblings make it unlikely that they can be part of the same circle of outside friends.

The sample sizes in this study, substantial though they are, did not permit testing the full array of subsystem connections. Did siblings become more disengaged from each other in families in which the parents were becoming more disengaged from the children? Does sibling conflict reflect marital conflict? Do parent-child relationships mediate the effects of sibling conflict on children's adjustment? Or is the reverse true? These issues remain to be explored.

Few researchers would have had the courage to embark on an enterprise of the scope that this project represents. Assessments have been done of parents, target children, and their siblings at three points in time. Information gathered from parents, children, and teachers has been supplemented by in-home observations of family interactions. The samples of each type of family are large enough to permit analysis by sex of child. It is breathtaking to see that this team not only attempted such an enterprise but brought it off so successfully. We are greatly in their debt.

References

Block, J. H., Block, J., & Gjerde, P. F. (1986). The personality of children prior to divorce: A prospective study. *Child Development,* **57,** 827–840.

Buchanan, C. M., Maccoby, E. E., & Dornbusch, S. M. (1991). Caught between parents: Adolescents' experience in divorced homes. *Child Development,* **62,** 1008–1029.

Cherlin, A. J., Furstenberg, F. F., Chase-Lansdale, P. L., Kiernan, K. E., Robins, P. K., Morrison, D. R., & Teitler, J. O. (1991). Longitudinal studies of effects of divorce on children in Great Britain and the United States. *Science,* **252,** 1386–1389.

Jaffe, P., Wolfe, D. A., & Wilson, S. K. (1990). *Children of battered women.* Newbury Park, CA: Sage.

Johnston, J. R., Kline, M., & Tschann, J. M. (1989). Ongoing post-divorce conflict in families contesting custody: Effects on children of joint custody and frequent access. *American Journal of Orthopsychiatry,* **59,** 576–592.

Maccoby, E. E., & Mnookin, R. H. (in press). *Dividing the child: The social and legal dilemmas of custody.* Cambridge, MA: Harvard University Press.

CONTRIBUTORS

E. Mavis Hetherington (Ph.D. 1958, University of California, Berkeley) is the James M. Page Professor of Psychology at the University of Virginia. She is currently the associate editor of *Abnormal Child Psychology* and a past editor of *Child Development* and a past associate editor of *Developmental Psychology*. She is noted for her research in childhood psychopathology, personality and social development, and stress and coping of children and families. She is currently collaborating with Robert Plomin of Pennsylvania State University and David Reiss of George Washington University. Together, they are investigating the relations between genetics, nonshared environment, and children's depression and conduct disorders.

W. Glenn Clingempeel (Ph.D. 1980, University of Virginia) is an associate professor of psychology at Francis Marion College and the codirector of the Family Psychology Institute in Florence, South Carolina. His research interests include the effects of marital transitions on family relationships and children's social development. He is particularly interested in grandparent-grandchild relationships and stepfathers' relationships with all their children.

Edward R. Anderson (Ph.D. 1989, University of Virginia) is an assistant professor in the Department of Human Development and Family Studies at Texas Tech University. His research interests include adolescent development, sibling relationships, stress and coping, and longitudinal research methodology.

James E. Deal (Ph.D. 1987, University of Georgia) is an assistant professor of psychology at the University of Arizona. He is currently investigating the integration of marital and parental roles in couples with preschool children.

Margaret Stanley Hagan (Ph.D. 1989, University of Virginia) is an assistant professor of psychology at the University of North Carolina at Charlotte. She is currently investigating factors related to resiliency and coping with normative and nonnormative life transitions. She is particularly interested in how family temperament and support factors contribute to coping.

E. Ann Hollier (Ph.D. 1989, University of Virginia) is the vice president for information systems and research with Maguire Associates. She specializes in media research for educational television and institutional research for colleges and universities.

Marjorie S. Lindner (M.A. 1990, University of Virginia) is a doctoral candidate at the University of Virginia. She is currently investigating stepchildren's relationships with their three parents, religion as it affects the marital relationship, and conceptual and statistical models of stress and coping.

Layne D. Bennion (M.S. 1989, Utah State University) is a doctoral candidate at the University of Virginia. His current research interests include family process, social support, and issues of observational coding and reliability.

Jeanne Cavanaugh Brown (M.A. 1986, University of Virginia) is a research analyst in demographics at the University of Virginia's Center for Public Service.

Marlene Eisenberg (Ph.D. 1991, University of Virginia) is a research scientist at the University of Virginia. She is currently investigating the interrelations among child care, work, family life, and social policy.

Thomas G. O'Connor (B.A. 1989, University of Rochester) is a doctoral candidate at the University of Virginia. His research interests include family systems theory and family process in nondivorced and remarried families.

Alyson M. Rice (B.A. 1988, University of Virginia) is a senior lab technician at the University of Virginia. She is currently involved in the implementation of an observational coding system being used to examine the relation between nonshared environment and children's depression and conduct disorders.

Eleanor E. Maccoby (Ph.D. 1950, University of Michigan) is professor emerita of psychology at Stanford University. Her research has focused on gender differentiation in childhood and on parent-child interaction. Her most recent work (with law professor Robert H. Mnookin) is on custodial arrangements for the children of divorcing families and is reported in the forthcoming *Dividing the Child: The Social and Legal Dilemmas of Custody.*

STATEMENT OF EDITORIAL POLICY

The *Monographs* series is intended as an outlet for major reports of developmental research that generate authoritative new findings and use these to foster a fresh and/or better-integrated perspective on some conceptually significant issue or controversy. Submissions from programmatic research projects are particularly welcome; these may consist of individually or group-authored reports of findings from some single large-scale investigation or of a sequence of experiments centering on some particular question. Multiauthored sets of independent studies that center on the same underlying question can also be appropriate; a critical requirement in such instances is that the various authors address common issues and that the contribution arising from the set as a whole be both unique and substantial. In essence, irrespective of how it may be framed, any work that contributes significant data and/or extends developmental thinking will be taken under editorial consideration.

Submissions should contain a minimum of 80 manuscript pages (including tables and references); the upper limit of 150–175 pages is much more flexible (please submit four copies; a copy of every submission and associated correspondence is deposited eventually in the archives of the SRCD). Neither membership in the Society for Research in Child Development nor affiliation with the academic discipline of psychology are relevant; the significance of the work in extending developmental theory and in contributing new empirical information is by far the most crucial consideration. Because the aim of the series is not only to advance knowledge on specialized topics but also to enhance cross-fertilization among disciplines or subfields, it is important that the links between the specific issues under study and larger questions relating to developmental processes emerge as clearly to the general reader as to specialists on the given topic.

Potential authors who may be unsure whether the manuscript they are planning would make an appropriate submission are invited to draft an outline of what they propose and send it to the Editor for assessment.

This mechanism, as well as a more detailed description of all editorial policies, evaluation processes, and format requirements, is given in the "Guidelines for the Preparation of *Monographs* Submissions," which can be obtained by writing to Wanda C. Bronson, Institute of Human Development, 1203 Tolman Hall, University of California, Berkeley, CA 94720.